modern chairs

Charlotte & Peter Fiell

modern chairs

TASCHEN

KÖLN LONDON LOS ANGELES MADRID PARIS TOKYO

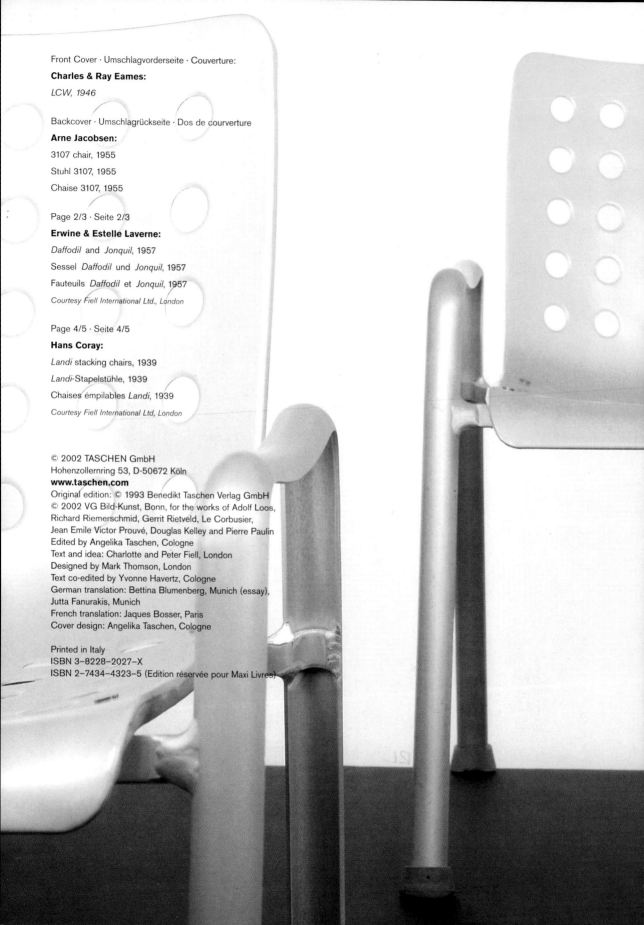

Front Cover · Umschlagvorderseite · Couverture:
Charles & Ray Eames:
LCW, 1946

Backcover · Umschlagrückseite · Dos de courverture
Arne Jacobsen:
3107 chair, 1955
Stuhl 3107, 1955
Chaise 3107, 1955

Page 2/3 · Seite 2/3
Erwine & Estelle Laverne:
Daffodil and *Jonquil*, 1957
Sessel *Daffodil* und *Jonquil*, 1957
Fauteuils *Daffodil* et *Jonquil*, 1957
Courtesy Fiell International Ltd., London

Page 4/5 · Seite 4/5
Hans Coray:
Landi stacking chairs, 1939
Landi-Stapelstühle, 1939
Chaises émpilables *Landi*, 1939
Courtesy Fiell International Ltd, London

© 2002 TASCHEN GmbH
Hohenzollernring 53, D-50672 Köln
www.taschen.com
Original edition: © 1993 Benedikt Taschen Verlag GmbH
© 2002 VG Bild-Kunst, Bonn, for the works of Adolf Loos,
Richard Riemerschmid, Gerrit Rietveld, Le Corbusier,
Jean Emile Victor Prouvé, Douglas Kelley and Pierre Paulin
Edited by Angelika Taschen, Cologne
Text and idea: Charlotte and Peter Fiell, London
Designed by Mark Thomson, London
Text co-edited by Yvonne Havertz, Cologne
German translation: Bettina Blumenberg, Munich (essay),
Jutta Fanurakis, Munich
French translation: Jaques Bosser, Paris
Cover design: Angelika Taschen, Cologne

Printed in Italy
ISBN 3-8228-2027-X
ISBN 2-7434-4323-5 (Edition réservée pour Maxi Livres)

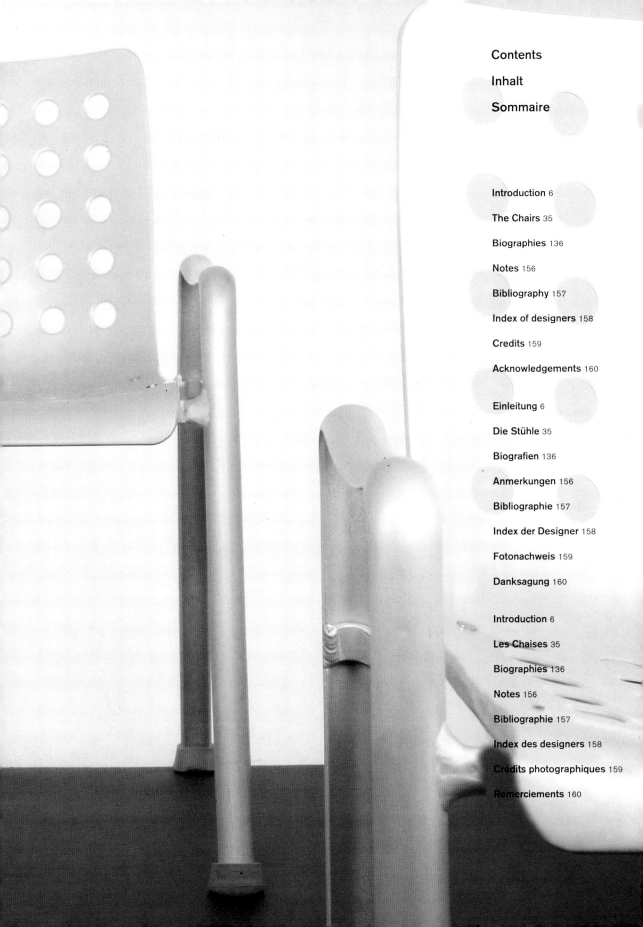

Contents
Inhalt
Sommaire

Marcel Breuer:

Wassily club chair, *Model No. B3*, 1925

Wassily-Stuhl, *Modell Nr. B3*, 1925

Chaise *Wassily, modèle n° B3*, 1925

Courtesy Sotheby's, New York

The chair as a twentieth century icon

Der Stuhl als Ikone des 20. Jahrhunderts

Le siège, icône du xxème siècle

In 1873, Dr. Christopher Dresser wrote, "A chair is a stool with a back-rest, and a stool is a board elevated from the ground by supports."[1]

This definition of the chair seems absurdly simplistic today, for over the last hundred years the chair has been subject to a succession of revolutionary transformations, uniquely emerging as an eloquent symbol of our highly complex society. The enduring success of a particular chair design can be evaluated by how skilfully its creator has synthesized aesthetics and function while addressing a specific need. The relevance of an individual design may also be gauged by how well it expresses the spirit of the age in which it was created. Chairs sustain a far greater physical and psychological relationship with their users than do tables or case pieces. For this reason, the design of chairs has to be seen as set apart from that of other furniture. Since the beginning of civilization humans have required something to sit on – and as societies evolve, so does the chair. As a symbolic object, therefore, the chair has few equals – in the form of a throne or the electric chair, it potently expresses power and authority. The chair is an object steeped in connotations; it confers status on its user, it can possess varying degrees of intellectual content.

Im Jahre 1873 schrieb Dr. Christopher Dresser: »Ein Stuhl ist ein Hocker mit einer Rückenlehne, und ein Hocker ist ein Brett, das durch Stützen vom Boden abgehoben ist.«[1]

Diese Definition des Stuhls kommt uns heute fast lächerlich einfältig vor, denn der Stuhl hat im Laufe der letzten hundert Jahre eine Reihe von so revolutionären Wandlungen erfahren, daß er zu einem einzigartigen und beredten Sinnbild unserer überaus komplexen Gesellschaft geworden ist. Ob einem bestimmten Stuhl dauerhafter Erfolg beschieden ist, hängt davon ab, wie gut es seinem Schöpfer gelungen ist, Ästhetik und Funktionalität miteinander zu vereinen und dabei den spezifischen Verwendungszweck nicht aus den Augen zu verlieren. Die Bedeutung eines bestimmten Entwurfs läßt sich auch daran messen, wie treffend er den Geist seiner Entstehungszeit widerspiegelt. Stühle stehen in einer wesentlich engeren physischen und psychologischen Beziehung zu ihren Benutzern als Tische oder Schränke. Deshalb nimmt der Entwurf von Stühlen eine Sonderstellung gegenüber dem übrigen Möbeldesign ein. Seit den Anfängen der Zivilisation haben Menschen etwas gebraucht, worauf sie sitzen konnten – und mit den Gesellschaftsformen entwickelt sich auch der Stuhl. Deshalb

En 1873, Christopher Dresser écrivait: «Un siège est un tabouret avec un dossier et un tabouret est une planche surélevée du sol par le moyen de supports.»[1]

Si cette définition peut sembler absurdement simpliste aujourd'hui c'est que le siège a été soumis à une telle succession de transformations révolutionnaires durant ces cent dernières années qu'il est en fait devenu un symbole de notre société dans toute sa complexité. Le succès durable d'un modèle peut s'évaluer au savoir-faire de son créateur, qui sait réaliser la synthèse de l'esthétique et du fonctionnalisme tout en apportant une réponse à un besoin spécifique, et sa pertinence peut se juger à la manière dont il exprime son époque. Les sièges entretiennent en effet avec leurs utilisateurs une relation physique et psychologique beaucoup plus importante que celle d'une table ou d'un meuble de rangement et c'est pour cette raison que leur création doit être considérée à part de celle des autres éléments du mobilier. Depuis les débuts de la civilisation, les hommes ont toujours eu besoin de quelque chose pour s'asseoir et le siège a évolué de la même façon que la société. En tant qu'objet symbolique, sa puissance n'a que peu d'équivalents. Ainsi, par exemple, sous la forme d'un trône ou d'une chaise électrique, il sait exprimer le pou-

More than any other type of furniture, the chair can be seen as a barometer of social change. While its primary function as an object to sit on remains constant, the specific purposes for which some chairs are designed are mutable. The hall chair, for instance, is all but obsolete today, whereas the operator's chair undergoes continual research and development. The chair more accurately mirrors the social and economic contexts within which design has evolved in the twentieth century, because it best expresses the essence of specific decorative styles. It is also particularly susceptible to the evanescent influences of taste and popular consumerism. In times of economic austerity rationally designed chairs and other durable products will by necessity prevail in the marketplace, while in periods of relative prosperity there is a general tendency towards the anti-rationalism of ornamentation and exaggerated forms.

Chairs are "territorialized" by us in our daily lives; at home, members of a family each have their own particular chair in which they prefer to sit . At work, chairs are used to represent status; manufacturers commonly supply seating systems that incorporate a single standard model which can be variously upgraded – the less costly receptionist's chair is efficiently adapted into an executive's chair with the addition of luxury options. So prevalent and subtle is this symbolism of power that frequently its existence is only registered subconsciously. Chairs also reflect the aspirations and socio-political viewpoints of their owners, laying bare their personalities and social class. More than any other furniture type, the chair offers an insight into the souls of men.

Arne Jacobsen:

Plywood chair, 1955

Sperrholzstuhl, 1955

Chaise contreplaqué, 1955

Courtesy Whitechapel Art Gallery, London

hat der Stuhl als symbolhafter Gegenstand kaum seinesgleichen – in Gestalt eines Throns oder des elektrischen Stuhls ist er ein unmißverständlicher Ausdruck von Macht und Autorität. Der Stuhl ist ein bedeutungsreiches Objekt: Er kann seinem Benutzer Rang verleihen, er kann in unterschiedlichem Maße geistige Inhalte verkörpern.

Mehr als jedes andere Möbelstück kann der Stuhl als Indikator des sozialen Wandels gelten. Zwar bleibt seine Grundfunktion als Sitzmöbel bestehen, doch ist die spezifische Verwendung, für die Stühle entworfen werden, veränderbar. Der Dielenstuhl beispielsweise ist heute völlig veraltet, während der Schreibtischstuhl auf wissenschaftlicher Basis ständig weiterentwickelt wird. Der Stuhl ist ein verläßlicher Spiegel des sozialen und ökonomischen Kontexts, in dem das Design des 20. Jahrhunderts sich entfaltet hat, denn in ihm kommt das Charakteristische bestimmter Einrichtungsstile am deutlichsten zum Ausdruck. Er erweist sich überdies als besonders sensibel für die flüchtigen Einflüsse von Geschmack und Massenkonsum. In Zeiten angespannnter Wirtschaftslage werden stets Stühle mit eindeutig rationalem Design und andere dauerhafte Produkte den Markt beherrschen, während Zeiten relativen Wohlstands durch eine allgemeine Tendenz zum Antirationalismus des Ornamentalen und der übersteigerten Formen gekennzeichnet sind.

In unserem Alltagsleben haben Sitzmöbel für uns etwas von einem »Revier«; zu Hause hat jedes Familienmitglied seinen Lieblingsplatz. Am Arbeitsplatz sind Stühle Rangabzeichen; Hersteller bieten in der Regel Programme an, bei denen sich ein einziges Standardmodell beliebig aufrüsten läßt – aus dem weniger kostspieligen Stuhl für die Empfangsdame wird in der Luxusausführung im Handumdrehen ein Chefsessel. Diese Machtsymbolik ist so weit verbreitet und so subtil, daß man sie oft nur unterschwellig wahrnimmt. Stühle können auch etwas über die Zielvorstellungen und soziopolitischen Standpunkte ihrer Besitzer aussagen, deren Charakter und soziale Herkunft sie offenbaren. Mehr als jedes andere Möbelstück verschafft uns der Stuhl einen Einblick in die menschliche Seele.

voir, l'autorité et la justice. C'est un objet extraordinairement connoté qui peut conférer un statut social ou hiérarchique à son utilisateur, offrir différents niveaux de signification.

Plus que n'importe quel autre type de meuble, le siège peut être considéré comme un baromètre des changements sociaux. Alors que sa première fonction – un objet fait pour s'asseoir – est restée immuable, les buts dans lesquels certains sièges sont conçus évoluent: la cathèdre, par exemple, est aujourd'hui totalement obsolète alors que la chaise de la standardiste fait l'objet de recherches et de développements continus. Le siège reflète avec une grande précision les contextes économiques et sociaux de l'évolution du design au XXème siècle et nul mieux que lui n'exprime l'essence même de chaque style décoratif tout en restant particulièrement sensible aux influences éphémères du goût et de la grande consommation. En période d'austérité économique, les sièges conçus selon des critères rationnels seront appréciés par le marché, tandis qu'en phase de relative prospérité se déploiera une certaine tendance à l'anti-rationalisme, à l'ornementation et aux formes exagérées.

Nous intégrons avec facilité les sièges à notre «territoire». A la maison, chaque membre de la famille dispose de son propre siège sur lequel il préfère s'asseoir. Au travail, les sièges sont des symboles de statut hiérarchique. Très couramment, les fabricants en proposent des lignes qui évoluent à partir d'un modèle de base, la chaise moins coûteuse de la réceptionniste se transformant habilement en fauteuil de dirigeant grâce à quelques options de luxe. Si fort et si subtil est ce symbolisme du pouvoir qu'il n'est souvent perçu qu'inconsciemment. Les sièges révèlent également les aspirations, l'appartenance à une classe sociale et les opinions sociopolitiques de leurs propriétaires. Plus que n'importe quel autre meuble, le siège offre une regard sur l'âme humaine.

Architects and chair design

Architekten und Stuhldesign

Les architectes et la conception du siège

In the quest for a greater unity of design, architects have historically created furniture for specific interiors within their buildings. Although once regarded as subordinate to architecture, the design of furniture and especially that of chairs became a separate discipline when its manufacture was transferred from the domain of the craftsman to that of the industrial process. This shift in the method of production demanded a professional approach to design. Architects, with their background knowledge of engineering, were especially well placed to develop new furniture products that were both functional and aesthetically pleasing within the constraints of modern manufacturing technology. Additionally, furniture design appealed to architects, for through it, more easily than with architecture, they could express their design philosophies in three dimensions. Peter Smithson writes, "It could be said that when we design a chair, we make a society and a city in miniature. Certainly this has never been more true than in this century. One has a perfectly clear notion of the sort of city, and the sort of society envisaged by Mies van der Rohe, even though he has never said much about it. It is not an exaggeration to say that the Miesian city is implicit in the Mies chair".[2]

As a potentially mass-produced and

In ihrem Bemühen um die Schaffung eines einheitlichen Gesamtentwurfs haben Architekten seit jeher entsprechende Möbel für ihre Gebäude entworfen. Obwohl die Gestaltung des Mobiliars einst als der Architektur untergeordnet betrachtet wurde, hat sich der Entwurf von Möbeln, und vor allem von Stühlen, zu einer eigenen Disziplin ausgebildet, als die Herstellung aus dem Bereich des Handwerks in die industrielle Fertigung verlagert wurde. Diese grundlegende Veränderung in der Produktionsweise erforderte eine professionelle Umstellung im Design. Architekten waren aufgrund ihres technischen Wissens und ihrer Konstruktionserfahrung besonders befähigt, neue Möbel zu entwerfen, die sowohl ästhetisch als auch funktional ansprechend waren und gleichzeitig den Erfordernissen der modernen industriellen Fertigung entsprachen. Außerdem kam der Möbelentwurf den Architekten besonders entgegen, weil sie hierin leichter als in der Architektur ihre Entwerferphilosophie in drei Dimensionen zum Ausdruck bringen konnten. Peter Smithson schreibt: »Man könnte sagen, wenn wir einen Stuhl entwerfen, schaffen wir eine Gesellschaft und eine Stadt in miniature. Sicherlich ist dies noch nie so deutlich gewesen wie in diesem Jahrhundert. Man bekommt eine ganz klare Vorstellung von der Art Stadt und der

Historiquement, dans le cadre de leurs recherches d'une plus grande unité de conception, les architectes ont créé des meubles pour l'intérieur des bâtiments qu'ils construisaient. Bien que considéré à une époque comme subordonné à l'architecture, le dessin de meuble et spécialement celui du siège devint une discipline à part lorsque sa fabrication passa du domaine de l'artisan et de son atelier à celui de la production industrielle. Cette modification des méthodes de production réclamait une approche professionnelle du design. Grâce à leurs connaissances techniques, les architectes étaient particulièrement bien placés pour mettre au point de nouveaux meubles à la fois fonctionnels et esthétiques dans le cadre des contraintes technologiques d'une fabrication industrialisée. De plus, la création de meubles exerçait sur eux une forte attraction car ils y voyaient la possibilité d'exprimer leur philosophie d'une conception en trois dimensions plus aisément qu'avec l'architecture. Peter Smithson écrit: «On peut dire que lorsque nous dessinons un siège, nous édifions une société et une ville en miniature. Et ceci n'a sans doute jamais été aussi évident qu'au cours de ce siècle. On possède une notion parfaitement claire du type de société et de cité envisagé par Mies van der Rohe, même s'il ne s'est

9

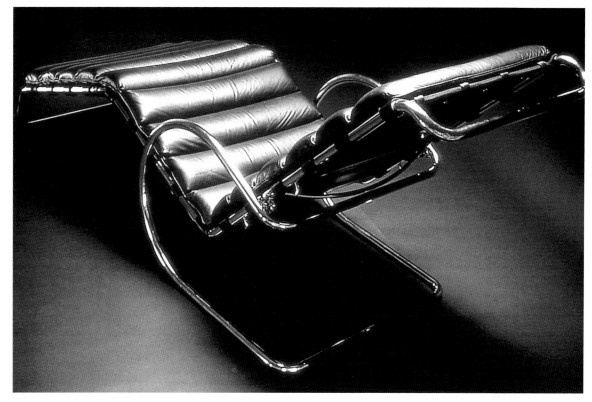

Ludwig Mies van der Rohe:
Chaise longue, *Model No. 241*, 1931
Chaiselongue, *Modell Nr. 241*, 1931
Chaise longue, *modèle n° 241*, 1931
Courtesy Knoll Group, New York

thereby more accessible microcosm of the ideological aspirations of the architect, the chair has not surprisingly led many architects to become better known for their furniture designs than for their buildings. Since the 1940s, designers' names have become synonymous with the chairs they have created: for example, the *Mies chair*, the *Eames chair* and the *Le Corbusier chaise longue*.

Art Gesellschaft, die Mies van der Rohe im Auge hatte, wenn er selbst sich dazu auch nicht weiter geäußert hat. Es ist keine Übertreibung zu sagen, daß die Mies-Stadt im kleinen im Mies-Stuhl enthalten ist.«[2]

Darum ist es nicht überraschend, daß der Stuhl als potentielles Massenprodukt und als ein leichter zugänglicher Mikrokosmos der ideologischen Anliegen des Architekten dazu beigetragen hat, daß viele Architekten durch ihre Möbelentwürfe bekannter geworden sind als durch ihre Gebäude. Seit den 40er Jahren des 20. Jahrhunderts sind Designernamen zu Synonymen geworden für die Stühle, die sie entworfen haben: so der *Mies-Stuhl*, der *Eames-Stuhl* und die *Le-Corbusier-Chaiselongue*.

jamais beaucoup exprimé sur ce sujet. Ce n'est pas exagérer que de dire que la ville miesienne est implicite dans les sièges de Mies.»[2]

Image en réduction des aspirations idéologiques de l'architecte, susceptible d'une production en masse et d'accès relativement aisé, il n'est pas surprenant que la création de sièges ait finalement abouti à ce que de nombreux architectes soient plus connus pour leurs meubles que pour leurs bâtiments. Depuis les années 40, certains noms de créateurs sont devenus synonymes de sièges, par exemple la *Chaise de Mies*, la *Chaise des Eames* ou la *Chaise longue de Le Corbusier*.

The examples we have selected for this survey of the history of the modern chair have been almost exclusively designed by the avant-garde. Those chairs that have no direct bearing on the evolution of Modernism may be considered essentially anti-rational within the context of the classical definition of design. In production or sales terms, modern (with a small "m") designs such as these have only made up a small percentage of the market. Nevertheless, some anti-rational chair designs can be regarded as extremely influential, through either their innovative use of materials and technology, or the aesthetic, political and intellectual agendas they set, while expressing the spirit of the age in which they were created. An analogy could be made with the effect of haute couture on high-street fashion. It should be noted, however, that the concept of rationalism is fluid – what appears to be a rational solution in one era may be considered anti-rational in another. As the needs and concerns of society change, so do designers' and manufacturers' responses to them. To a varying degree, therefore, all design is ephemeral.

The Modern chair is quintessentially an industrial product which has an ancestry that can be traced back to the second quarter of the nineteenth century. Mod-

˙Die Beispiele, die wir für diesen Überblick über die Geschichte des modernen Stuhls ausgewählt haben, zählen fast ausschließlich zur Avantgarde des Möbeldesigns. Diejenigen Stühle, die nicht unmittelbar zur Entwicklung des Modernismus beigetragen haben, bezeichnen wir als antirational, wohl verstanden vor dem Hintergrund der klassischen Definition von Design. Bezüglich der Produktions- oder Verkaufszahlen machen solche neuzeitlich-modischen Entwürfe nur einen kleinen Prozentsatz des Gesamtmarktes aus. Dennoch haben sich manche antirationalen Stuhlentwürfe als höchst einflußreich erwiesen, sei es durch ihre innovative Verwendung des Materials und der Technologie, sei es durch die ästhetische, politische und intellektuelle Aktualität, die sie umsetzen, indem sie den Zeitgeist zum Ausdruck bringen, in dem sie geschaffen wurden.

Der moderne Stuhl ist ein klassisches Beispiel für ein Industrieprodukt, dessen Vorläufer bis in das zweite Viertel des 19. Jahrhunderts zurückverfolgt werden können. Modernismus ist kein Stil, sondern eine weltanschauliche Bewegung, die eine klassische und menschenwürdige Ideologie propagiert, die auch auf das Möbeldesign angewandt werden kann. Die rationalen Dogmen des Modernismus lauten:

Les exemples illustrant cette histoire du siège moderne sont presque tous l'œuvre de créateurs d'avant-garde. Ces sièges qui n'ont pas de lien direct avec l'évolution du Modernisme peuvent être qualifiés d'anti-rationnels par rapport à la définition classique du design. En termes de production ou de vente, les créations de ce type ne représentent qu'une faible part du marché. Néanmoins, certains de ces modèles ont pu exercer une très grande influence, que ce soit pour leur utilisation de matériaux nouveaux ou de technologies avancées, leur esthétique ou les enjeux politiques ou intellectuels qu'ils soulèvent en exprimant l'esprit de leur époque. Une analogie pourrait être tracée avec la haute-couture et son effet sur la mode de la rue. Il faut noter qu'en tant que concept, le rationalisme peut varier et que ce qui apparaît comme rationnel à un certain moment peut sembler anti-rationnel quelques temps plus tard. Dans une certaine mesure tout design est éphémère.

Le siège moderne est par essence un produit industriel dont l'origine remonte au second quart du XIXème siècle. Le Modernisme n'est pas un style, mais un mouvement philosophique, une idéologie d'essence classique et humaniste applicable à la création de mobilier. Les principes rationalistes du Modernisme sont: l'unification

11

ernism is not a style but a philosophical movement which promotes a classical and humanizing ideology that can be applied to furniture design. The rational tenets of Modernism are: the unification of the physical and the spiritual, the harmonizing of functionalism and aesthetics, internationalism derived through abstraction for greater universality of appeal, innovation, social morality, truth to materials, revealed construction and the responsible use of technology. Design, or as it was referred to in the post-war years, "Good Design", is necessarily a Modernist approach that has little to do with style and everything to do with correctly perceiving social needs.

Within Modernism, there are two distinct approaches to design; geometric abstraction and organic abstraction. The former was widely promoted by the pioneers of the Modern Movement, such as Marcel Breuer, Ludwig Mies van der Rohe and Le Corbusier. The latter approach was founded in the work of pre-World War II Scandinavian designers, initially derived from the teachings of Kaare Klint while he was professor of furniture design at the Academy of Fine Arts, Copenhagen, in the 1920s. Unlike his Bauhaus contemporaries, who urged their students to dissociate themselves from previous styles, Klint believed that his students benefited from studying the decorative arts of the past. The designs that result from this method "do not reveal a craving for newness, but are a restatement of classical solutions combining comfort and dignified simplicity".[3] As such, the work of Alvar Aalto and more significantly the later chair designs of Eero Saarinen and Charles Eames have to be seen as evolutionary in the forms they adopted, while revolutionary in the new production techniques they employed. Although both forms of Modernism are holistic in their intent, organic rationalism is informed by the natural world while the symmetry of rectilinear rationalism is drawn from the classical canons of proportion and formal geometry. Though originally derived from the study of human anatomy, geometric formalism is aesthetically idealizing, extremely rigid and if too strictly adhered to can be perceived as inhuman and thereby alienating.

die Vereinigung des Physischen und des Geistigen, die Harmonisierung des Funktionalen und des Ästhetischen; Internationalismus, der auf Abstraktion beruht, die eine universellere geschmackliche und formale Akzeptanz bewirken soll; wesentlich sind außerdem Innovation, gesellschaftliche Moralität, materialgerechte Verarbeitung, Sichtbarmachung der Konstruktion und verantwortungsbewußter Umgang mit der Technologie. Design, oder wie man es in den Nachkriegsjahren gar nannte, »gutes Design«, verfolgt notwendigerweise ein neuzeitlich-zeitgemäßes Anliegen, das wenig mit Stil zu tun hat, sondern ganz und gar darauf ausgerichtet ist, die gesellschaftlichen Bedürfnisse richtig zu erkennen.

Im Modernismus gibt es zwei unterschiedliche Auffassungen und Richtungen des Designs: die geometrische und die organische Abstraktion. Die erste wurde weitgehend von den Pionieren der modernistischen Bewegung wie Marcel Breuer, Ludwig Mies van der Rohe und Le Corbusier vertreten. Letztere wurde von skandinavischen Designern in der Zeit vor dem Zweiten Weltkrieg begründet, die sie wiederum aus den Lehren von Kaare Klint weiterentwickelt hatten, der in den 20er Jahren Professor für Möbeldesign an der Kunstakademie in Kopenhagen war. Anders als seine Zeitgenossen vom Bauhaus glaubte Klint, daß seine Studenten davon profitieren würden, wenn sie sich mit den dekorativen Künsten aus der Vergangenheit eingehend auseinandersetzten. Die Entwürfe, die aus diesen Lehren hervorgegangen sind, »enthüllen nicht eine krampfhafte Suche nach Neuerungen, sondern sind eine Neuformulierung klassischer Lösungen, die in sich Komfort und würdevolle Einfachheit verbinden«.[3] In diesem Sinne müssen die Arbeiten Aaltos und noch signifikanter die späten Stuhlentwürfe von Eero Saarinen und Charles Eames als evolutionär in ihren übernommenen Formen angesehen werden, hingegen sind sie revolutionär in ihren neuen Produktionstechniken. Wenn auch beide Formen des Modernismus in ihrer Zielsetzung ganzheitlich sind, ist doch der organische Rationalismus von der natürlichen Welt geprägt, während die Symmetrie des geradlinigen Rationalismus ihre Wurzeln aus dem klassischen Kanon von Proportion und formaler Geometrie bezieht. Obwohl sich der geometrische Formalismus ursprünglich aus dem Studium der menschlichen Anatomie entwickelt hat, impliziert er ästhetische Idealisierung, und darin wirkt er einseitig; zu strikt an die Gesetze der Geometrie gebunden, wird er sogar als inhuman und entfremdend angesehen.

du physique et du spirituel, l'harmonisation du fonctionnalisme et de l'esthétique, l'internationalisme dû à une abstraction permettant une plus grande universalité de séduction, l'innovation, la morale sociale, l'authenticité de l'utilisation des matériaux, la mise en évidence de la construction et l'utilisation responsable de la technique. Le design, ou comme on disait dans les années d'après-guerre, le «Good Design» se réfère nécessairement à une approche moderniste qui n'a que peu de rapports avec le style et se trouve étroitement liée à la juste perception des besoins sociaux.

Au sein du Modernisme, coexistent deux approches distinctes du design: l'abstraction géométrique et l'abstraction organique. Les pionniers du mouvement moderniste, comme Marcel Breuer, Ludwig Mies van der Rohe et Le Corbusier, furent les avocats de la première. La seconde approche est née des travaux de designers scandinaves de la période précédant la Seconde Guerre mondiale, eux-mêmes influencés par l'enseignement de Kaare Klint, professeur à l'Académie des Beaux-Arts de Copenhague, dans les années vingt. A la différence de ses contemporains du Bauhaus qui pressaient leurs étudiants de rompre avec les styles antérieurs, Klint pensait qu'il fallait savoir tirer parti de l'étude des arts décoratifs du passé. Les créations issues de cette méthode «ne révèlent pas un goût pour la nouveauté mais une relecture des solutions classiques, combinant la recherche du confort et une digne simplicité».[3] Dans cet esprit, l'importance des travaux d'Alvar Aalto et, de façon encore plus significative, les sièges plus tardifs d'Eero Saarinen et de Charles Eames relèvent non seulement d'une évolution formelle mais aussi d'une révolution dans les techniques de production. Bien que les deux écoles du Modernisme soient holistiques dans leur propos, le rationalisme organique s'inspire de l'univers naturel tandis que le rationalisme symétrique et rectiligne s'inspire plutôt des canons classiques de proportions et de géométrie. Bien qu'issu au départ de l'étude de l'anatomie de l'homme, le formalisme géométrique tend vers un idéal esthétique extrêmement rigide qui, poursuivi avec trop de rigueur, peut être perçu comme déshumanisant et aliénant.

The use of new technology and materials, frequently developed in other areas of industry and applied to furniture production, has fundamentally shaped the changes that have occurred in chair design this century. How industrial innovation can influence furniture design was identified by George Nelson when defining two diametrically opposed chair types – "the shocking and the soothing".[4] The "shocking" demands attention through the use of contrasts, often, but not exclusively, by manipulating unusual forms or materials, while the "soothing" represents an understated and harmonious unity of design.

Nelson also defined three main influences in modern chair design: "the handicrafted look"," the machine look" and "the biomorphic look".[5] The chair that adopts the handicraft look does not necessarily rely upon craftsmanship in its production and can be made exclusively by machine. Such chairs, which are often only finished by hand, rely on vernacular forms, for example Hans Wegner's *Peacock chair* of 1947. The analysis and subsequent "updating" of existing furniture types originated in the Arts and Crafts movement, whose chief protagonist, William Morris, concluded that evolutionary designs were based on function rather than superfluous ornament.

Die Verwendung neuer Technologien und Materialien, die häufig in anderen Bereichen der Industrie entwickelt und erst dann auf die Möbelproduktion angewandt worden sind, hat grundlegend die Veränderungen bestimmt, die sich im Stuhldesign des 20. Jahrhunderts abgezeichnet haben. In welchem Maße industrielle Innovation das Möbeldesign beeinflussen kann, hat George Nelson in seiner Definition zweier diametral entgegengesetzter Stuhltypen auf den Begriff gebracht: »der Schockierende und der Schmeichelnde«.[4] Der »Schockierende« erfordert Aufmerksamkeit, denn er basiert auf Kontrasten, die häufig, aber nicht ausschließlich, daraus resultieren, daß ungewöhnliche Formen oder Materialien zusammengebracht werden, während der »Schmeichelnde« eine maßvolle und harmonische Einheit des Entwurfs zeigt.

Nelson hat darüber hinaus die drei wesentlichen Einflüsse im modernen Stuhldesign definiert: den »Handwerks-Look«, den »Maschinen-Look« und den »biomorphen Look«.[5] Der Stuhl, der ein handgefertigtes Aussehen hat, muß nicht unbedingt handwerklich hergestellt worden sein, in manchen Fällen kann er sogar ausschließlich maschinell gefertigt sein. Diese Stuhltypen, die meist nur ihren letzten Schliff von Hand erhalten haben, sind

L'utilisation de nouvelles technologies et de nouveaux matériaux dans la production de mobilier, fréquemment mis au point d'ailleurs pour d'autres secteurs industriels, a exercé un rôle fondamental dans les changements qu'a connus la conception des sièges au cours de ce siècle. Le niveau d'influence de l'innovation industrielle a été précisé par George Nelson dans sa tentative de définition de deux types de sièges diamétralement opposés: «le choquant et l'apaisant».[4] Le «choquant» attire l'attention en recourant à des contrastes obtenus souvent, mais pas exclusivement, par la manipulation de formes ou de matériaux inhabituels, tandis que «l'apaisant» repose sur une unité de dessin discrète et harmonieuse.

Nelson définit également les trois principales directions stylistiques du design du siège moderne: le style «artisanal», le style «mécaniste» et le style «biomorphique».[5] Les sièges qui adoptent le style artisanal n'ont pas été forcément réalisés par un artisan et dans certains cas peuvent même avoir été exclusivement fabriqués à la machine. Ils sont d'ailleurs souvent finis à la main et s'inspirent de formes vernaculaires, tels le fauteuil *Peacock* de Hans Wegner (1947). L'étude et la «modernisation» de types de meubles existants trouvent leur origine dans le mouvement

The "machine" look is effected either through truly mechanized means of production or by handcrafting representations of the industrial process which express the machine aesthetic. Ludwig Mies van der Rohe's *Barcelona chair* of 1929 is a good example of this type, for although it appears machine-made, it was originally produced almost entirely by hand. Conversely, a chair like the *Polyprop*, designed by Robin Day in 1963, not only looks machine-made but also its design was wholly determined by the most efficient means of standardized industrial production.

Nelson's final category, the "biomorphic look", can be produced by machine or hand using abstracted "biological or organic form – neither homely like the handicraft object nor rigid like the machine form – but amorphous and flowing like living tissue".[6] This type of design was initially influenced by contemporary abstract sculpture in the late 1940s. Ironically, the materials best able to express the abstract essence of nature are synthetic media such as plastic and foam rubber.

Throughout most of this century, the trend in the production of general domestic furniture has been away from the workshop/studio and into the factory. With markets continuing to diversify, however, a

häufig aus regionalen und volkstümlichen Formen entwickelt worden wie etwa Hans Wegners *Pfauenstuhl* von 1947. Studium, Auswertung und zeitgemäße Umsetzung bestehender Möbeltypen, die ihren Ursprung im »Arts and Crafts Movement« haben, einer handwerklich-kunsthandwerklichen Bewegung, deren Kopf William Morris war, haben zu dem Schluß geführt, daß evolutionäres Design auf Funktionalität beruht und nicht auf überflüssigem Ornament.

Der »Maschinen-Look« wird entweder durch rein mechanische Produktionsmittel erzielt oder durch handwerkliche Nachahmung des industriellen Fertigungsprozesses, der die Maschinenästhetik zum Ausdruck bringt. Mies van der Rohes *Barcelona-Stuhl* von 1929 ist ein gutes Beispiel für diesen Typus, denn obwohl er aussieht, als sei er maschinell hergestellt, wurde er ursprünglich fast völlig von Hand gefertigt. Im Gegensatz dazu sieht ein Stuhl wie der *Polyprop*, den Robin Day 1963 entworfen hat, nicht mehr maschinengefertigt aus, sondern auch sein Design ist vollständig bestimmt durch die effizientesten Mittel standardisierter Industrieproduktion. Nelsons dritte Kategorie, der »biomorphe Look«, kann von Maschine oder von Hand hergestellt werden, wobei abstrahierte

Arts and Crafts, dont le principal protagoniste, William Morris, estimait que les projets évolutionnistes devaient plutôt s'appuyer sur la fonction que sur l'ornement inutile.

Le style «mécaniste» résulte, quant à lui, de moyens de production mécanisés ou de versions artisanales du processus industriel traduisant une esthétique mécaniste. La *chauffeuse Barcelona* de Ludwig Mies van der Rohe (1929) en est un bon exemple. Bien qu'elle donne l'impression d'avoir été produite en usine, elle était réalisée à l'origine presque entièrement à la main. Inversement, une chaise comme la *Polyprop* de Robin Day (1963), semble non seulement avoir été fabriquée à la machine mais sa conception a été entièrement déterminée par la recherche des moyens les plus efficaces d'aboutir à une standardisation industrielle de sa production.

La dernière catégorie de Nelson, le style «biomorphique», peut s'obtenir à la machine ou à la main «... à travers des formes biologiques ou organiques pas aussi sensibles que les produits de l'artisanat ni aussi rigides que ceux de la machine, mais lisses comme un tissu vivant.»[6] Cette sorte de conception fut influencée par la sculpture abstraite con-

Paolo Ruffi:
La Cova, 1973
La Cova, 1973
La Cova, 1973
Courtesy Poltronova, Milan

Knoll International advertisement for Eero Saarinen's *Tulip* chair

Werbefoto der Firma Knoll International für Eero Saarinens *Tulip*-Stuhl

Knoll International publicité pour la chaise *Tulip* d'Eero Saarinen

Courtesy Knoll Group, New York

reversal of this trend is becoming increasingly apparent. To cope with the popular demand for greater individuality, major manufacturers are currently producing limited editions and short batch runs of antirational chair designs, often utilizing low-tech methods of production for the domestic market, while concentrating their research and development budgets on the large and highly lucrative office-furnishings sector. The introduction of Herman Miller's revolutionary *Action Office II* system in 1968 represents one of the most significant benchmarks from which the great divergence of the contract and domestic markets can be measured. Prior to this, a higher percentage of chairs and other furnishings were conceived as multi-functional, efficiently bridging in many successful cases the contract and domestic markets.

»biologische oder organische Formen« verwendet werden, »die weder schlicht und hausbacken wie ein Handwerksobjekt wirken noch strikt und starr wie eine Maschinenform, sondern amorph und fließend wie aus lebendem Stoff«.[6] Diese Art von Design wurde von der zeitgenössischen abstrakten Skulptur Ende der 40er Jahre beeinflußt. Ironischerweise sind synthetische Materialien wie Kunststoff und Schaumgummi am besten geeignet, das abstrakte Wesen der Natur zum Ausdruck zu bringen.

Im Laufe des 20. Jahrhunderts hat sich die Herstellung des häuslichen Mobiliars immer mehr von den Werkstätten und Kunsthandwerkerateliers in die Fabriken verlagert. Je mehr sich jedoch heute unsere Märkte erweitern, desto deutlicher ist eine Umkehrung dieses Trends spürbar. Um der immer stärker um sich greifenden Forderung nach Individualität gerecht zu werden, produzieren große Hersteller immer häufiger limitierte Auflagen und nur kurzfristig produzierte Modelle von antirationalen Stuhlentwürfen, für die häufig Low-Tech-Methoden bei der Produktion angewandt werden, vor allem für das heimische Mobiliar, während sie Forschung und Entwicklung wesentlich auf den höchst lukrativen Büromöbelsektor konzentrieren. Die Einführung von Herman Millers revolutionärem *Action-Office-II*-System im Jahr 1968 markiert einen der bedeutsamsten Schnittpunkte, von dem aus das starke Auseinanderdriften des Firmen- und des Privatkundenmarktes bemessen werden kann. Vor dieser Wende wurde ein größerer Prozentsatz von Stühlen und anderen Möbeln als multifunktional angesehen, so daß man in vielen erfolgreichen Fällen von einer Brücke zwischen diesen beiden Marktbereichen sprechen könnte.

temporaine à la fin des années 40. D'une façon ironique, les matières synthétiques comme le plastique et le caoutchouc mousse sont les mieux adaptées pour exprimer le caractère abstrait de la nature.

Pratiquement tout au long de ce siècle, la production de meubles pour la maison s'est peu à peu éloignée de l'atelier pour se rapprocher de l'usine, même si, à la suite de la diversification continue des marchés, un renversement de cette tendance s'opère actuellement. Pour s'adapter à la forte demande de plus d'individualisme, les grands fabricants produisent maintenant pour le marché de la maison certains modèles non classiques en éditions limitées ou en petites séries, souvent selon des méthodes très traditionnelles, mais concentrent leurs investissements de recherche et de développement sur le secteur plus vaste et plus rentable de l'équipement de bureau. L'introduction du système révolutionnaire d'Herman Miller, *Action Office II*, (1968), représente l'une des dates décisives à partir de laquelle se constate la divergence des marchés de la maison et du bureau. Auparavant, une grande proportion de sièges et autres meubles s'adaptait avec bonheur aux besoins de la clientèle privée comme à ceux des entreprises.

Michael Thonet:

Steam-bent chairs, c. 1836 – 40

Bugholzstühle, um 1836 – 40

Chaises cintrée, vers 1836 – 40

Courtesy Gebrüder Thonet, Vienna

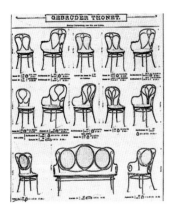

Page from Gebrüder Thonet
catalogue, Vienna, 1904

Seite aus dem Katalog der
Gebrüder Thonet, Wien, 1904

Page du catalogue des Gebrüder
Thonet, Vienne, 1904

During the second half of the nineteenth century, the chair became an industrialized product, mainly as a result of the pioneering research into the steam-bending of wood laminates and later solid wood by Michael Thonet. With the material and structural continuity of his early steam-bent laminated chairs, Thonet set an important precedent in the evolution of the Modern chair – "the elimination of the extraneous, the unification of the essential, the celebration of the natural, the quest for the comfortable, and the popularization of the beautiful".[7] His company, Gebrüder Thonet, manufactured the first truly mass-produced chairs using the newly patented techniques for steam-bending solid wood. These products, however, were not structurally or materially unified, being made in component form for later assembly. Primarily intended for cafés and bars, these innovative chairs were highly successful, owing mainly to the plethora of recently opened coffee houses in Vienna. Thonet's chairs, such as the *Model No. 14*, did not particularly differ in style from the mainly handcrafted contemporary domestic seat furniture and can, therefore, only be seen as Modern in terms of their method of manufacture. Between 1859 and 1914, an astounding 40 million *Model No. 14* chairs were produced, with Thonet employing

In der zweiten Hälfte des 19. Jahrhunderts wurde der Stuhl ein Industrieprodukt, was vor allem der Pionierleistung von Michael Thonet zu verdanken ist, dem es gelungen war, Schichtholz und später auch massives Holz mit Dampf zu biegen. Durch die kontinuierliche Weiterentwicklung von Material und Konstruktion seiner frühen dampfgebogenen Schichtholzstühle hat Thonet einen wichtigen Ausgangspunkt für die Entwicklung des modernen Stuhls markiert – durch die »Eliminierung des Unwesentlichen, die Vereinigung des Wesentlichen, die Zelebrierung des Natürlichen, die Suche nach der Bequemlichkeit und die Verbreitung des Schönen«.[7] In seiner Firma, Gebrüder Thonet, wurden die ersten wirklich massenproduzierten Stühle hergestellt, unter Verwendung der neu patentierten Technik zur Dampfformung von massivem Holz. Diese Produkte wurden aus Einzelteilen zum späteren Zusammensetzen gefertigt. Diese neuen, höchst erfolgreichen Stühle waren vor allem für Cafés und Bars bestimmt und bald aus den zahlreichen Kaffeehäusern nicht mehr wegzudenken. Thonets Stühle, wie etwa das *Modell Nr. 14*, unterschieden sich nicht wesentlich im Stil von den weitgehend handwerklich hergestellten zeitgenössischen Wohnsitzmöbeln; sie können nur bezüglich ihrer Herstellung als modern

Pendant la seconde moitié du XIXème siècle, le siège est devenu un produit industriel, grâce principalement aux avancées décisives dues à Michael Thonet dans le domaine du cintrage à la vapeur de lamellés de bois et, plus tard, de bois massif. En réussissant à se rapprocher avec succès d'une réelle unité de structure et de matériaux, Thonet introduisit un important précédent dans l'évolution du siège: «L'élimination de l'inutile, l'unification de l'essentiel, la célébration du naturel, la recherche du confort et la diffusion de la beauté.»[7] Sa société, Thonet Frères, fut la première a vraiment fabriquer des sièges en série grâce à ses nouvelles techniques qu'il avait fait breveter. Ils étaient cependant encore réalisés en plusieurs éléments séparés puis assemblés. Conçus pour des cafés, ces sièges novateurs connurent un vif succès. Au plan du style, les sièges de Thonet, comme le *modèle n° 14*, ne sont pas fondamentalement différents des sièges de l'époque réalisés selon des méthodes artisanales et ne peuvent donc être considérés comme modernes qu'au regard de leur méthode de fabrication. De 1859 à 1914, le chiffre étonnant de 40 millions de *modèle n° 14*, furent produits, tandis que Thonet employait plus de 25 000 personnes dans soixante usines implantées dans toute l'Europe. Cette

25,000 people in sixty factories scattered across Europe. This incredible capacity was achieved through the implementation of a factory line system of production which separated the stages of the manufacturing process. Systemized production meant that a worker had little part in the creative process or contact with the product through to its completion.

During the nineteenth century, furniture manufacturers generally used technical innovations in industry to mimic handcrafted items. These products were thus neither true to the materials nor the technology they employed in their manufacture. By mid-century, however, it was being acknowledged in certain quarters that beauty could lie in function and honestly expressed materials rather than extraneous ornament. At a meeting of the Freemasons of the Church in 1849, Mr. William Smith Williams delivered a lecture entitled "Importance of the Study of Design" suggesting that, "The adaptation of the thing to its purpose, so far from producing ugliness, tends to beauty, and it also induces new forms. The problem to be solved is simply this: given the use and material of the article, to find a beautiful shape. In the commonest, rudest, and oldest implements of husbandry – the plough, the scythe, the sickle – we have examples of simple yet beautiful curves. The most elementary and simple of forms, if well-proportioned and of graceful contour, are the most pleasing".[8]

Growing sentiments such as these, combined with some acknowledgement of the deceptive use of the industrial process, culminated in a rejection of the machine and the formation of the Arts and Crafts Movement, whose advocates initially proposed handcrafted methods of production which could be operated through a guild system. Although virtuous in its aspirations, this approach failed in its objective of providing the masses with well-designed and affordable furniture. William Morris was forever frustrated by the fact that most of his business was conducted through a private clientele composed of the privileged classes. When asked why he was in such an agitated mood while working on the interior scheme of a house owned by Sir Louther Bell, Morris fiercely replied, "It is only that I spend my life ministering to the swinish luxury of the rich."[9] Although Morris must have recognized that his ideology was flawed in practice, he did make a significant contribution towards the foundations of Modernism in that his designs were based on a reductivist aesthetic. The promotion of vernacular forms and handcrafted techniques made honesty and

angesehen werden. Zwischen 1859 und 1914 wurden nicht weniger als vierzig Millionen Stück vom *Modell Nr. 14* hergestellt, und Thonet beschäftigte inzwischen 25 000 Mitarbeiter in sechzig Fabriken, die über Europa verstreut lagen. Diese unglaubliche Produktionskapazität konnte dadurch möglich werden, daß ein Fabrikationssystem eingeführt wurde, in dem die einzelnen Stadien der Herstellung in verschiedenen Fabriken vorgenommen wurden. Diese systematisierte Reihenproduktion bedeutete für den Arbeiter, daß er nur geringen Anteil am kreativen Prozeß und nur wenig Kontakt mit dem Produkt auf dem Weg bis zu seiner Fertigstellung hatte.

Im späten 19. Jahrhundert verwandten Möbelfabrikanten technische Neuerungen in der Industrie dazu, handwerklich hergestellte Gegenstände nachzuahmen. Diese Produkte waren also weder materialgetreu, noch entsprachen sie der Technologie, die in den Fabrikationsstätten verwandt wurde. In der Mitte des Jahrhunderts wurde jedoch von mancher Seite anerkannt, daß Schönheit auch in der Funktion liegen dürfe und auch im solide verarbeiteten, klar zur Geltung gebrachten Material, nicht aber im überflüssigen Ornament. Bei einem Treffen der Freimaurer im Jahre 1849 hielt William Smith Williams eine Rede mit dem Titel »Die Bedeutung des Studiums des Designs«, in der er folgendes sagte: »Die Anpassung des Stils an seinen Zweck, weit entfernt von der Herstellung von Häßlichkeit, strebt nach Schönheit, und sie führt zur Gestaltung neuer Formen. Das Problem, das es zu lösen gilt, ist ganz einfach dies: Verwendungszweck und Material des Gegenstands vorausgesetzt, muß eine schöne Form gefunden werden. Bei den gebräuchlichsten, gröbsten und ältesten Geräten der Landwirtschaft – dem Pflug, der Sense, der Sichel – haben wir Beispiele für einfache und doch schöne geschwungene Formen. Die elementarsten und einfachsten Formen sind, sofern sie gut proportioniert und elegant in ihren Umrissen sind, die gefälligsten.«[8]

Zunehmend wurden solche Ansichten populär, und außerdem wurde der industrielle Fortschritt immer mehr als Enttäuschung empfunden. Dies gipfelte schließlich in einer Ablehnung der Maschinen, und aus dieser abweisenden Haltung formierte sich das »Arts and Crafts Movement«, eine Bewegung zur Erhaltung und Förderung des Handwerks und Kunsthandwerks, deren Verfechter für Herstellungsmethoden eintraten, die durch organisierte Gilden am Leben erhalten werden sollten. So ehrgeizig dieses Vorhaben auch war, es scheiterte an seiner Zielset-

incroyable capacité de production fut permise par la mise au point d'un système de chaîne de production qui séparait les diverses étapes de la production. Mais la rationalisation de la production signifiait aussi qu'un ouvrier n'avait plus guère de rôle créatif ou même de contact avec le produit.

A la fin du XIXème siècle, les fabricants de meubles, se contentaient généralement de tirer parti des progrès de l'industrie pour reproduire les articles jusquelà faits à la main. Ces produits n'étaient donc pas «authentiques» que ce soit dans leurs matériaux ou leur technologie. Vers le milieu du siècle cependant, on commença à prendre conscience dans certains cercles que la beauté pouvait naître d'une réponse adéquate à une fonction et de l'utilisation honnête des matériaux plutôt que d'une ornementation superfétatoire. En 1849, lors d'une réunion de francsmaçons, William Smith Williams put ainsi tenir une conférence intitulée «L'importance de l'étude du dessin» qui suggérait que: «L'adaptation d'une chose à son objet, loin de produire de la laideur, tend vers la beauté et induit également de nouvelles formes. Le problème à résoudre est tout simplement celui-ci: étant donné l'usage et les matériaux dont est fait l'objet, il s'agit de lui trouver une forme superbe. Dans les accessoires les plus communs, les plus grossiers et les plus anciens de l'agriculture, comme une charrue, une faux, ou une faucille, nous trouvons des exemples de courbes simples et cependant magnifiques. Les formes les plus simples et les plus élémentaires, si elles sont bien proportionnées et de contour gracieux, sont les plus plaisantes.»[8]

La diffusion de ce type de raisonnement et quelques déceptions rencontrées par l'industrialisation culminèrent pour certains dans un rejet de la machine et expliquent la naissance du mouvement Arts and Crafts, qui se fit au départ le défenseur de méthodes artisanales de production dans le cadre d'un système corporatiste. Bien que vertueuse dans ses aspirations, cette approche échoua dans son objectif d'offrir aux masses des meubles bien dessinés et de prix abordable. William Morris fut à jamais frustré de ce que l'essentiel de son travail soit surtout apprécié par les classes privilégiées. A quelqu'un qui lui demandait les raisons de sa nervosité alors qu'il travaillait sur l'aménagement intérieur d'une maison appartenant à Sir Louther Bell, il répliqua avec fureur: «C'est parce que je passe ma vie à travailler pour le sale luxe des riches.»[9] Bien que Morris ait reconnu l'échec pratique de ses idées, il a néanmoins apporté

simplicity in design desirable to society's affluent elite.

Charles Voysey, a later proponent of the Arts and Crafts Movement, argued that it was the manufacturers' inappropriate use of the machine and not the machine itself that was to blame for the production of poor quality, excessively embellished objects in the High Victorian style. He believed that if the machine was used responsibly it could provide high-quality furniture at a reasonable cost. Although Voysey did produce furniture such as this, the machine was never wholeheartedly accepted in Britain. Nevertheless, for all its inbuilt contradictions, the Arts and Crafts Movement expanded the debate on design reform and, by doing so, influenced the Glasgow School, the Wiener Werkstätte, the American Arts and Crafts Movement and the architect Frank Lloyd Wright, all of which had an impact on the origins of the Modern Movement.

The Glasgow School can be seen as an offshoot of the Arts and Crafts Movement in Britain for, although it shared many of the same principles, such as truth to materials and revealed construction, it employed different forms. The abstracted, geometric and elongated chairs designed by Charles Rennie Mackintosh in the latter part of his career were highly influential on the Continent, where they were exhibited to great acclaim. Predominantly three-dimensional spatial exercises, the uncanny appearance of these chairs led Mackintosh and his followers to be dubbed "the spook school".[10]

Josef Hoffmann and other Wiener Werkstätte designers also used pared down geometric forms which were customarily pierced with square or rectangular motifs. This abstraction of form into linear planes, as so manifest in Josef Hoffmann's *Sitzmaschine* of c. 1908, was to have some bearing on later designers, especially Gerrit Rietveld. The Deutsche Werkbund, of which Hoffmann was a member, was founded in 1907 in opposition to the perceived backwardness of the prevalent Art Nouveau style with its excessive ornamentation. The members of this group urged "the improvement of industrial products through the combined efforts of artists, industrialists and craftsmen" in an effort to promote a more meaningful mode of design. In 1908, a member of the group, Adolf Loos, wrote a seminal paper entitled, "Ornament und Verbrechen" ("Ornament and Crime") which asserted the notion that the inordinate use of applied decoration could lead to the debasing of society and ultimately to crime. Later, in 1924, the Werkbund published

zung, die Massen mit gut gestalteten und erschwinglichen Möbeln zu versorgen. William Morris war sehr bald zutiefst über die Tatsache enttäuscht, daß der größte Teil seiner Unternehmung durch eine private Klientel aufrechterhalten wurde, die zur privilegierten Klasse gehörte. Als er gefragt wurde, warum er sich in einer so aufgewühlten Verfassung befände, während er mit der Innenausstattung eines Hauses beschäftigt war, das sich im Besitz von Sir Louther Bell befand, antwortete Morris grimmig: »Das kommt daher, weil ich mein Leben damit verbringe, zum saumäßigen Luxus der Reichen beizutragen.«[9] Obwohl Morris erkennen mußte, daß seine Ideologie in der Praxis scheitern mußte, leistete er sehr wohl einen bedeutenden Beitrag zur Grundlegung des Modernismus, vor allem hinsichtlich seiner Gestaltungsprinzipien, die auf einer reduktionistischen Ästhetik basierten. Seine Förderung volkstümlicher, regionaler Formen und handwerklicher Techniken bewirkte, daß Strenge und Einfachheit der Gestaltung auch für die wohlhabende Gesellschaftsschicht zu einem wünschenswerten Prinzip wurden.

Charles Voysey, ein späterer Förderer des »Arts and Crafts Movement«, gab zu bedenken, daß es an dem unangemessenen Umgang der Hersteller mit den Maschinen läge und nicht an der Maschine selbst, die also nicht für die schlechte Qualität und exzessiv verzierte Objekte im hochviktorianischen Stil verantwortlich gemacht werden könnte. Er war überzeugt, daß die Maschine, wenn sie verantwortungsvoll eingesetzt würde, qualitativ hochwertige Möbel zu angemessenen Preisen produzieren könnte. Obwohl Voysey seine Möbel unter dieser Voraussetzung herstellte, wurde die Maschinenproduktion in England niemals mehr voll akzeptiert. Trotz all seiner Widersprüchlichkeit gelang es dem »Arts and Crafts Movement«, die Debatte über die Design-Reform über ihre Grenzen hinaus auszudehnen; sie beeinflußte die Glasgow School, die Wiener Werkstätte, das amerikanische »Arts and Crafts Movement« und den Architekten Frank Lloyd Wright, die alle einen wichtigen Beitrag zur Entstehung des »Modern Movement« geleistet haben.

Die Glasgow School kann als ein Ableger des »Arts and Crafts Movement« in Großbritannien angesehen werden; sie machte sich viele Gestaltungsprinzipien zu eigen, etwa die materialgerechte Verarbeitung und die Offenlegung der Konstruktion, sie bediente sich dabei aber unterschiedlicher Formen. Die abstrakten, geometrischen und langgestreckten Stühle, die Charles Rennie Mackintosh in der

une contribution significative au Modernisme à travers sa recherche d'une esthétique épurée. Par ailleurs, la promotion des formes vernaculaires et des techniques artisanales sensibilisèrent l'élite aisée à l'authenticité et la simplicité du design.

Charles Voysey, défenseur plus tardif du mouvement Arts and Crafts soutint quant à lui que c'était l'utilisation inappropriée de la machine pour produire – mal – des objets excessivement décorés dans le goût victorien et non la machine elle-même qui était à blâmer. Il pensait qu'utilisée de façon responsable, elle pouvait produire des meubles de haute qualité à faible coût. Bien que Voysey ait réussi à produire des meubles dans cet esprit, la machine ne fut jamais vraiment bien acceptée en Grande-Bretagne. En dépit de ses contradictions internes, le mouvement réussit cependant à diffuser le débat sur la réforme du design et, ce faisant, influença l'Ecole de Glasgow, les Wiener Werkstätte, le mouvement américain Arts and Crafts et l'architecte Frank Lloyd Wright, qui tous jouèrent un rôle important dans les origines du mouvement moderniste.

L'Ecole de Glasgow peut être considérée comme une branche des Arts and Crafts britanniques même si, bien que ces deux mouvements aient partagé de nombreux principes dont la vérité des matériaux et la mise en évidence de la construction, elle suivit des chemins différents. Les chaises «abstraites», géométriques et élongées que Charles Rennie Mackintosh dessina dans la dernière partie de sa carrière eurent beaucoup d'influence sur le continent où elles furent exposées. Exercices de style en trois dimensions, leur apparence étrange fit que l'on qualifia vite Mackintosh et ses suiveurs d'«école des fantômes».[10]

Josef Hoffmann et d'autres designers des Wiener Werkstätte utilisèrent également des formes géométriques épurées, ajourées de motifs rectangulaires ou carrés. Ce traitement de la forme selon des plans rectilignes, si manifeste dans la *Sitzmaschine* d'Hoffmann (vers 1908) devait avoir une certaine influence sur des designers ultérieurs, en particulier Gerrit Rietveld. Le Deutsche Werkbund, dont Hoffmann était membre, fut fondé en 1907 par opposition au caractère considéré comme rétrograde d'un Art nouveau surdécoré alors au sommet de sa gloire. Les membre de ce groupe appelaient de leurs vœux «l'amélioration des produits industriels grâce aux efforts combinés d'artistes, d'industriels et d'artisans» pour tenter de promouvoir un mode de design plus significant. En 1908, Adolf Loos, membre du groupe, écrivit un article remarqué: 19

Frank Lloyd Wright:
Chair designed for Midway
Gardens, 1914

Stuhl, entworfen für Midway
Gardens, 1914

*Chaise dessinée pour Midway
Gardens, 1914*

Courtesy Cassina, Milan

Gerrit Rietveld:
Beugelstoel, 1927

Courtesy Fischer Fine Art Ltd., London

Spätphase seines Schaffens entworfen
hat, haben einen starken Einfluß auf den
Kontinent ausgeübt, wo sie unter großem
Beifall ausgestellt wurden. Diese Stühle
sind vor allem dreidimensionale Raum-
experimente, das heißt Umsetzungen von
Mackintoshs räumlichen Vorstellungen,
und ihr geradezu unheimliches Aussehen
hat dazu geführt, daß er und seine Anhän-
ger den Spitznamen »Die Spukschule«
erhielten.[10]

Josef Hoffmann und andere Designer
der Wiener Werkstätte benutzten ebenfalls beschnittene geometrische Formen,
die meist mit quadratischen oder recht-
eckigen Motiven durchsetzt waren. Diese
Abstrahierung der Form in linear geglie-
derte Flächen, wie sie bei Josef Hoffmanns
Sitzmaschine von ca. 1908 zu sehen ist,
sollte einige Auswirkung auf spätere Designer haben, vor allem auf Gerrit Rietveld.
Im Jahre 1907 wurde der Deutsche Werkbund gegründet, in dem Hoffmann Mitglied war. Die Gründung erfolgte in er-
klärter Opposition zu den als rückwärts
gewandt und veraltet empfundenen, aber
dennoch vorherrschenden Stilrichtungen
der Art Nouveau und des Jugendstils, die
sich exzessiver Ornamentierung bedienten.
Die Mitglieder dieses Bundes drangen auf
»die Verbesserung von Industrieprodukten
durch die vereinten Anstrengungen von
Künstlern, Industriellen und Handwerkern«
und setzten sich zum Ziel, dem Design
eine ernsthaftere Bedeutung beizumessen
und sich mehr auf die wesentlichen Elemente zu konzentrieren. 1908 verfaßte
Adolf Loos, Mitglied der Gruppe, ein
Grundsatzpapier mit dem Titel »Ornament
und Verbrechen«, in dem er die Behaup-
tung aufstellte, daß der wuchernde Gebrauch von dekorativen Elementen zum
Verderben der Gesellschaft und schließlich sogar zum Verbrechen führen könnte.
1924 veröffentlichte der Werkbund die
Schrift »Form ohne Ornament«, in der die
Illustrationen die Vorzüge eines Industriedesigns vorführten, das ausschließlich auf
Funktionalität basierte.

Die Architektur und das von Frank
Lloyd Wright entworfene Mobiliar basierten ebenfalls auf einfachen, geradlinigen
geometrischen Formen. Seine Vorliebe für
vollständig vereinheitlichtes Design sollte
auch in den späteren Arbeiten von Charles
Eames und Eero Saarinen von vorrangiger
Bedeutung werden. Wahrscheinlich von
noch größerer Bedeutung ist Wrights Pio-
nierarbeit für ein einheitliches Design im
Hinblick auf George Nelson, auf den er
einen entscheidenden Einfluß bei der Entwicklung integrierter Möbelsysteme für
den Wohnraum und den Arbeitsplatz
ausübte.

«Ornament und Verbrechen» (Ornementation et crime) dans lequel il affirmait que le
recours désordonné à une décoration arti-
ficielle pouvait mener à la désagrégation
de la société et, en dernier recours, au
crime. Plus tard, en 1924, le Werkbund
publia «Form ohne Ornament» (Forme
sans ornementation) dans lequel les illustrations démontraient les vertus d'un design industriel essentiellement fondé sur
la fonction.

L'architecture et le mobilier de Frank
Lloyd Wright reposaient également sur
une géométrie simple et rectiligne. Sa
préférence pour une conception globale-
ment unificatrice devait être de première
importance pour les travaux ultérieurs de
Charles Eames et d'Eero Saarinen. Mais
peut-être plus remarquable encore est
l'exploration par Wright de cette approche
globalisante du design qui se retrouvera
dans le concept de George Nelson de
systèmes de mobilier intégré pour la maison et les lieux de travail.

Le *fauteuil rouge-bleu* de Gerrit
Rietveld (1917/18) est généralement considéré comme le premier siège vraiment
moderne. Bien que Rietveld n'ait pas fait
appel à de nouveaux matériaux ou de nouvelles techniques dans sa conception, il
ouvrit la porte à une nouvelle réflexion sur
la façon dont un siège pouvait être conçu.
Avec ses plans géométriques nettement
marqués, le *fauteuil rouge-bleu* remettait
en question le besoin traditionnel de ressorts et de rembourrage. Ce remarquable
dessin, qui brisait tant de règles établies,
contestait avant tout le recours à une di-
versité de matériaux. L'utilisation volontaire
de panneaux de bois de taille standardisée
et la simplicité de l'assemblage étaient
révolutionnaires dans le climat de l'époque
où les fabricants se faisaient une gloire de
leurs techniques artisanales. Il est important de noter que sa facilité de construction le rendait susceptible d'une production à grande échelle. Cependant, son
esthétique était trop avant-gardiste pour
plaire à un vaste public. Son dessin suggérait qu'un fauteuil ne devait pas forcément posséder le «poids» matériel et visuel
associé au luxe et au coût élevé des
meubles traditionnels. Après avoir réalisé
un premier modèle en frêne naturel, Rietveld décida de peindre le suivant pour la
maison Schröder-Schrader (1924). Le
siège et le dossier furent rouge et bleu, la
coupe des extrémités en jaune et la structure en noir. Il plaça ensuite le siège sur un
sol noir et contre un mur noir pour donner
l'impression que les parties siège et dossier flottaient dans l'espace. Cette recherche d'une plus grande transparence
structurelle allait devenir l'un des signes

"Form ohne Ornament" ("Form without Ornament"), in which illustrations demonstrated the virtues of industrial designs based solely on function.

The architecture and furniture of Frank Lloyd Wright was also based on simple, rectilinear geometry. His preference for unified design was to be of primary significance to the later work of Charles Eames and Eero Saarinen. Perhaps even more importantly, however, Wright's pioneering approach to design influenced George Nelson's concept of integrated furniture systems for the home and the workplace.

The Red-and-blue-chair designed by Gerrit Rietveld in 1917/18 is generally regarded as the first truly Modern chair. Although Rietveld did not incorporate new materials or construction techniques in the chair's design, he gave rise to a new insight into how a chair could be conceived – with its simple geometric planes the Red-and-blue-chair questioned the need for traditional springing and upholstery. This remarkable design, which broke all pre-existing rules, essentially contested the use of anything but a minimum of materials. The intentional use of roughly cut wood of standard sizes and the simplistic joining of elements were revolutionary in a climate in which mainstream manufacturers prided themselves on their conventional craft-based techniques. Importantly, the ease of its construction made it viable for full-scale mass-production. However, its aesthetics were too avant-garde for popular appeal. The design suggested that a chair did not have to possess the visual and material weight that associated traditional furniture with luxury and high cost. Initially, the chair was constructed of natural beech, and later, in 1924, for the interior of the Schröder-Schrader house, Rietveld painted the seat and back blue and red, and the cut ends yellow, while staining the supporting structure black. He then placed the chair on a black floor and against a black wall to create the impression that the seat and back sections were floating in air. This quest for a greater structural transparency was to become one of the central endeavours of Modernism. The date of the Red-and-blue-chair is highly significant, for it was "a natural turning point in modern history. It was a moment at which – after cubism, abstraction, Dada – art could never be the same again; at which – after the massive displacements of the First World War – society could never be the same again; at which – after the terrible destruction of economic means – the techniques of architecture and the objectives of industrial design could never be the same again."[11]

Der von Gerrit Rietveld 1917/18 entworfene Rot-Blau-Stuhl wird allgemein als der erste wirklich moderne Stuhl angesehen. Obwohl Rietveld bei seinem Entwurf keine neuen Materialien oder Konstruktionstechniken angewandt hat, eröffnete er mit diesem Modell neue Einsichten für die Gestaltung von Stühlen – mit seinen einfachen geometrischen Flächen stellte der Rot-Blau-Stuhl die Notwendigkeit traditioneller Federung und Polsterung grundsätzlich in Frage. Dieser bemerkenswerte Entwurf, der mit allen bestehenden Regeln brach, sollte vor allem beweisen, daß man mit einem Minimum an Material auskommen konnte. Die Verwendung von grob zugeschnittenem Holz in standardisierter Größe und die höchst einfache Verbindung der Elemente galten als revolutionär, denn bis dahin herrschte ein Klima, in dem die weithin anerkannten Hersteller ihre konventionellen, vom Handwerk entlehnten Techniken priesen. Es ist von besonderer Bedeutung, daß die einfache Konstruktion dieses Stuhls ihn bestens geeignet machte für eine voll technisierte Massenproduktion. Doch seine Ästhetik war zu avantgardistisch für den allgemeinen Geschmack. Das Design brachte zum Ausdruck, daß ein Stuhl nicht das optische und materielle Gewicht in Anspruch zu nehmen habe, das vor allem solche traditionellen Möbelstücke für sich beanspruchen – oder das man ihnen beimißt – die gemeinhin mit Luxus und hohen Preisen in Verbindung gebracht werden. Ursprünglich war der Stuhl aus naturbelassenem Buchenholz gebaut, doch später, im Jahre 1924, malte Rietveld für die Innenausstattung des Schröder-Schrader-Hauses Sitz und Lehne blau und rot an, die abgeschnittenen Enden gelb und die tragende Struktur schwarz. Er stellte den Stuhl auf einen schwarzen Fußboden und vor eine schwarze Wand, um den Eindruck zu erwecken, daß Sitz und Lehne in der Luft schwebten. Dieses Bemühen um eine größere Transparenz der Konstruktion sollte zu einem zentralen Anliegen des Modernismus werden. Der Zeitpunkt, zu dem der Rot-Blau-Stuhl entstand, ist höchst bezeichnend, denn es war »ein natürlicher Wendepunkt in der modernen Zeitgeschichte. Es war ein Zeitpunkt, zu dem die Kunst – nach Kubismus, reiner Abstraktion und Dada – nicht mehr das sein konnte, was sie gewesen war; ein Moment, in dem auch die Gesellschaft – nach den massiven Umwälzungen durch den Ersten Weltkrieg – nicht mehr dieselbe bleiben konnte; ein Zeitpunkt, zu dem – nach der entsetzlichen Zerstörung der wirtschaftlichen Mittel – die Technik und die Architektur und die Zielsetzungen des

Mart Stam:

Side chair and table, 1926/27

Stuhl und Tisch, 1926/27

Chaise et table, 1926/27

*from Werner Gräff, "Innenräume",
Verlag Dr. Fr. Wedekind, Stuttgart, 1928*

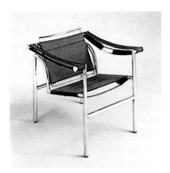

Le Corbusier:

Basculant chair,
Model No. B301, c. 1929

Basculant-Stuhl,
Modell Nr. B301, um 1929

Chaise *Basculant*,
modéle n°. B301, vers 1929

Courtesy Sotheby's, New York

21

This culture of turmoil demanded new solutions to existing problems but did not offer significant industrial innovation, unlike the period following the Second World War. Instead, progress had to be made ideologically rather than technically. The *Red-and-blue-chair* was shown at a general exhibition at the Bauhaus in 1923, and as "a three-dimensional realization of the philosophy of the De Stijl movement"[12] it was the first chair to express a radical Modern ideology. The design disseminated the movement's vision of utopia, the basis of which was founded in Dutch puritanism. The members of De Stijl advocated the purification of art and design through abstracted cubism, or as Piet Mondrian described it, Neo-Plasticism, which in its search for honesty and beauty would bring harmony and enlightenment to humanity.

Although the potential mass-production of modern furniture through the application of new technology was first explored at the Bauhaus, the founding fathers of the Modern Movement, such as Ludwig Mies van der Rohe and Marcel Breuer, still primarily viewed furniture as integral to unified architectural schemes. Their designs, such as the *Barcelona chair* of 1929 and the *Wassily chair* of 1925, were initially created within the context of specific interior plans – the German Pavilion at the Barcelona International Exhibition of 1929 and the painter Wassily Kandinsky's staff accommodation at the Dessau Bauhaus. Ironically, chair designs such as these, which very much appear to be machine-made, were labour-intensive to produce and, therefore, costly to manufacture – an aspect that ran counter to Bauhaus philosophy. It was realized that the true mass-production of democratic Modern furniture would only be possible if a form of mechanized standardization was adopted. However, it was not until the post-World War II years that it was economically or technically feasible to achieve this on a wide scale.

Modern architecture and design that addressed the pressing requirement for public housing and low-cost furnishings was the central theme explored at the Deutsche Werkbund exhibition, "Die Wohnung" ("The Dwelling") held at the Weissenhofsiedlung in 1927. A year earlier, all the architects who were to take part in the exhibition met in Stuttgart. At this gathering of kindred spirits, the Dutch architect Mart Stam presented drawings of a prototype chair that incorporated the architectural cantilever principle. Visually simpler while structurally and materially more unified than those with four legs, Stam's chair

Industriedesigns nicht mehr dieselben sein konnten«.[11] In dieser Zeit der Umwälzungen verlangten Kunst und Kultur nach neuen Lösungen für die bestehenden Probleme, doch sie bewirkten keine nennenswerten industriellen Neuerungen, wie es in der Zeit nach dem Zweiten Weltkrieg der Fall war. Jetzt mußte der Fortschritt eher auf ideologischer als auf technischer Ebene stattfinden. Der *Rot-Blau-Stuhl* wurde 1923 auf einer Ausstellung im Bauhaus gezeigt; als »eine dreidimensionale Realisierung der Philosophie der De-Stijl-Bewegung«[12] war er der erste Stuhl, der auf radikale Weise die Ideologie der Modernität zum Ausdruck brachte. Der Stuhlentwurf propagierte die utopische Vision der Bewegung, die ihre Wurzeln im niederländischen Puritanismus hatte. Die Mitglieder von De Stijl setzten sich für die Reinheit von Kunst und Design ein und entwickelten aufgrund dieser Haltung einen abstrakten Kubismus, oder, wie Piet Mondrian es nannte, einen Neoplastizismus, der in seinem Streben nach Strenge und Schönheit der Menschheit Harmonie und Klarheit bringen sollte.

Es war am Bauhaus, wo die Möglichkeit der Massenproduktion moderner Möbel durch die Anwendung neuer Technologien zuerst erforscht wurde; doch es waren die Gründungsväter der Moderne wie Ludwig Mies van der Rohe und Marcel Breuer, die als erste das Mobiliar als einen integralen Bestandteil einer einheitlichen architektonischen Planung ansahen. Ihre Stuhlentwürfe, etwa der *Barcelona-Stuhl* von 1929 und der *Wassily-Stuhl* von 1925, waren ursprünglich als Elemente bestimmter innenarchitektonischer Konzeptionen geplant – der eine für den deutschen Pavillon auf der Weltausstellung von 1929 in Barcelona, der andere für die Mitarbeiterrunde des Malers Wassily Kandinsky am Dessauer Bauhaus. Ironischerweise sind Stuhlentwürfe wie diese, die so aussehen, als seien sie maschinell gefertigt, sehr arbeitsintensiv in der Herstellung und verursachen daher hohe Kosten – ein Gesichtspunkt, der der Bauhausphilosophie zuwiderlief. Man war sich darüber im klaren, daß eine sinnvolle Massenproduktion moderner Möbel nur dann möglich wäre, wenn eine Form von mechanisierter Standardproduktion erreicht werden könnte. Es dauerte jedoch noch bis in die Jahre nach dem Zweiten Weltkrieg, bis es ökonomisch und technisch möglich war, dies in größerem Umfang zu verwirklichen.

Moderne Architektur und Design, die speziell auf die drängenden Bedürfnisse des sozialen Wohnungsbaus und kostengünstiger Möbel ausgerichtet waren,

distinctifs du Modernisme. La date de création du *fauteuil rouge-bleu* est très significative car elle marque «une inflexion naturelle de l'histoire moderne. Ce fut le moment – avec le cubisme, l'abstraction pure, Dada – après lequel l'art ne pouvait plus jamais être le même; après lequel, si l'on pense aux grands mouvements de population de la Première Guerre mondiale, la société n'allait plus jamais être la même, et, après les terribles destructions du conflit, les techniques de l'architecture et les objectifs du design industriel n'allaient plus jamais être les mêmes».[11] Cette culture de crise réclamait de nouvelles solutions mais ne proposait pas d'innovations industrielles significatives, à la différence de l'après-Seconde Guerre mondiale. Le progrès allait emprunter des voies idéologiques plutôt que techniques. Le *fauteuil rouge-bleu* fut présenté lors d'une grande exposition du Bauhaus en 1923. Matérialisation en trois dimensions de la philosophie du mouvement De Stijl[12], il fut le premier à exprimer une idéologie radicalement moderne. Le design fit connaître la vision utopique de ce mouvement qui prenait ses racines dans le puritanisme néerlandais. Les membres de De Stijl réclamaient la purification de l'art et du design grâce au cubisme abstrait ou, comme le déclara Piet Mondrian, le néo-plasticisme qui allait apporter l'harmonie et illuminer l'humanité à travers sa recherche de la vérité et de la beauté.

Bien que la problématique de la production de meubles en série grâce aux progrès de la technique ait été initialement explorée par le Bauhaus, les pères fondateurs du mouvement moderniste, comme Ludwig Mies van der Rohe et Marcel Breuer, considéraient encore essentiellement le mobilier comme part intégrante de leurs projets architecturaux pris dans leur globalité. La chauffeuse *Barcelona* de 1929 et le fauteuil *Wassily* de 1925 furent d'abord créés pour des aménagements intérieurs spécifiques, en l'occurrence le pavillon allemand de la Foire Internationale de Barcelone de 1929 et les bureaux de Wassily Kandinsky au Bauhaus de Dessau. Ironiquement, ces projets semblent devoir beaucoup à la machine, alors qu'ils demandaient de nombreuses heures de travail augmentant considérablement leur prix et les éloignant de ce fait de la philosophie du Bauhaus. On comprit alors qu'une véritable production en série de mobilier moderne démocratique ne pouvait être possible que si l'on adoptait une forme de standardisation autorisant la mécanisation. Mais pourtant ce ne fut pas avant la fin de la Seconde Guerre mondiale qu'il fut économiquement ou techniquement

was the first of its kind. Such was the magnitude of this breakthrough in design that its significance is comparable in sculpture to Michelangelo's realization of the first full unsupported contraposto since Antiquity in his "David".

At the Weissenhof exhibition, Stam first displayed his cantilevered side chair which was being produced by the L.&C. Arnold company in rigid cast tubular steel, reinforced with metal rods. Controversially, Ludwig Mies van der Rohe also exhibited a cantilevered chair, the *Model No. MR10*, a refined version of Stam's precedent which later became known as the Weissenhof chair. The more elegant *MR10* was constructed of resilient bent tubular steel which allowed a greater degree of flexibility, affording the sitter comfort without the need of springing or upholstery. A year later, Marcel Breuer produced two further cantilevered chairs, the *Model No. B32*, known as the *Cesca* (named after his daughter, Francesca) and the *Model No. B33*, which was highly derivative of Stam's earlier design. Reputedly inspired by the handlebars of his newly purchased Adler bicycle, it was Breuer who had first incorporated resilient tubular steel in the design of chairs with his *Model No. B3 Wassily chair* of 1925. With this landmark design, Breuer paid homage to the linearity and reductivist aesthetics of Gerrit Rietveld's earlier *Red-and-blue-chair*.

Even if cost-efficient industrial mechanisms had been in place to facilitate the high-volume manufacture of Modernist furniture, it is highly debatable whether the masses for whom these designs were intended would have embraced them with widespread enthusiasm. Tubular metal, for instance, was still generally associated with industry and did not, therefore, mesh with the working classes' bourgeois aspirations. The Modern designs of the Bauhaus were not only too avant-garde for industrial production, but also too forward-looking and aesthetically challenging for widespread public acceptance. The philosophical morality promoted by the Bauhaus, however, formed the bedrock on which Modernism would grow into an international movement. In the 1930s, several important members of the Bauhaus emigrated from Germany to the United States of America via Britain, disseminating Modernist ideology and widely influencing the next generation of architects and designers.

A less stringent form of geometric rationalism was adopted by the pioneers of the so-called "International Style" in France – Le Corbusier, Pierre Jeanneret and Charlotte Perriand. These designers

bildeten das zentrale Thema auf der Ausstellung »Die Wohnung«, die der Deutsche Werkbund 1927 in der Weißenhof-Siedlung ausrichtete. Ein Jahr zuvor hatten sich alle Architekten, die an dieser Ausstellung teilnehmen sollten, in Stuttgart getroffen. Bei dieser Zusammenkunft von Gleichgesinnten präsentierte der niederländische Architekt Mart Stam Zeichnungen von einem Stuhlprototypen, der auf dem architektonischen Prinzip der freitragenden Fläche beruhte. Stams Stuhl wirkte optisch einfacher als herkömmliche Stühle mit vier Beinen, und gleichzeitig wirkte er einheitlicher in Konstruktion und Material; es war der erste Stuhl in dieser Art. Dieser Entwurf bedeutete für das Design einen derart entscheidenden Durchbruch, daß er in seiner Bedeutung zu vergleichen ist mit Michelangelos Verwirklichung der ersten vollkommen ungestützten Kontrapost-Skulptur seit der Antike, mit seinem »David«.

Auf der Weißenhof-Ausstellung führte Stam seinen Stuhl mit freitragender Sitzfläche zum erstenmal vor; er wurde von der Firma L. & C. Arnold aus unelastischem Stahlrohr, das mit Metallstäben verstärkt war, hergestellt. Als Gegenentwurf stellte auch Ludwig Mies van der Rohe einen freitragenden Stuhl aus, das *Modell Nr. MR10*, eine veredelte Version von Stams Vorläufer, der später als der *Weißenhof-Stuhl* bekannt wurde. Der eleganter wirkende *MR 10* war aus federndem, gebogenem Stahlrohr gebaut, das eine stärkere Biegsamkeit gestattete und den Sitzkomfort erhöhte, ohne daß eine Federung oder Polsterung notwendig war. Ein Jahr später produzierte Marcel Breuer zwei weitere freitragende Stühle, das *Modell Nr. B32*, das als *Cesca* (benannt nach seiner Tochter Francesca) bekannt ist, und das *Modell Nr. B33*, das deutlich aus Stams früherem Entwurf abgeleitet war. Breuer war angeblich durch die Lenkstange seines neuerworbenen Adler-Fahrrades dazu angeregt worden, als erster federndes Stahlrohr für seine Stuhlentwürfe zu verwenden, und so entwickelte er 1925 sein *Modell Nr. B3 Wassily*. Dieser Stuhl bedeutete einen Markstein im Design. Breuer erwies damit seine Reverenz an die Linearität und reduktionistische Ästhetik von Gerrit Rietvelds früherem *Rot-Blau-Stuhl*.

Selbst wenn kostengünstige industrielle Fertigungsverfahren zur Verfügung gestanden hätten, um die aufwendige Herstellung moderner Möbel zu erleichtern, so ist es doch höchst fraglich, ob die Massen, für die diese Entwürfe gedacht waren, sie mit der entsprechenden Begeisterung aufgenommen hätten. Stahlrohr wurde

possible d'y arriver, du moins à grande échelle.

L'architecture et le design modernes, qui répondaient aux besoins pressants du public en logements et en mobilier économiques, furent le thème central de l'exposition du Deutsche Werkbund «Die Wohnung», (l'habitation) qui se tint à la cité de Weissenhof en 1927. Un an plus tôt, tous les architectes qui devaient y prendre part se rencontrèrent à Stuttgart. A cette réunion, le Néerlandais Mart Stam montra le dessin d'un prototype de siège en porte-à-faux. D'aspect et de structure plus simples que les modèles classiques à quatre pieds et faisant appel à un nombre de matériaux réduit, cette chaise était la première de ce type. Telle fut l'importance de cette percée du design que l'on peut comparer sa signification à la sculpture du David de Michel-Ange, premier «contraposto» sans aucun soutien.

A l'exposition de Weissenhof, Stam présenta donc sa chaise en porte-à-faux, produite par la L.& C. Arnold Company en tubes de fonte d'acier rigide renforcés de tiges de métal. Ludwig Mies van der Rohe exposa également son *modèle n° MR10*, une version raffinée de celui de Stam et qui prit plus tard le nom de Weissenhof. Plus élégant, le *MR10*, était construit en tube d'acier cintré flexible, qui permettait davantage de souplesse et offrait à la personne assise un réel confort malgré l'absence totale de ressorts ou de rembourrage. Un an plus tard, Marcel Breuer sortit deux autres sièges en porte-à-faux, le *modèle n° B32*, connu sous le nom de Cesca (d'après le prénom de sa fille, Francesca) et le *modèle n° B33*, très directement dérivés du modèle initial de Stam. Inspiré, d'après ce que l'on disait, par le guidon de son nouveau vélo Adler, Breuer avait été le premier à se servir de tube d'acier flexible pour la fabrication d'un siège, dès son *modèle n° B3 Wassily* en 1925. A travers cette création d'importance historique, Breuer rendait hommage à la linéarité et au minimalisme du *fauteuil rouge-bleu* de Rietveld.

Même si la structure industrielle capable de fabriquer les meubles modernistes en grande série avait été en place, on peut se demander si les masses auxquelles ces créations étaient destinées les auraient adoptées avec enthousiasme. Le tube de métal, par exemple, rappelait le plus souvent l'industrie et s'associait mal, pour cette raison, aux aspirations bourgeoises des classes travailleuses. Les projets modernistes du Bauhaus n'étaient pas seulement trop avant-gardistes pour la production industrielle de l'époque mais également trop avancés et esthétiquement trop

collaborated on many projects, including several chair designs such as the *Grand Confort* and the *Model No. 2072 chaise longue*. Like their German counterparts, they used a combination of tubular metal and leather in their designs. However, their use of these materials was less utilitarian in nature. Influenced by the contemporary Art Deco style, these designs bear the unmistakable hallmark of Parisian chic. Nevertheless, the interior schemes and chair designs of Le Corbusier, Jeanneret and Perriand must be considered Modern, for they encapsulate many of the same principles as their Bauhaus counterparts yet in a less doctrinaire way. By associating luxury and style with industrial materials, the Modern chair became more desirable to the affluent and increasingly sophisticated furniture-buying public.

Unlike those at the Bauhaus, Scandinavian designers such as Alvar Aalto and, slightly later, Bruno Mathsson relied on the use of natural woods and other organic materials in their approach to Modernism. Aalto made a significant contribution to the history of the Modern chair with his bent laminated wood *Paimio chair* of 1931/32. Where the design required greater pliancy, such as in the scrolls of the seat and back, Aalto removed several layers of veneer, thereby increasing the material's malleability. The Scandinavian's gentler and more tactile form of rationalism was well received in America and Britain during the 1930s and 1940s.

Importantly, the prominent Finnish architect, Eliel Saarinen emigrated to the United States in 1923 and a year later took up a visiting professorship at the University of Michigan – one of the main furniture-producing regions in America. In 1927, the Cranbrook Foundation was established by the philanthropist and newspaper proprietor, George G. Booth, and in 1932, Eliel Saarinen became the director of the Cranbrook Academy of Arts. As the democratic counterpart to the Bauhaus, Cranbrook was founded with the intention of bringing unity to the arts. Both institutions operated studios and workshops dedicated to the teaching of the various disciplines within the fine and applied arts and an exchange of ideas between these fields of study was strongly promoted. The Cranbrook Academy of Arts was the pre-eminent design institute in America during the inter-war years, with many of its alumni and staff becoming leaders in their fields of design and architecture. The significance of Eliel Saarinen's directorship of Cranbrook cannot be overstated, for he inculcated the principles of Modernism to a small but extremely

immer noch weitgehend als Material zur industriellen Verarbeitung angesehen und ließ sich daher kaum mit den bürgerlichen Sehnsüchten der arbeitenden Klasse in Einklang bringen. Das moderne Design des Bauhauses war nicht nur zu avantgardistisch für die industrielle Produktion, sondern auch zu sehr in die Zukunft gerichtet; außerdem bedeutete es ästhetisch eine zu große Herausforderung für die breite Akzeptanz des Publikums. Doch die moralischen Grundlagen einer Weltanschauung, die vom Bauhaus propagiert wurde, bildeten das Fundament, auf dem der Modernismus sich zu einer internationalen Bewegung auswachsen sollte. In den 30er Jahren emigrierten viele bedeutende Mitglieder des Bauhauses über England in die Vereinigten Staaten und verbreiteten ihre Ideologie der Moderne. Sie übten einen weitreichenden Einfluß auf die folgende Generation von Architekten und Designern aus.

Eine weniger stringente Form des geometrischen Rationalismus wurde von den Pionieren des sogenannten »internationalen Stils« in Frankreich entwickelt; zu ihnen gehörten Le Corbusier, Pierre Jeanneret und Charlotte Perriand. Diese Architekten und Designer arbeiteten bei vielen Projekten zusammen und entwarfen mehrere Stühle, etwa den *Grand Confort* und das *Modell Nr. 2072 Chaise Longue*. Wie ihre deutschen Kollegen verwendeten sie in ihren Entwürfen eine Kombination aus Metallrohr und Leder. Jedoch war die Verwendung dieser Materialien bei ihnen weniger zweckgebunden. Sie unterlagen noch immer den Einflüssen des zeitgenössischen Art-Déco-Stils, und daher weisen diese Entwürfe unverkennbar die Merkmale des pariserischen Chics auf. Dennoch kann man die Innenausstattungen und Stuhlentwürfe von Le Corbusier, Jeanneret und Perriand als modern bezeichnen, denn sie beruhen in vieler Hinsicht auf denselben Prinzipien, denen auch ihre Bauhaus-Kollegen folgten, wenn auch in der französischen Variante auf weniger doktrinäre Weise. Indem sie bei ihren Entwürfen Luxus und Stil mit Industriematerial wie etwa Stahlrohr in Verbindung brachten, wurde der moderne Stuhl auch für das wohlhabende und zunehmend anspruchsvollere Publikum zum begehrenswerten Kaufobjekt.

Im Unterschied zu den Mitgliedern des Bauhauses wandten sich skandinavische Designer wie Alvar Aalto und, etwas später, Bruno Mathsson, bei ihrer Auseinandersetzung mit dem Modernismus natürlichen Materialien zu, vor allem der Verwendung von Naturhölzern. Aalto leistete mit seinem *Paimio-Stuhl* von 1931/32 aus

Charles & Ray Eames:

Plywood lounge chair (prototype), 1946

Sessel aus Schichtholz (Prototyp), 1946

Fauteuil en bois lamellé (prototype), 1946

Courtesy Eames Office, Venice, California

gebogenem Schichtholz einen wichtigen Beitrag zur Geschichte des modernen Stuhls. An den Stellen, wo die Konstruktion größere Biegsamkeit erforderte, etwa in den Vertiefungen von Sitz und Rückenlehne, entfernte Aalto mehrere Schichten des Furniers und erhöhte so die Geschmeidigkeit des Materials. Die weichere und taktilere Spielart des skandinavischen Rationalismus wurde in den 30er und 40er Jahren in Amerika und England sehr gut aufgenommen. Ein folgenreiches Ereignis war die Emigration des prominenten finnischen Architekten Eliel Saarinen im Jahre 1923 in die Vereinigten Staaten; ein Jahr später übernahm er eine Gastprofessur an der Universität von Michigan – in einer der wichtigsten möbelproduzierenden Regionen Amerikas.

1927 gründete der Zeitungsverleger und Mäzen George G. Booth die Cranbrook Foundation; im Jahr 1932 wurde Eliel Saarinen Direktor der Cranbrook Kunstakademie. Cranbrook, das man als demokratisches Gegenstück zum Bauhaus bezeichnen kann, wurde mit dem Ziel gegründet, eine Einheit in die Künste zu bringen. Beide Institutionen unterhielten Ateliers und Werkstätten, die dafür bestimmt waren, in den verschiedenen Disziplinen innerhalb der schönen und angewandten Künste zu unterrichten, und es wurde größter Wert darauf gelegt, daß ein Ideenaustausch zwischen diesen beiden Bereichen stattfand. Die Cranbrook Academy of Arts war die beste und einflußreichste Schule für Design in Amerika in den Jahren zwischen den Kriegen, und viele ihrer Studenten und Lehrer wurden die führenden Köpfe in ihren Bereichen von Design und Architektur. Man kann Eliel Saarinens Leistung als Direktor der Cranbrook Academy gar nicht hoch genug einschätzen, denn er vermittelte einer kleinen, äußerst talentierten Gruppe von jungen Männern und Frauen die Prinzipien des Modernismus. Es war diese Generation von Designern, die einige der wichtigsten und beispielhaftesten Neuerungen in die Geschichte des Stuhldesigns einführte: Sie trieb die moralischen Überzeugungen des Modernismus weiter voran und brachte sie in drei Dimensionen in massenhafter Verbreitung zum Ausdruck; die Anwendung künstlerisch anspruchsvoller Technologie blieb dabei oberstes Gebot.

Der Zweite Weltkrieg hatte enorme Auswirkungen auf die Möbelindustrie, vor allem in den Vereinigten Staaten. Da in der Kriegszeit Forschung und Entwicklung in erheblichem Maße in kriegswichtige Produktionsbereiche investiert wurden, vor allem in die Luftfahrtindustrie, hatte dies für die Nachkriegszeit zur Folge, daß

osés pour être acceptés par le grand public. La morale philosophique du Bauhaus, cependant, constituait une base solide sur laquelle le Modernisme allait s'épanouir et devenir un mouvement international. Dans les années 30, plusieurs membres importants du Bauhaus émigrèrent d'Allemagne vers les Etats-Unis en passant par l'Angleterre et diffusèrent l'idéologie moderniste qui allait influencer profondément la génération suivante d'architectes et de designers.

Une forme moins rigoureuse de rationalisme géométrique fut adoptée par les pionniers français du «Style international». Le Corbusier, Pierre Jeanneret et Charlotte Perriand collaborèrent sur de nombreux projets dont plusieurs sièges, le *Grand Confort* et la chaise longue *modèle n° 2072*. Comme leurs homologues allemands, ils utilisaient une association de tubes de métal et de cuir mais dans un esprit moins utilitaire. Influencées par le style Art déco de l'époque, ces créations portent la marque indélébile de l'élégance parisienne. Néanmoins, les projets d'aménagement intérieurs et de sièges de Le Corbusier, Jeanneret et Perriand doivent être considérés comme modernistes, car ils font la synthèse de nombreux principes du Bauhaus quoique d'une façon moins doctrinaire. En mariant le luxe et le style à des assemblages de matériaux industriels comme le tube d'acier, le siège moderne put alors séduire une clientèle aisée qui commença à acheter des meubles de plus en plus sophistiqués.

A la différence de ceux du Bauhaus, les designers scandinaves comme Alvar Aalto et, légèrement plus tard, Bruno Mathsson suscitèrent une approche moderniste différente qui faisait appel au bois et à d'autres matériaux naturels. Aalto apporta une contribution significative à l'histoire du siège moderne avec sa chaise de bois lamellé cintré, la *Paimio* (1931/32). Aux endroits où son dessin réclamait un cintrage techniquement audacieux, comme dans les enroulements du siège et du dossier, Aalto fit enlever plusieurs couches de placage pour augmenter la souplesse du matériau. Cette forme de rationalisme scandinave plus douce et plus tactile fut bien reçue en Amérique et en Grande-Bretagne tout au long des années 30 et 40. Il est important de noter que le grand architecte finlandais Eliel Saarinen émigra vers les Etats-Unis en 1923 et devint, un an plus tard, professeur invité à l'Université du Michigan, l'une des premières régions américaines pour la production de meubles.

En 1927, le propriétaire de journaux et philanthrope George G. Booth créa la

talented group of young men and women. It was this generation of designers who would set some of the most important precedents in the history of chair design by carrying forward the moral certainties of Modernism and expressing them in three dimensions on a mass scale through the application of state-of-the-art technology.

The Second World War had an enormous impact on the furniture industry, particularly in the United States. The dramatic increase in wartime research and development in other manufacturing fields, especially the aircraft industry, meant that after the war furniture designers and manufacturers had the opportunity of applying the latest and most efficient technology to the peacetime production of durable products. During this period, the interdisciplinary science of ergonomics, founded by Kaare Klint in 1917, was still in its infancy, with wartime research having been conducted by the military into what was then known as "human engineering".[13] After 1945, designers for the first time were able to quantify data which provided a new insight into the relationship between man and machine. Chairs could adopt forms that were more suited to accommodating the human body. The seat and back of the plywood series of chairs designed by Charles and Ray Eames, for example, were moulded in a way that closely followed the line of the seated body, thus affording a high degree of comfort without the use of padding. During the war, the Eameses' research into the production of low-cost wood laminates and mouldings led to a commission by the US Navy to design and produce leg splints, arm splints and stretchers in moulded plywood. Using their specially developed "Kazam" machines, so named because of the noise they made when operated, the Eameses were the first designers to mould plywood into three-dimensional compound curves – a technical breakthrough that would have enormous implications for chair design.

In postwar America and slightly later in Europe, there was a huge demand for domestic furniture at the same time as much of the Western World was enjoying an unprecedented economic boom. This era was a hopeful and forward-looking period in history, with many designers firmly believing that science and technology could bring about a brave new world. During this period many architect-designers concentrated their talents on the development of innovative furniture rather than on architectural projects. As a consequence, enlightened manufacturing companies, such as Herman Miller and

Möbeldesigner und -hersteller nun die Möglichkeit hatten, die neuesten und wirkungsvollsten Technologien auf die Herstellung bestimmter dauerhafter Produkte für friedliche Zwecke anzuwenden. Zu dieser Zeit steckte die interdisziplinäre Wissenschaft der Ergonomie, die 1917 von Kaare Klint begründet worden war, noch in ihren Kinderschuhen; zumal die Forschungen der Kriegszeit, die von Militärs betrieben wurden, zu dem geführt hatten, was man dann »human engineering« (Menschenmanipulation) nannte.[13] Nach 1945 sahen sich Designer zum erstenmal in der Lage, Daten auszuwerten, die neue Einsichten in die Beziehung zwischen Mensch und Maschine brachten. Das machte es ihnen möglich, Stühle so zu formen, daß sie besser geeignet waren, eine Paßform für den menschlichen Körper zu bilden. Zum Beispiel bei der Serie von Sperrholzstühlen nach Entwürfen von Charles und Ray Eames waren Sitz und Rückenlehne so geformt, daß sie genau den Umrissen des sitzenden Körpers angepaßt waren, so daß sie dem Sitzenden ein hohes Maß an Bequemlichkeit verschafften, ohne daß eine Polsterung erforderlich war. Während des Krieges führte die Forschung der Eames-Brüder im Bereich der kostengünstigen Schichthölzer und Formbretter dazu, daß sie von der US-Marine den Auftrag erhielten, Bein- und Armschienen und Tragbahren aus geformtem Sperrholz zu entwerfen und zu produzieren. Unter Verwendung ihrer speziell entwickelten »Kazam«-Maschinen – ein lautmalerischer Name – formten sie als erste Designer komplexe dreidimensionale Ausbuchtungen in Sperrholz; dies bedeutete einen technischen Durchbruch, der unabsehbare Folgen für das Stuhldesign haben sollte.

Im Amerika der Nachkriegszeit und wenig später auch in Europa bestand eine gewaltige Nachfrage nach Haushalts- und Wohnraummöbeln, denn zugleich erlebte der größte Teil der westlichen Welt einen nie dagewesenen wirtschaftlichen Aufschwung. Diese Ära war eine hoffnungsvolle und vorwärtsgewandte Periode in der Geschichte, und viele Designer glaubten fest daran, daß Wissenschaft und Technik eine schöne neue Welt hervorbringen würden. In dieser Zeit konzentrierten viele Architekten-Designer ihr Talent ganz auf die Entwicklung innovativer Möbel und weniger auf architektonische Entwürfe. Das hatte zur Folge, daß aufgeklärte und weitsichtige Möbelhersteller wie etwa Herman Miller und Knoll International in der Lage waren, einem großen Publikum revolutionäre, kostengünstige und qualitativ hochwertige moderne Möbel anzubieten.

Cranbrook Foundation et, en 1932, Eliel Saarinen devint le directeur de la Cranbrook Academy of Arts. Equivalent démocratique du Bauhaus, Cranbrook fut fondé dans l'intention de militer pour une vision unificatrice dans les arts. Les deux institutions disposaient de même de studios et d'ateliers consacrés à l'enseignement de diverses disciplines et multipliaient les échanges entre les beaux-arts et les arts appliqués. La Cranbrook Academy of Arts fut l'institut de design prééminent de l'Amérique de l'entre-deux-guerres et beaucoup de ses anciens étudiants et de ses animateurs occupèrent une place de premier plan dans leur domaine d'activité. L'importance de la direction d'Eliel Saarinen ne doit pas être négligée, car il inculqua les principes du Modernisme à un groupe d'étudiants et d'étudiantes peu nombreux mais extrêmement talentueux. Ce fut de cette génération de designers qu'allaient sortir certains des modèles qui, en traduisant la philosophie du Modernisme et en particulier la volonté de production à grande échelle et celle de recourir à des technologies d'avant-garde, allaient exercer un rôle fondamental dans l'histoire du siège.

La Seconde Guerre mondiale exerça un impact énorme sur l'industrie du meuble et avant tout aux Etats-Unis. L'important accroissement de la recherche et du développement dans certains domaines d'activités, en particulier l'industrie aéronautique, signifiait qu'après la guerre, les designers et les fabricants de mobilier allaient avoir la possibilité d'appliquer les technologies le plus récentes et les plus efficaces à la production de biens de consommation durables. Par ailleurs, pendant cette période, la science interdisciplinaire de l'ergonomie, fondée par Kaare Klint en 1917, fit des débuts prometteurs à l'occasion de certaines recherches militaires sur ce que l'on appelait alors l'«human engineering».[13] Après 1945, les designers purent pour la première fois disposer de données quantifiables qui leur donnaient une nouvelle vision des relations entre l'homme et la machine. Ceci déboucha sur des formes de sièges mieux adaptées au corps humain. Le siège et le dossier de la série «Contreplaqué» de Charles et Ray Eames, par exemple, furent moulés selon une technique qui suivait au plus près la ligne d'un corps assis, assurant un meilleur degré de confort sans avoir recours au rembourrage. Pendant la guerre, les recherches des Eames dans le domaine de la production économique de lamellés et de moulages de bois furent encouragées par une commande de l'US Navy pour la conception et la fabrication de gouttières

Knoll International, were able to offer the general public revolutionary, low-cost, yet high-quality, Modern furniture.

In the 1950s, through the emergence of a new Scandinavian-influenced approach to Modernism, ergonomics and advanced technology, particularly in the plastics industry, the chair uniquely became more unified in design. Unlike the geometric formalism adhered to by the early Modern Movement, which at best only offered the possibility of structural and material unity, a truly functional unification of the chair with its user could be realized through an organic approach to design. More concerned with the way people actually sat than with how they were compelled to sit according to convention, Eero Saarinen and Charles Eames, after intensive research in the late 1940s and early 1950s, developed several seminal chair designs in fibreglass-reinforced plastic that achieved a hitherto unrealized organic unity of design. Concurrently in Italy, designers such as Marco Zanuso began exploring the potential of foam rubber as a suitable material for upholstery, and its successful application led to a new confidence of expression in chair design. By the mid 1950s, the chair became more sculptural in form to better accommodate the human body while counteracting the geometric regularity of the novel and increasingly prevalent built-in storage units. In doing so, the chair became one of the central points of the modern interior.

The mass-production of low-cost durable products for the huge domestic and contract requirement after the Second World War was viewed as an essential and, therefore, worthy social objective. Throughout the 1950s manufacturers in both Europe and the United States emphasized in their marketing strategies the quality, cost efficiency and universality of their products. With domestic interiors becoming generally smaller in scale, individual chair designs were by necessity multi-functional, being used for such purposes as writing, dining and lounging. This concern for flexibility enabled companies in America, such as Knoll International and Herman Miller, to seat dominant market shares as their seat furniture in particular could be used successfully within both domestic and contract environments.

With the rise and celebration of popular culture in the 1960s, the status of the chair was profoundly altered by the avant-garde: it became a disposable product. In this age of booming consumerism, when it was believed that built-in obsolescence would increase productivity and thereby economic prosperity, the modern chair

Durch einen neuen, von Skandinavien beeinflußten Zugang zur Moderne, durch den Einsatz von Ergonomie und fortschrittlicher Technologie, vor allem in der Kunststoffindustrie, wurde der Stuhl in den 50er Jahren einheitlicher im Design. Im Gegensatz zum geometrischen Formalismus, dem die Verfechter des frühen Modernismus anhingen, der aber bestenfalls nur die Möglichkeit einer Vereinheitlichung von Konstruktion und Material bot, konnte nun durch die Auseinandersetzung mit den organischen Bedingungen des Designs eine wirklich funktionale Verbindung des Stuhls mit seinem Benutzer erreicht werden. Entwerfer wie Eero Saarinen und Charles Eames beschäftigten sich nunmehr mit der Frage, wie die Leute tatsächlich saßen, als mit der Frage, wie sie der Konvention entsprechend zu sitzen hatten. Nach ausgedehnten Studien in den späten 40er und frühen 50er Jahren entwickelten sie mehrere zukunftsweisende Stuhlentwürfe in fiberglasverstärktem Kunststoff, durch den sie eine unübertroffene organische Einheit erreichten. Zur gleichen Zeit begannen in Italien Designer wie Marco Zanuso, die Möglichkeiten von Schaumgummi als geeignetem Polstermaterial näher zu beleuchten; die erfolgreiche Verwendung dieses Materials führte zu einer ganz neuen Perspektive in der Formensprache des Stuhldesigns. In der Mitte der fünfziger Jahre wurde der Stuhl skulpturaler in seiner Gestaltung und setzte zugleich einen Gegenakzent gegen die geometrische Regelmäßigkeit der neu aufgekommenen und immer beliebter werdenden Einbaumöbel. In seiner Funktion als Raumakzent wurde der Stuhl zum Blickpunkt des modernen Innenraums.

Die Massenproduktion von dauerhaften Tiefpreisprodukten für den riesigen häuslichen und professionellen Bedarf nach dem Zweiten Weltkrieg wurde als eine wesentliche und daher notwendige Zielsetzung angesehen. Sowohl europäische als auch amerikanische Hersteller setzten in den 50er Jahren in ihren Vermarktungsstrategien auf Qualität, günstige Preise und weltweiten Vertrieb ihrer Produkte. Da die Wohnungseinrichtungen zu jener Zeit im allgemeinen bescheidenere Ausmaße hatten, erwies es sich als sinnvoll, multifunktionale Stühle zu entwerfen, die sowohl zum Schreiben als auch zum Essen und für den Wohnbereich zu verwenden waren. Dieses Bedürfnis nach Flexibilität ermöglichte es Firmen in Amerika, zum Beispiel Knoll International und Herman Miller, sich beherrschende Marktanteile zu sichern, da vor allem ihre Sitzmöbel sowohl im privaten häuslichen Bereich als auch in Büros und professio-

et de civières en contreplaqué moulé. Utilisant des machines spécialement mises au point à cet effet, les «Kazam», ainsi nommées pour le bruit qu'elles faisaient, les Eames furent les premiers designers à mouler le contreplaqué selon des formes complexes tridimensionnelles, percée technique qui allait avoir d'énormes implications sur le design du siège.

Dans l'Amérique d'après-guerre et légèrement plus tard en Europe, alors que la plupart des pays du monde occidental connaissaient une expansion économique sans précédent, se dessinait une énorme demande pour le mobilier de maison. Cette époque était pleine d'espoir et de croyance en l'avenir et de nombreux designers pensaient fermement que la science et la technologie réunies pouvaient conduire au meilleur des mondes. Pendant cette période, de nombreux architectes-designers s'orientèrent vers la mise au point de meubles innovateurs plutôt que de projets architecturaux. C'est ainsi que des entreprises particulièrement éclairées, comme Herman Miller et Knoll International furent en mesure d'offrir à un vaste public des meubles modernes de haute qualité à un coût relativement raisonnable. Au cours des années cinquante, profitant de la convergence de la nouvelle approche scandinave, de l'ergonomie et des nouvelles techniques, en particulier de l'industrie des plastiques, le siège fit du progrès décisifs vers son unification conceptuelle. A la différence du formalisme géométrique auquel adhéraient les tenants historiques du mouvement moderniste, qui ne pouvait qu'offrir au mieux une plus grande unité de structure et de matériaux, une véritable symbiose du siège et de son utilisateur était enfin à portée de la main grâce à l'approche organique. Plus intéressés par la façon dont les gens s'assoient réellement que par la manière dont les conventions leur enseignent de s'asseoir, Eero Saarinen et Charles Eames, après des recherches intensives à la fin des années 40 et au début des années 50, mirent au point plusieurs sièges en matériaux plastiques renforcés de fibre de verre qui atteignirent à une cohérence de design jusque-là inconnue. Dans le même temps, en Italie, des designers comme Marco Zanuso commencèrent à explorer le potentiel de la mousse de caoutchouc dans le rembourrage et leurs réussites ouvrirent de nouvelles possibilités d'expression à la conception du siège. Vers le milieu des années 50, il prit des formes plus sculpturales pour mieux s'adapter au corps humain tout en jouant un rôle de contrepoint face à la sécheresse géométrique des rangements intégrés, de plus en plus

became just another short-lived gimmick as expendable as a paper dress. Peter Murdoch and Peter Raacke, among others, challenged the tradition that associated furniture with high cost and permanence by producing designs constructed of paperboard and cardboard. Aimed at a youth-based and socially liberated market, the chair was no longer seen as a durable product for the home, but as a lifestyle accessory subject to the ephemeral demands of fashion. This approach was exploited in Italy through the introduction of novel seating formats such as the inflatable *Blow chair* designed by Scolari, D'Urbino, Lomazzi and De Pas in 1967, the *Sacco* beanbag designed by Gatti, Paolini & Teodoro in 1968 and the vacuum-packed *Up* series designed by Gaetano Pesce in 1969. These revolutionary innovations combined with the increasing availability of "flat-pack" or "knock-down" furniture greatly simplified the act of purchasing – one could now literally buy a chair off the shelf.

In Britain during the 1960s, fuelled by the emergence of colour supplement magazines, there was a reaction against the rational austerity of "Good Design" which had until then been widely promoted, not least by the Government, as "good" taste. Having been forced to accept an unrelenting State form of Modernism and a steady diet of Scandinavian functionalism for a decade, the British public longed for something more exciting and less responsible. Through a media explosion and the early manifestations of the Global Village, this decade first witnessed the manipulative capabilities of the manufacturer to design the consumer to fit the product. While the design and manufacture of attention-grabbing evanescent and gimmicky products flourished, popular culture and rampant consumerism became widespread throughout America and, slightly later, Europe. In Italy, furniture manufacturers realized that the only way to maintain their already prominent position within the market was to accelerate research and development projects with more funding. "Concept factories" were established by companies such as Cassina, Zanotta, Poltronova and Artemide with the objective of creating new seating formats. The quest for technical novelty for its own sake ensured that considerable advances were made, especially in the area of injection-moulded plastics. With the advent of thermoplastics such as Polypropylene and ABS, first applied to furniture production in 1963 and 1967 respectively, a new world of possibilities was opened to the manufacturer of Modern furniture. During this period of

nellen Bereichen erfolgreich Verwendung fanden.

Mit dem Aufkommen und der Verherrlichung der Popkultur in den 60er Jahren erfuhr der Status des Stuhls durch die Avantgarde eine grundlegende Veränderung: Er wurde zum Wegwerfprodukt. In diesem Jahrzehnt des Konsumbooms war man überzeugt, daß die in dem Produkt mitgelieferte schnelle Veraltung die Produktivität und damit den ökonomischen Wohlstand erhöhen würde; der moderne Stuhl wurde zu einem weiteren kurzlebigen Werbegag, ebenso entbehrlich wie ein Papierkleid. Peter Murdoch, Peter Raacke und andere Designer forderten die Tradition heraus, die Möbel mit hohen Kosten und langer Haltbarkeit in Verbindung gebracht hatte, indem sie Stühle entwarfen, die aus Pappkarton und Pappdeckeln gebaut waren. Zielgruppen waren junge Leute und ein sozial unabhängiger Markt, der den Stuhl nicht länger als ein dauerhaftes Produkt für die Inneneinrichtung betrachtete, sondern als ein Life-Style-Accessoire, das den vergänglichen Bedürfnissen der Mode unterworfen war. Diese Ideen fanden in Italien großen Anklang und wurden sofort in neue Entwürfe umgesetzt, zum Beispiel den aufblasbaren *Blow-Stuhl* nach Entwürfen von Scolari, D'Urbino, Lomazzi und De Pas aus dem Jahr 1967, den *Sacco*-Bohnensack, entworfen von Gatti, Paolini und Teodoro im Jahr 1968, und die vakuumverpackten *Up*-Serien nach Entwürfen von Gaetano Pesce von 1969. Diese revolutionären Neuerungen und das wachsende Angebot an »Flachpack«- oder »Zusammenklapp«-Möbeln vereinfachten das Einkaufen ganz erheblich – jetzt konnte man buchstäblich den Stuhl aus dem Regal nehmen.

In Großbritannien erhob sich in den 60er Jahren eine spürbare Abwehr gegen die rationale Nüchternheit des »Guten Designs«, das bis dahin stark gefördert worden war, zumal von der Regierung, die es als »guten Geschmack« propagierte. Dem britischen Volk war ein Jahrzehnt lang eine phantasielose, staatlich geförderte Form von Modernität und eine ständige Versorgung mit skandinavischem Funktionalismus aufgenötigt worden, und nun sehnte es sich nach aufregenderen und weniger einengenden Produkten. Durch das explosionsartige Anwachsen der Medien und die ersten Anzeichen einer weltweiten Verstädterung wurde man sich in den 60er Jahren der manipulativen Fähigkeiten der Fabrikanten bewußt, die den Verbraucher so »umzuprogrammieren« verstanden, daß er sich ihrem Produkt anpaßte. Während Entwurf und Herstellung von kurzlebigen Blickfang- und Wegwerf-

Piero Gilardi:
Model *Pavé*, 1965
Modell *Pavé*, 1965
Modèle *Pavé*, 1965
Courtesy Gufram, Turin

Gruppo Strum:
Pratone (Big Meadow), 1962
Courtesy Gufram, Turin

Robert Venturi:

Sheraton chair, 1984

Stuhl *Sheraton*, 1984

Chaise *Sheraton*, 1984

Courtesy Knoll Group, New York

George Sowden:

Oberoy chair designed for
Memphis, 1981

Sessel *Oberoy*, entworfen für
Memphis, 1981

Fauteuil *Oberoy*, dessinée pour
Memphis, 1981

Courtesy Memphis, Milan

produkten ihre Blüten trieben, verbreiteten sich die Popkultur und eine hemmungslose Konsumlust über ganz Amerika und später auch über Europa. In Italien hatten die Möbelhersteller bald begriffen, daß die einzige Möglichkeit, ihre bereits beherrschende Marktposition zu behaupten, darin bestand, Forschung und Entwicklung ihrer Projekte durch höhere Investitionen zu beschleunigen. Firmen wie Cassina, Zanotta, Poltronova und Artemide richteten sogenannte »Konzeptionsfabriken« ein mit dem Ziel, neue Sitzmöbelformate zu entwickeln. Die Suche nach technischen Neuerungen um jeden Preis bewirkte, daß beachtliche Fortschritte erzielt wurden, vor allem im Bereich gespritzter Kunststofformen. Durch das Aufkommen von Thermokunststoffen wie Polypropylen und ABS, die erstmals 1963 beziehungsweise 1967 bei der Möbelherstellung verwandt wurden, eröffnete sich eine neue Welt der Möglichkeiten für die Hersteller moderner Möbel. In dieser Zeit erneut auflebender Aktivitäten in der italienischen Möbelindustrie spielten Designer wie Vico Magistretti, Marco Zanuso und Joe Colombo eine Vorreiterrolle; ihren ausgefallenen modernen Stuhlentwürfen ist es zu verdanken, daß Kunststoff als luxuriöses und hochwertiges Material einen gehobenen Status erhielt. Der erste Stuhl, der als vorbildliches Einzelstück Furore machen sollte, wurde von Verner Panton entworfen, der bezeichnenderweise aus Skandinavien stammte. Mit seinem freischwingenden *Stapelstuhl* von 1960, der erst 1968 in die Produktion ging, verwirklichte Panton Eero Saarinens bisher nicht umgesetzte Vorstellung einer vollkommenen Einheitlichkeit des Designs.

Das immer stärkere Auseinanderdriften des Möbelmarktes in Wohnbereich und Büroausstattung in den späten 60er und frühen 70er Jahren hatte zur Folge, daß, wenn auch in begrenztem Umfang, immer eigenwilligere avantgardistische Wohnmöbel hergestellt wurden. Ein extremes Beispiel für diese Entwicklung war das Auftauchen höchst surrealistischer Möbel, die von den Popskulpturen des Künstlers Claes Oldenburg inspiriert waren. Sie bestanden aus geformtem Polyurethan-Schaum, überdimensioniert in der Größe und als Einzelstücke gedacht; zu ihnen gehörte *Capitello*, ein Stuhlentwurf von Studio 65 aus dem Jahr 1971, der alle bisherigen Vorstellungen vom Aussehen eines Stuhls über Bord warf. Doch dies war bereits die Dämmerzeit der Popkultur, und als sich in der Mitte der 70er Jahre die Ölkrise abzuzeichnen begann, wandte sich die öffentliche Meinung immer stärker gegen die Exzesse der allgemeinen Konsumlust.

à la mode. Ce faisant, il devint l'un des principaux points d'attraction esthétique de l'habitation moderne.

Après la Seconde Guerre mondiale, la production en série de produits durables et économiques pour répondre aux énormes besoins des marchés domestiques et de l'équipement de bureau fut considérée comme un véritable projet de société. Tout au long des années 50, les fabricants, que ce soit en Europe ou aux Etats-Unis, mirent en valeur dans leurs stratégies de commercialisation le coût et la polyvalence de leurs produits. Avec des logements dont la taille s'était généralement réduite, les sièges devinrent par nécessité multifonctionnels, utilisés aussi bien pour écrire et se détendre que pour manger. Ce souci de la polyvalence permit à des sociétés américaines, comme Knoll International et Herman Miller, de s'assurer des parts importantes du marché, en particulier grâce à des sièges utilisables aussi bien à la maison que dans l'entreprise.

Avec l'explosion de la culture pop dans les années 60, le statut du siège fut profondément modifié par l'avant-garde: il devint un produit que l'on pouvait jeter. En cette période de folie de consommation, où l'on pensait que l'obsolescence programmée allait permettre d'accroître la production et donc la prospérité économique, le siège devint un gadget supplémentaire, d'aussi peu de valeur qu'une robe en papier. Peter Murdoch et Peter Raacke, entre autres, défièrent la tradition du mobilier de prix que l'on conservait pendant des générations en lançant des modèles en carton. Destinés à un public jeune et socialement libéré, ces sièges n'étaient plus considérés comme des produits durables, mais comme des accessoires de style de vie sujets aux foucades éphémères de la mode. Cette approche fut exploitée en Italie qui vit apparaître des types de sièges entièrement nouveaux, comme le fauteuil gonflable *Blow* de Scolari, D'Urbino, Lomazzi et De Pas en 1967, le *Sacco*, fauteuil-sac dessiné par Gatti, Paolini et Teodoro en 1968, et la gamme *Up*, emballée sous vide, dessinée par Gaetano Pesce en 1969. Ces innovations révolutionnaires combinées à l'envahissement des meubles en kit, à monter soi-même, simplifiaient grandement l'acte d'achat et l'on pouvait littéralement choisir son siège comme n'importe quel autre produit de grande consommation.

En Grande-Bretagne, les années 60 virent se dessiner une réaction animée par les suppléments en couleur de la grande presse, contre l'austérité du rationalisme du «Good Design». Celui-ci était alors largement soutenu par l'Etat pour lequel il

renewed vigour within the Italian furniture industry, designers such as Vico Magistretti, Marco Zanuso and Joe Colombo were instrumental in establishing the status of plastics as materials of quality and luxury through their sophisticated Modern chair designs. The first chair to achieve a crucial single-piece construction, however, was designed by Verner Panton, ironically a Scandinavian. With his cantilevered *Stacking chair* of 1960, which was not fully manufactured until 1968, Panton accomplished Eero Saarinen's unrealized ambition of total design unity.

One of the results of the ever-growing divergence of the domestic and contract markets in the late 1960s and early 1970s was the production, though limited, of increasingly expressive avant-garde furniture for the home. An extreme example of this was the appearance of highly surreal furniture inspired by the Pop Art sculptures of Claes Oldenburg. Constructed of moulded polyurethane foam, oversized and out-of-context designs, such as *Capitello* created by Studio 65 in 1971, completely altered previously held perceptions of what a chair could look like. These were the twilight years, however, of Pop Culture, and when the reality of the mid-1970s oil crisis dawned there was an enormous backlash of public opinion against the excesses of popular consumerism.

The global recession of the 1970s hailed a more austere and conscientious approach to design within the industrial mainstream – the chair was now more commonly seen as equipment for sitting. Dwindling markets and cost constraints, which compelled designers and manufacturers to return to a rational approach to design, prompted the minority style known as High Tech. As somewhat of a reinterpretation of Modern Movement rationalism, High Tech furniture, such as Rodney Kinsman's *Omkstak chair* of 1971, integrated utilitarian industrial materials while expressing a machine aesthetic. In less talented designers' hands than Kinsman's, however, the High Tech style, which is limited by geometric formalism, is characterless and bland.

The pervasive conservatism within the furniture industry during the 1970s, however, fuelled the emergence of several radical design groups in Italy with decidedly utopian aspirations. Global Tools, Superstudio, Archizoom and Gruppo Strum all questioned the assumptions of Modernism and signalled a mode of design based on spontaneous creativity and philosophical pluralism. Their design "projections" were a means of subversion in a mainstream immobilized by economic constraints and

Mit der weltweiten Rezession in den 70er Jahren besann man sich in der Industrieproduktion wieder auf einen nüchterneren und vernünftigeren Aspekt des Designs. Der Stuhl wurde jetzt vor allem als praktisches Sitzmöbel angesehen. Schrumpfende Märkte und Kostendämpfungen, durch die Designer und Hersteller gezwungen waren, sich wieder auf das Machbare zu besinnen, förderten das Klima für eine neue Stilrichtung, genannt High Tech, die wiederum nur von einer Minderheit angenommen wurde. High-Tech-Möbel wie etwa Rodney Kinsmans Stuhl *Omkstak* aus dem Jahr 1971 waren eine Art Neuinterpretation des rationalen Modernismus; sie bestanden aus zweckdienlichen, industriell gefertigten Materialien und brachten eine Maschinenästhetik zum Ausdruck. Wenn jedoch weniger talentierte Designer als Kinsman ans Werk gingen, geriet der High-Tech-Stil, der sich durch geometrischen Formalismus auszeichnet, ins Beliebige, er wurde langweilig und charakterlos.

Doch in den 70er Jahren machte sich in der Möbelindustrie zunehmend ein Konservatismus breit, der in Italien mehrere radikale Designergruppen auf den Plan rief, die entschieden utopische Ziele vor Augen hatten. Vereinigungen wie Global Tools, Superstudio, Archizoom und Gruppo Strum stellten die Errungenschaften des Modernismus radikal in Frage und propagierten eine Richtung im Design, die auf spontane Kreativität und weltanschaulichem Pluralismus basierte. Ihre Designprojekte waren als Mittel gedacht, die gängige Hauptrichtung zu unterwandern, die durch wirtschaftliche Beschränkungen und intellektuelle Apathie zum Stillstand gekommen war. Gegengruppen wie diese, die sich zum üblichen Design in Opposition setzten, hielten die Debatte über modernes Design lebendig und ebneten den Weg für die Einrichtung des Studios Alchimia im Jahre 1976. Alessandro Mendini war der führende Kopf dieser höchst einflußreichen Designergruppe, die die Trennung von Kunst und Design von Grund auf in Frage stellte. Seine »Neuentwürfe« von Joe Colombos *4867*-Stuhl, den er mit einem falschen Marmorüberzug versah, und Gio Pontis *Superleggera*, den er respektloserweise mit Bootsflaggen verzierte, machten sich über die Anspruchshaltung des »Guten Designs« lustig. Das Studio Alchimia, das sich bei all seinen Entwürfen um die physikalische Funktion am wenigsten scherte, unterlegte diese Designs mit sozialen und politischen Kommentaren – der Stuhl war nun zu einem symbolischen und provokanten Objekt geworden. Das Studio Alchimia verkündete lautstark seine

était devenu le «bon goût». Soumis à une version officielle de Modernisme et à un régime sévère de fonctionnalisme scandinave pendant dix ans, le public britannique avait envie de quelque chose de plus enthousiasmant et de moins sérieux. Sous la pression des médias et des premières manifestations du «village global», cette décennie fut tout d'abord le champ d'expérience de la capacité des fabricants à manipuler le consommateur pour qu'il s'adapte à leurs produits. Un design tout de séduction et une abondante production industrielle de meubles aussi superficiels qu'éphémères, contribuèrent à la diffusion de la culture pop et du goût pour la consommation aux Etats-Unis puis, légèrement plus tard, en Europe. En Italie, les fabricants de meubles réalisèrent que la seule façon de maintenir leur position déjà prééminente sur le marché était d'accélérer la recherche et le développement. «Des usines-concept» furent construites par des sociétés comme Cassina, Zanotta, Poltronova et Artemide dans le but de créer de nouveaux standards de sièges. La recherche de la nouveauté technique à tout prix déboucha sur des progrès considérables, en particulier dans le domaine de l'injection plastique. Avec l'arrivée des thermoplastiques, tels le polypropylène (1963) et l'ABS (1967), de nouvelles possibilités s'ouvrirent. Pendant cette période de vigueur renouvelée de l'industrie du meuble italienne, des designers comme Vico Magistretti, Marco Zanuso et Joe Colombo et leurs créations sophistiquées jouèrent un rôle fondamental dans la montée en puissance des plastiques enfin reconnus comme matériaux de qualité et même de luxe. Le premier siège à avoir été produit en une seule opération, fut cependant l'œuvre de Verner Panton, un Scandinave. Avec sa chaise en porte-à-faux, la *Stacking Chair* de 1960, qui ne fut réellement produite qu'à partir de 1968, il réalisa l'ambition inaboutie d'Eero Saarinen d'unité totale du design.

L'un des résultats de la divergence grandissante entre les marchés de la maison et du bureau de la fin des années 60 et du début des années 70 fut la production, quoique limitée, d'un mobilier pour la maison de plus en plus avant-gardiste et expressionniste avec, pour exemple extrême, l'apparition de meubles surréalistes inspirés par les sculptures pop de Claes Oldenburg. Souvent en mousse de polyuréthane moulée, sur-dimensionnées et hors contexte, ces créations, comme le *Capitello* du Studio 65 (1971), modifièrent complètement les perceptions que l'on avait pu avoir jusqu'alors d'un siège. Mais la pop culture en était déjà à son crépus-

intellectual apathy. Counter-design groups such as these kept the Modern design debate lively and paved the way for the establishment of Studio Alchimia in 1976. Alessandro Mendini was the leading propagandist of this highly influential design group, which challenged the distinctions between art and design. His "redesigns" of Joe Colombo's *4867* chair, to which he applied a faux marble finish, and Gio Ponti's *Superleggera*, to which he wryly attached yachting ensigns, mocked the pretensions of Good Design. With physical function the least of its considerations, Studio Alchimia infused these designs with social and political commentary – the chair had been intentionally transformed into a symbolic object. Blatantly anti-commercial and self-consciously intellectual in content, Studio Alchimia exploited decorative embellishment to mark what it believed to be the death of Modernism.

Founded in 1981, the Memphis design studio was central to the promotion of post-modernism within the decorative arts. Like its anti-design paradigm, Studio Alchimia, Memphis created furniture that ran against the accepted tenets of design and culture, using decoration, however, for its own sake and not for the promotion of a coherent ideology. Borrowing ornamental references from previous styles, Memphis successfully popularized anti-design, contributing to its general acceptance within the furniture industry's mainstream.

Against the background of a credit-fuelled economic boom and the perceived failure of Modernism, post-modernism emerged in the 1980s in response to the demand for a new mainstream international style. Divorcing industry from design and relating it more to fine art, post-modern furniture designers viewed styling rather than functionalism as paramount in importance. Often employing visual puns and decorative motifs borrowed from historic styles amalgamated in a single design, post-modern furniture, unlike that of the Pop era, was intended to possess a physical durability through the use of expensive materials and lavish construction. While drawing inspiration from eclecticism rather than consumerism, post-modern designers acknowledged the architect and critic Charles Jenck's rallying cry for double-coding mixed references and hybrid themes. Ultimately, these anti-design sentiments led to the kitsch vulgarity of Las Vegas being lauded for its honesty, while furniture designers created *Mickey meets Sheraton* chairs. A new visual language had indeed been created but at the expense of any real meaning or value to the consumer.

antikommerziellen und bewußt intellektuellen Anliegen und wucherte mit Dekor und Zierwerk, um deutlich ins Auge springen zu lassen, was es für den Tod der Moderne hielt.

Das 1981 gegründete Memphis-Design-Studio hatte eine zentrale Bedeutung für das Aufkommen der Postmoderne in der dekorativen Kunst. Wie der Protagonist des Anti-Design, Studio Alchimia, schuf Memphis Möbel, die den gängigen und allgemein anerkannten Strömungen in Design und Kultur zuwiderliefen; es verwendete den Dekor jedoch um seiner selbst Willen und nicht zur Propagierung einer stimmigen Ideologie. Memphis entlehnte ornamentale Elemente aus früheren dekorativen Stilen und machte Anti-Design populär; es trug sogar dazu bei, daß es in der gängigen industriellen Möbelmode akzeptiert wurde.

Vor dem Hintergrund eines durch Kredite gespeisten Wirtschaftsbooms und dem endgültig konstatierten Scheitern der Moderne kam in den 80er Jahren die Postmoderne auf, die ursprünglich eine Bewegung in der Architektur war; sie war die Antwort auf die Forderung nach einer neuen, international akzeptierten Stilrichtung. Postmoderne Möbeldesigner praktizierten eine klare Trennung zwischen Industrie und Design, das sie wieder mehr der Kunst annähern wollten; sie sahen die stilistische Gestaltung als ihre wichtigste Aufgabe an, nicht den Funktionalismus. Sie verwendeten häufig optische Spielereien und dekorative Motive, die sie von historischen Stilen entlehnt hatten und in einem postmodernen Design zu etwas Neuem verschmolzen; anders als in der Pop-Ära sollten postmoderne Möbel von dauerhafter Haltbarkeit sein, was durch die Verwendung teurer Materialien und aufwendiger Konstruktionen erreicht wurde. Die postmodernen Designer gewannen ihre Inspiration mehr aus dem Eklektizismus als aus dem Konsumbedürfnis der Menschen, denn sie hörten auf die lautstarke Forderung des Architekten und Kritikers Charles Jenck, die nach vielfältig verschlüsselten Verweisen und der Vermischung unterschiedlicher Themen verlangte. Letztlich führten diese Anti-Design-Theorien zu dem vulgären Kitsch von Las Vegas, der für seine Aufrichtigkeit gelobt wurde, während Möbeldesigner Stühle entwarfen wie *Mickey meets Sheraton*. Diese neue optische Sprache blieb aber für den Verbraucher letztlich ohne besonderen Wert.

In den 80er Jahren kam mit dem allgemeinen wirtschaftlichen Wohlstand ein Pluralismus im Design auf, der auch vom Verbraucher akzeptiert wurde und eine

cule. Avec la crise du pétrole du milieu des années 70 se manifesta une réaction massive de l'opinion contre les excès de la société de consommation.

La récession générale des années 70 déboucha sur une approche plus austère et plus responsable du design devenu «industriel», le siège étant tout simplement considéré comme un équipement pour s'asseoir. La mauvaise santé des marchés et l'accroissement des contraintes de coût forcèrent les designers et les fabricants à revenir à une approche rationnelle du design et donnèrent naissance à un nouveau style de modernité, le High Tech. Sorte de réinterprétation du rationalisme moderniste, le mobilier High Tech, comme la chaise *Omkstak* de Rodney Kinsman (1971), intégrait des matériaux industriels et exprimaient une esthétique mécaniste. En des mains moins talentueuses, cependant, ce style limité par son formalisme géométrique se révélera vite sans caractère.

En Italie, par réaction, le conservatisme affirmé de l'industrie du meuble pendant les années 70 fit éclore plusieurs groupes de design radical aux aspirations résolument utopistes. Global Tools, Superstudio, Archizoom et Gruppo Sturm remirent en question les certitudes du Modernisme et installèrent un mode de design reposant sur la créativité spontanée et le pluralisme philosophique. Leurs «projections» de design étaient autant de moyens de subversion dans un courant principal immobilisé par des contraintes économiques et l'apathie intellectuelle. Des groupes d'anti-design permirent ainsi au débat sur la modernité de continuer et ouvrirent la voie à l'apparition du Studio Alchimia en 1976. Alessandro Mendini fut le premier propagandiste de ce groupe de design très influent qui défiait les distinctions entre art et design. Ses «redesigns» de la *chaise 4867* de Joe Colombo à laquelle il appliqua une finition de faux-marbre et de la *Superleggera* de Gio Ponti, qu'il décora avec humour de symboles de yachting, se moquaient des prétentions du «Good Design». La fonction étant son moindre souci, le Studio Alchimia formulait à travers ses œuvres des commentaires politiques et sociaux au bénéfice desquels le siège était alors transformé en objet-symbole provocant, profondément anti-commercial et d'un intellectualisme affiché. Le Studio Alchimia exploita l'ornementation pour marquer ce qu'il pensait être la mort de la modernité.

Fondé en 1981, le Groupe Memphis a joué un rôle central dans la promotion du post-modernisme dans le domaine des arts décoratifs. Comme son équivalent de

By the mid 1980s an accepted pluralism in design emerged, with the general economic prosperity sustaining an ever greater stylistic diversification in the decorative arts. Working outside of the industrial process, independent designers explored unconstrained spontaneous creativity, producing ever more fanciful chair designs while the patrons of avant-garde furniture became increasingly concerned with expressing their own individuality through the acquisition of these pieces. Producing highly poetic "one-off" and batch production furniture, comprising mainly chairs, designers such as Ron Arad, Tom Dixon, Danny Lane and André Dubreuil flourished, becoming internationally renowned. In this period of relative excess, specialized furniture galleries were established to exhibit these experimental and challenging designs. The reticence of mainstream manufacturers to become involved with such anti-rationalism, regarded as of limited appeal even within the high-end domestic furniture market, ebbed in the mid 1980s as the work of many independent designers began to receive considerable recognition by the international design press.

Avant-garde designers working within the industry, such as Philippe Starck, continually produced new chair designs to sate the public's desire for novelty during the 1980s. Like the 1960s, this was a decade when domestic furniture design followed fashion rather than the quest for solutions to real needs. Well-established manufacturers were content to fund the production of anti-rational furniture which grabbed the attention of the press, thus indirectly publicizing the company's static range, which often consisted of contract seating and systems products. This publicity-motivated funding, coupled with an increasing competition for the spotlight, meant that many manufacturers were distracted from concentrating their resources on the worthwhile research and development of more ecologically conscious products.

The beginning of the 1990s, however, has seen a shift of attitude in the approach of some designers and manufacturers towards the production of environmentally sound furniture design. Philippe Starck's *Louis 20 chair* for instance, is an innovative construction of recyclable materials, while the highly rational *Ensemble chair* by Alfred Homann, with an even wider functional application, is primarily constructed of a newly developed plastic that is also recyclable. Admirable as these designs are in addressing the environmental concerns of today, the most effective guiding

immer größere stilistische Vielfalt in der dekorativen Kunst bewirkte. Unabhängige Designer, die außerhalb der industriellen Fertigungsprozesse tätig waren, loteten die Möglichkeiten ihrer freien Kreativität aus und produzierten immer witzigere Möbelentwürfe, während die Initiatoren der Avantgarde-Möbel zunehmend dazu übergingen, ihre Individualität durch den Erwerb solcher Stücke zum Ausdruck zu bringen. Designer wie Ron Arad, Tom Dixon, Danny Lane und André Dubreuil produzierten höchst poetische »Unikate« und Möbelentwürfe in begrenzter Stückzahl, vor allem Stühle, und erwarben sich damit internationales Ansehen. In dieser Zeit exzessiver Kreativität entstanden in ganz Europa spezielle Möbelgalerien, in denen diese experimentellen und provokanten Designs ausgestellt wurden. Die Möbelhersteller der gängigen Marken zeigten große Zurückhaltung, sich mit solch antirationalen Produkten einzulassen, denn sie wurden als wenig erfolgversprechend für den Markt angesehen, selbst in der gehobenen Klasse; diese Zurückhaltung löste sich Mitte der 80er Jahre allmählich auf, als die Arbeit vieler unabhängiger Designer große Anerkennung durch die internationale Designpresse erhielt.

Avantgarde-Designer wie Philippe Starck, die für die Industrie tätig waren, produzierten unablässig neue Stuhlentwürfe, um das Bedürfnis des Publikums nach Neuerungen in den 80er Jahren zu befriedigen. Wie die 60er Jahre war auch dies ein Jahrzehnt, in dem sich Wohnmöbel-Design mehr nach der Mode richtete als nach der Befriedigung tatsächlich bestehender Bedürfnisse. Hersteller mit gefestigten Marktpositionen förderten mit Vorliebe die Produktion antirationaler Möbel, die die Aufmerksamkeit der Medien auf sich zogen und dadurch indirekt Reklame machten für das fest umrissene Firmenprogramm, das häufig aus Bürositzmöbeln und Einbausystemen bestand. Diese publicity-orientierte Förderung, gepaart mit einem wachsenden Wettbewerb um das Rampenlicht, hatte zur Folge, daß viele Hersteller ihre Forschungsmittel nun nicht mehr ausschließlich auf die Entwicklung ökologisch sinnvoller Produkte konzentrierten.

Zu Beginn der 90er Jahre ließ sich jedoch eine Veränderung in der Haltung mancher Designer und Hersteller feststellen: Ihr Interesse galt nun verstärkt der Produktion umweltfreundlicher Möbel. So ist Philippe Starcks Stuhl *Louis 20* eine innovative Konstruktion aus recyclefähigem Material, und ebenso ist der höchst funktionale *Ensemble-Stuhl* von Alfred Homann, der einen breiteren

l'anti-design, Studio Alchimia, Memphis créa des meubles qui allaient à l'encontre des règles ambiantes, utilisant cependant le décor pour lui-même et non pour la promotion d'une idéologie cohérente. Empruntant ses références ornementales à d'anciens styles décoratifs, Memphis popularisa avec succès l'anti-design et contribua à le faire accepter par l'industrie du meuble.

C'est sur un fond d'expansion économique à crédit et d'échec patent du Modernisme que le post-modernisme émergea dans les années 80. Il se fit d'abord remarquer en architecture où il apportait une réponse à l'attente impatiente d'un nouveau grand style international. Poussant au divorce de l'industrie et du design qu'ils tiraient vers les beaux-arts, les designers post-modernes attachaient une importance majeure au style, au détriment du fonctionnalisme. Employant souvent d'un même élan astuces visuelles et motifs décoratifs empruntés, le mobilier postmoderne, à la différence de celui de la période pop, se voulait posséder une certaine durabilité en employant des matériaux chers et des constructions sophistiquées. Tirant leur inspiration de l'éclectisme plutôt que de la société de consommation, les designers post-modernes se reconnurent dans les textes de l'architecte et critique Charles Jenck qui défendait un mélange de références à double codage et de thèmes hybrides. Ces attitudes antidesign firent, par exemple, que l'esthétique de Las Vegas, se vit portée aux nues pour son «honnêteté», tandis que des créateurs dessinaient des chaises portant des noms comme *Mickey au Sheraton*. Un nouveau langage visuel s'était bien créé mais aux dépens de toute réelle signification ou de toute valeur pour le consommateur.

Vers le milieu des années 1980, émergea dans le monde du design un pluralisme nouveau qui allait de pair avec une prospérité économique retrouvée et une diversification stylistique artistique de plus en plus marquée. Loin de l'univers industriel, des designers indépendants se moquant des contraintes, dessinèrent des sièges pleins de fantaisie qui plaisaient à une clientèle d'avant-garde heureuse d'exprimer sa personnalité à travers l'acquisition de ces œuvres. Produisant des pièces très poétiques en exemplaire unique ou en édition très limitée – essentiellement des sièges d'ailleurs – des designers comme Ron Arad, Tom Dixon, Danny Lane et André Dubreuil se firent connaître dans le monde entier. Pendant cette période, marquée de nombreux excès, des galeries spécialisées dans le mobilier s'ouvrirent dans toute l'Europe pour exposer des

principle in confronting the longer term ecological requirement would be to simply make less last longer. To quote Marcel Breuer – "A piece of furniture, (and above all the chair), is not an arbitrary composition: it is a necessary component of our environment… the outward expression of our everyday needs; it must be able to serve both those needs that remain constant and those which vary. This variation is possible only if the very simplest and most straightforward pieces are used; otherwise changing will mean buying new pieces. Let our dwelling have no particular 'style', but only the imprint of the owner's character."[14]

Verwendungsspielraum zuläßt, hauptsächlich aus einem neuentwickelten Kunststoff konstruiert, der ebenfalls recyclefähig ist. So bewundernswert diese Entwürfe in ihrem Bemühen um eine umweltfreundliche Verarbeitung auch sind, müßte doch der Grundgedanke bei der Umsetzung heutiger ökologischer Erfordernisse sein, eine Langzeitplanung im Auge zu behalten, nach dem Motto: weniger, aber haltbarer. Um Marcel Breuer zu zitieren: »Ein Möbelstück (und vor allem ein Stuhl) ist keine beliebige Komposition: Es ist ein notwendiger Bestandteil unserer Umwelt… der äußere Ausdruck unserer alltäglichen Bedürfnisse; er müßte in der Lage sein, sowohl jene Bedürfnisse zu befriedigen, die gleich bleiben, als auch solche, die sich verändern. Diese Wechselbeziehung ist nur möglich, wenn die einfachsten und unkompliziertesten Möbelstücke verwendet werden; andernfalls würde Veränderung bedeuten, neue Stücke zu kaufen. Unser Wohnzimmer sollte keinen speziellen › Stil ‹ haben, sondern nur die persönliche Note des Besitzers zum Ausdruck bringen.«[14]

projets audacieux et souvent expérimentaux. La réticence des fabricants à s'impliquer dans ce mouvement qu'ils considéraient comme d'intérêt limité, même pour le marché du meuble domestique de luxe, cessa vers le milieu des années 80 lorsque le travail de nombreux designers indépendants commença à se faire reconnaître par la presse internationale du design.

Des designers d'avant-garde proches de l'industrie, comme Philippe Starck, produisirent de multiples modèles de sièges qui satisfaisaient le besoin de nouveauté du public. Comme pendant les années 60, le mobilier pour la maison suivit la mode plutôt que de chercher à répondre à des besoins réels. Des fabricants connus furent heureux d'utiliser ces meubles remarqués par la presse pour faire indirectement parler de leurs modèles plus classiques, en l'occurrence souvent des meubles ou des systèmes d'équipement pour le bureau. Ce financement à caractère publicitaire, couplé à une course effrénée pour la célébrité, empêcha en réalité de nombreux fabricants d'investir suffisamment dans une recherche valable pour des produits plus respectueux de l'environnement.

Le début des années 90, cependant, a vu un changement d'attitude dans l'approche écologique de certains designers et fabricants. La chaise *Louis 20* de Philippe Starck, par exemple, est réalisée à partir de matériaux recyclables, tandis que le siège *Ensemble* d'Alfred Homann, tout à fait rationnel et encore plus polyvalent, est essentiellement construit dans un nouveau plastique également recyclable. Aussi remarquables puissent être ces créations dans leur prise en compte des enjeux écologiques, on peut penser que la réponse la plus efficace à long terme, serait tout simplement d'arriver à faire durer ces meubles davantage. Pour citer Marcel Breuer: «Un meuble, et par dessus tout un siège, n'est pas une composition arbitraire: c'est une composante nécessaire de notre environnement … l'expression extériorisée de nos besoins de tous les jours; il doit être capable de servir à la fois les besoins qui ne changent pas et ceux qui peuvent varier. Cette variation n'est possible que si les éléments les plus simples et les plus sincères sont utilisés; autrement, le moindre changement voudra dire acheter de nouveaux meubles. Que nos habitations n'aient pas de ‹ style › particulier, mais reflètent simplement l'empreinte de la personnalité de leur propriétaire!»[14]

Alfred Homann:

Ensemble chair, 1992

Ensemble-Stuhl, 1992

Chaise *Ensemble*, 1992

Courtesy Fritz Hansen, Copenhagen

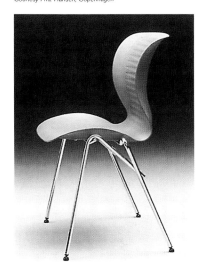

Ross Lovegrove:

FO8 chairs (prototype), 1991

FO8-Stühle (Prototyp), 1991

Chaises *FO8* (prototype), 1991

Courtesy Ross Lovegrove, London

The Chairs . Die Stühle . Les Chaises

1885–1992

Michael Thonet

1796–1871

Austria . Österreich . Autriche

Side chair, Model No. 14
c. 1885

Stuhl, Modell Nr. 14
um 1885

Chaise, modèle n° 14
vers 1885

Bent solid beechwood, moulded
laminated wood and solid
beechwood, with wooden seat

Rahmen aus Bugholz; Sitzfläche
aus geformtem Schichtholz

Cadre en hêtre cintré, siège en
bois lamellé moulé

**Gebrüder Thonet, Vienna,
after 1860**

Early *Model No. 14* variations,
c. 1855

Frühe Varianten des *Modells
Nr. 14*, um 1855

Premières variations du modèle
n° 14, vers 1855

Through its minimal use of materials
and suitability for mass-production,
Model No. 14 embodies some of the
principles associated with the Modern
Movement. The pared-down forms of
early Thonet chairs such as *Model
No. 14*, however, were simplified for
commercial reasons from contempor-
aneous period styles, Biedermeier in
particular[1], and, therefore, can only be
viewed as "modern" in terms of their
production method.

Mit seinem minimalen Materialaufwand
und seiner Eignung für die Massenproduktion verkörpert das *Modell
Nr. 14* einige Prinzipien der Moderne.
Allerdings sind die frühen Thonet-
Stühle mit ihrer klaren Linienführung, zu
denen dieses Modell zählt, eher als
»Sparversionen« zeitgenössischer
Nachahmungen historischer Stilarten
zu verstehen.[1] Sie wurden aus kommerziellen Gründen vereinfacht und
können daher nur in bezug auf die
Herstellungsmethode als »modern«
bezeichnet werden.

Parce qu'il utilise un nombre réduit de
matériaux et qu'il est adapté aux procédés de production en série, le
modèle n° 14 illustre certains des
principes du Mouvement moderniste.
Les formes dépouillées des premiers
sièges Thonet, tel ce *modèle n° 14*,
correspondaient en réalité à des versions simplifiées (pour des raisons
commerciales) des styles de l'époque,
en particulier le Biedermeier[1], et ne
peuvent guère être considérées
comme «modernes» qu'en termes de
méthodes de fabrication.

In 1852 the Shakers founded a factory in New Lebanon, New York, to produce furniture for sale outside their communities. The Shakers' belief that "regularity is beauty" and "beauty rests on utility" paralleled the ideals of the Arts and Crafts movement.[2]

1852 gründeten die Shaker in New Lebanon, New York, eine Möbelmanufaktur, in der sie Möbel für den Verkauf außerhalb ihrer Siedlungen herstellten. Ihre Überzeugungen – »Regelmäßigkeit ist Ordnung« und »Schönheit beruht auf Nützlichkeit« – standen im Einklang mit den Idealen der Arts-and-Crafts-Bewegung.[2]

En 1852, les Shakers créèrent un atelier à New Lebanon, dans l'Etat de New York, pour produire et vendre des meubles hors de leurs communautés. La croyance des Shakers que «la vérité est beauté» et que «la beauté repose sur l'utilité» rappelle les idéaux du mouvement Arts and Crafts.[2]

Licensed reissue of Shaker chairs

Lizensierter Nachbau der Shaker-Stühle

Rééditions des chaises Shaker

Licensed reissue of Shaker bench

Lizensierter Nachbau einer Shaker-Bank

Réédition de banc Shaker

Reconstruction of a Shaker interior

Rekonstruktion einer Inneneinrichtung der Shaker

Reconstruction d'un intérieur Shaker

Shaker

USA . Etats-Unis

Rocking-chair 1890

Schaukelstuhl 1890

Chaise à bascule 1890

Solid wood construction, rush seat

Holz massiv, Sitzfläche Binsengeflecht

Bois massif, siège en jonc tressé

Shaker Factory, New Lebanon, New York

Henry
van de Velde

1863–1957

Belgium . Belgien . Belgique

Bloemenwerf chair 1895

Stuhl Bloemenwerf 1895

Chaise Bloemenwerf 1895

Solid walnut frame with rush seat

Rahmen aus massivem Nußholz;
Sitzfläche aus Bastgeflecht

Cadre de noyer massif, siège en
raphia

Société van de Velde, Brussels

Henry van de Velde:

Solid padouk armchair with batik
upholstery, 1898/99

Armlehnstuhl aus massivem
Padouk-Holz, Polsterung mit
Batikbezug, 1898/99

Fauteuil en bois de santal massif,
revêtu de batik, 1898/99

This chair was designed for Van de
Velde's own house, Bloemenwerf, near
Brussels. He designed the house and
all its contents as part of an organic
and unified whole.

Den *Bloemenwerf*-Stuhl entwarf Van
de Velde für sein eigenes Haus in
Uccle bei Brüssel. Er hat es, einschließlich der Ausstattung, als
organisches, einheitliches Ganzes
konzipiert.

Cette chaise fut spécialement dessinée pour la propre maison de Van de
Velde, Bloemenwerf, à Uccle, près de
Bruxelles. Il conçut cette maison et
l'ensemble de son contenu comme un
tout organique et unifié.

Charles Rennie Mackintosh

1868–1928

Great Britain . Großbritannien .
Grande-Bretagne

Side chair 1897

Stuhl 1897

Chaise 1897

Solid oak construction with
upholstered seat

Rahmen aus Eiche massiv, Sitzfläche gepolstert

Cadre en chêne massif, siège
rembourré

**Manufacturer unknown
(reissued by Cassina, Italy,
from 1973)**

Charles Rennie Mackintosh:

Dining room. Drawing from the
collections of designs submitted
for the "House of an Art Lover"
competition, published by
Alexander Koch, 1901

Speisezimmer. Zeichnung aus
den von Alexander Koch veröffentlichten Entwurfsunterlagen für die
Ausschreibung zum »Haus eines
Kunstfreundes«, 1901

Salle à manger. Dessin provenant
des esquisses publiées par
Alexander Koch pour le
concours »Intérieur d'un
ami des artistes«, 1901

Reconstruction of a Mackintosh
room

Rekonstruktion eines Mackintosh-
Raums

Reconstruction d'une chambre de
Mackintosh

Designed for the Luncheon Room at Miss Cranston's Argyle Street Tea-Rooms, Glasgow, these high-backed chairs functioned as screens when placed around a table, affording greater privacy. "Given the diminutive stature of the Scotswomen who patronised this establishment at the turn of the century, the light passing through the pierce-work on the elliptical crest rails would have ideally imparted a halo-like glow about their heads… Mackintosh endowed these commanding chairs with a mystical quality through the manipulation of form."[3]

Die von Mackintosh für den Lunch Room in Miss Cranston's Tea-Rooms in der Argyle Street, Glasgow, entworfenen Stühle mit den hohen Rückenlehnen wirkten wie Wandschirme und schützten die Gäste vor neugierigen Blicken. »Bei der winzigen Statur schottischer Damen kann man sich gut vorstellen, daß der ovale Lichtschein, der durch die durchbrochenen Bekrönungen der Lehnen fiel, eine Art Heiligenschein um ihre Köpfe zeichnete… Mackintosh hat diese alles überragenden Stühle durch kunstvolle Gestaltung mit mystischer Qualität ausgestattet.«[3]

Spécialement créées pour la salle à manger de Miss Cranston's Tea-Rooms de Argyle Street, à Glasgow, ces chaises jouaient un rôle d'écran qui permettait aux clients de mieux s'isoler. «Etant donné la petite taille des clientes écossaises, la lumière qui filtrait à travers la découpe pratiquée dans l'écusson elliptique devait normalement envelopper leur tête d'une sorte de halo lumineux. Grâce à cette manipulation des formes, Mackintosh conféra à ces chaises une sorte de qualité mystique.»[3]

Adolf Loos

1870–1933

Austria . Österreich . Autriche

Chair c. 1898
Stuhl um 1898
Chaise vers 1898

Stained, bent beech frame with
woven cane seat

Rahmen Bugholz, gebeizt;
Sitzfläche aus Rohrgeflecht

Structure de hêtre cintré teinté,
siège canné

Jacob & Josef Kohn, Vienna

Although based on earlier precedents
set by Thonet[4], this chair, designed for
the Café Museum in Vienna, represents the first of a new generation of
architect-designed bent wood products. The Café Museum, designed by
Loos in 1899, was subsequently nick-
named the "Café Nihilismus" because
of its rather stark, undecorated interior
scheme.

Obwohl dieser speziell für das Café
Museum in Wien entworfene Stuhl von
Adolf Loos auf früheren Entwürfen von
Thonet[4] basiert, gehört er zu einer
neuen Generation von Bugholzmöbeln,
die von Architekten für einen bestimm-
ten Platz geschaffen wurden. Das Café
Museum, das Loos 1899 entworfen
hat, erhielt wegen seiner betont kargen
Innenausstattung den Spitznamen
»Café Nihilismus«.

Bien qu'inspirée de précédents sièges
de Thonet[4], cette chaise créée spécialement pour le Café Museum à
Vienne, représente le point de départ
de la nouvelle génération de meubles
en bois cintré dessinés par des architectes. Le Café Museum, créé par
Loos en 1899, fut rebaptisé «Café
Nihilisme» du fait d'un décor intérieur
particulièrement dépouillé.

Adolf Loos:
Café Museum, 1899

Richard Riemerschmid:

Music Room for the "Deutsche Kunstausstellung Dresden", 1899

Musikzimmer für die »Deutsche Kunstausstellung Dresden«, 1899

Le Salon de Musique pour la «Deutsche Kunstausstellung» de Dresde, 1899

Richard Riemerschmid:

Sketch for an armchair, 1899

Entwurfszeichnung für einen Armlehnsessel, 1899

Dessin pour un fauteuil, 1899

Richard Riemerschmid:

Beechwood chair, 1900

Stuhl aus massiver Buche, 1900

Chaise en hêtre massif, 1900

Richard Riemerschmid

1868–1957

Germany . Deutschland . Allemagne

Side chair 1899

Stuhl 1899

Chaise 1899

Solid oak frame with upholstered leather seat

Rahmen Eiche massiv; Sitzfläche gepolstert, mit Leder bezogen

Structure en chêne massif, siège rembourré, recouvert de cuir

Vereinigte Werkstätten für Kunst im Handwerk, Munich (also manufactured by Liberty & Co., London, after 1899)

Designed for the 1899 Dresden Art Exhibition, this elegant chair, which was intended for use by musicians, helped to establish Riemerschmid's reputation. The lack of arms allows the freedom of movement necessary when playing musical instruments. It is generally regarded as the most significant German Jugendstil chair design.

Dieser elegante Musikzimmerstuhl, den Riemerschmid für die Dresdner Kunstausstellung von 1899 entwarf, begründete seinen Ruf als Designer. Das Fehlen von Armlehnen ermöglichte optimale Bewegungsfreiheit beim Musizieren. Aufgrund seines Designs gilt dieser Stuhl im allgemeinen als das wichtigste Sitzmöbel des deutschen Jugendstils.

Dessiné pour l'Exposition artistique de Dresde en 1899, cet élégant siège de musicien contribua à établir la réputation de Riemerschmid. L'absence d'accoudoirs permet la liberté de mouvement nécessaire lorsque l'on joue d'un instrument. Il est généralement considéré comme le modèle de chaise le plus élaboré du Jugendstil allemand.

Koloman Moser

1868–1918

Austria . Österreich . Autriche

Wooden slatted chair 1902

Holzlattenstuhl 1902

Fauteuil en lattes de bois 1902

Painted beech frame with wicker-work seat

Rahmen Buche massiv, lackiert; Sitzfläche Korbgeflecht

Structure de hêtre peint avec siège en vannerie

Prag-Rudniker Korbwaren, Vienna

Josef Hoffmann:

Sanatorium Purkersdorf, 1904–06

Similar designs to this were exhibited at the Vienna Secession's 1903 exhibition of Gustav Klimt's work and were also used in the entrance lobby of Josef Hoffmann's sanatorium "Westend" in Purkersdorf. The chair's cubic form and restricted use of colour are signs of the mature Secessionist style and anticipate the geometric abstraction employed by Modern Movement designers in the 1920s and 1930s.

Ähnliche Entwürfe waren in der Klimt-Ausstellung der Wiener Sezession von 1903 und in der Eingangshalle des Sanatoriums Westend von Josef Hoffmann im niederösterreichischen Purkersdorf zu sehen. Die kubische Form und das zurückhaltende Farbkonzept sind typisch für den reifen Stil der Sezession und nehmen das geometrisch-abstrakte Design der Moderne der 20er und 30er Jahre vorweg.

Des modèles similaires avaient été présentés lors de l'Exposition des travaux de Gustav Klimt par la Sécession Viennoise et figuraient également dans l'entrée du sanatorium de Purkersdorf de J. Hoffmann. La forme cubique de ce siège et le recours limité à la couleur illustrent le style sécessionniste de la maturité et anticipent l'abstraction géométrique des créateurs modernistes des années 20 et 30.

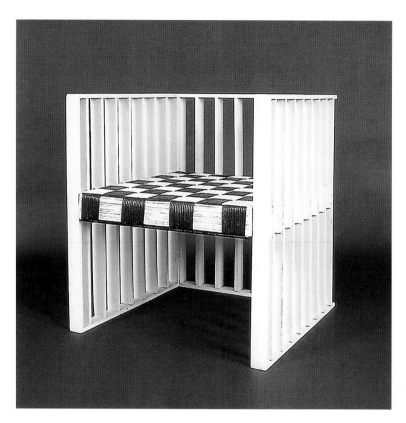

Koloman Moser:

Writing cabinet with integrated chair, Vienna, 1904

Schreibschrank mit integriertem Stuhl, Wien, 1904

Secrétaire avec fauteuil encastrable, Vienne, 1904

Koloman Moser:

Armchair, rear view, 1903

Armlehnsessel, Rückansicht, 1903

Fauteuil, vue de dos, 1903

Charles Rennie Mackintosh

1868–1928

Great Britain . Großbritannien .
Grande-Bretagne

Oak armchair c. 1903

Armlehnstuhl aus Eiche
um 1903

Fauteuil de chêne vers 1903

Stained, solid oak frames with
fabric-covered, upholstered
horsehair seats

Rahmen Eiche massiv, gebeizt;
Sitzflächen mit Roßhaar-
polsterung, mit Stoff bezogen

Structure de chêne massif teinté
avec sièges rembourrés de crin
de cheval et recouverts de tissu

Maker unknown

Charles Rennie Mackintosh:

Chair, 1903

Stuhl, 1903

Chaise, 1903

"From 1897 to 1916 (Mackintosh) was occupied with designing, decorating and furnishing a chain of Tea-Rooms, established in Glasgow by the Misses Cranston as part of a campaign started in the 1880s with the founding of the Glasgow Temperance Movement, to combat widespread daytime drunkenness. The Tea-Rooms were provided with billiard tables and smoking-rooms for the amusement of the customers but few, if any, of the Glasgow drunks patronised the new establishments with their elegant and original furniture and fittings."[5]

»Von 1897 bis 1916 war er (Mackintosh) mit dem Entwurf, der Ausstattung und der Einrichtung einer Kette von Tea-Rooms beschäftigt, die die Damen Cranston in Glasgow eröffnet hatten – im Rahmen der um 1880 gegründeten Glasgower Temperenzlerbewegung zur Bekämpfung der damals weit verbreiteten Trunksucht. Die Tea-Rooms waren zur Unterhaltung der Gäste mit Billardtischen und Rauchzimmern ausgestattet, aber nur wenige Glasgower Trunkenbolde, wenn überhaupt, besuchten die neuen eleganten Etablissements.«[5]

«De 1897 à 1916, Mackintosh dessine, décore et meuble une chaîne de salons de thé. Elle avait été créée à Glasgow par les demoiselles Cranston dans le cadre d'une campagne qui avait débuté dans les années 80 par la fondation d'une ligue de combat contre l'alcoolisme alors très répandu. Les salons de thé abritaient des billards et des fumoirs pour la distraction des clients, mais peu d'alcooliques de Glasgow – si jamais il y en eut – fréquentèrent ces établissements élégants, décorés et meublés avec originalité.»[5]

Charles Rennie Mackintosh:

Interior of Willow Tea-Rooms
c.1904

Inneneinrichtung der Willow-Tea-
Rooms, um 1904

Vue intérieure des Willow Tea-
Rooms, vers 1904

Frank Lloyd Wright

1869–1959

USA . Etats-Unis

Dining chair
c. 1904

Eßzimmerstuhl
um 1904

Chaise de salle à manger
vers 1904

Solid oak frame with fabric-
covered, upholstered seat

Rahmen Eiche massiv; Sitzfläche
gepolstert, mit Stoff bezogen

Structure de chêne massif,
avec siège rembourré recouvert
de tissu

Matthews Bros. Manufacturing
Co., Milwaukee, Wisconsin

The sophisticated design of this dining chair, designed for the Darwin D. Martin House in Buffalo, New York, shows Wright's preference for geometric regularity, simplicity and the harmonious synthesis of the American Arts and Crafts style with Japanese art and design.

Die elegant-einfache Gestaltung dieses Speisezimmerstuhls für das Haus von Darwin D. Martin in Buffalo, New York, demonstriert Wrights Vorliebe für geometrische Regelmäßigkeit, Einfachheit und die harmonische Verschmelzung des amerikanischen Arts-and-Crafts-Stils mit japanischer Kunst und japanischem Design.

Le dessin sophistiqué de cette chaise de salle à manger pour la maison Darwin D. Martin à Buffalo, New York, témoigne de la préférence de Wright pour la rigueur géométrique, la simplicité et la synthèse harmonieuse du style Arts and Crafts américain et des tendances du design japonais.

Frank Lloyd Wright:

Interior of the Darwin D. Martin
House, Buffalo, New York,
1904/05

Inneneinrichtung des Hauses von
Darwin D. Martin, Buffalo, New
York, 1904/05

Intérieur de la maison Darwin D.
Martin, Buffalo, New York,
1904/05

Frank Lloyd Wright:

High-backed side chair, c.1906

Stuhl mit hoher Rückenlehne,
um 1906

Chaise à haut dossier, vers 1906

44

Frank Lloyd Wright

1869–1959

USA . Etats-Unis

Office swivel chair 1904

Bürodrehstuhl 1904

Siège de bureau pivotant 1904

Painted steel frame with leather-covered upholstered seat, supported on a swivelling steel base terminating on castors

Rahmen aus lackiertem Stahl; Sitzfläche gepolstert, Lederbezug; drehbares Untergestell aus Stahl auf Rollen

Structure d'acier peint avec siège rembourré recouvert de cuir sur une base pivotante en acier montée sur roulettes

Von Dorn Iron Works Company, Cleveland, Ohio

Frank Lloyd Wright:

Interior of the Larkin Company Administration Building, Buffalo, New York, 1903–05

Das Innere des Verwaltungs-gebäudes der Larkin Company, Buffalo, New York, 1903–05

Intérieur de bureau de la Larkin Company, Buffalo, New York, 1903–05

Without architectural precedent, Frank Lloyd Wright's Larkin Company Administration Building in New York revolutionised the concept of the workplace environment, heralding the birth of the modern, integrated office. The Larkin Co. office chair was designed specifically for this project and its formal geometry was echoed throughout the surrounding building. Wright's intention with this regularity of form was to create a space that was both visually and functionally unified.

Mit seinem Bürogebäude für die Larkin Company in New York revolutionierte Frank Lloyd Wright die Gestaltung von Arbeitsplätzen und schuf eine moderne Bürolandschaft mit großen, ungeteilten Büroflächen. Den Bürostuhl für die Larkin Company hatte er speziell für dieses Projekt entworfen; seine streng geometrische Konstruktion korrespondierte mit den ihn umgebenden Gebäuden. Durch diese Regelmäßigkeit der Formen wollte Wright Räume schaffen, die visuell und funktionell eine Einheit bilden.

Sans précédent architectural connu, le Larkin Company Administration Building de Frank Lloyd Wright à New York révolutionne le concept de l'environnement du travail et annonce la naissance du bureau intégré moderne. Ce siège de bureau fut spécialement conçu pour ce projet et sa géométrie formelle faisait écho à l'architecture environnante. A travers cette rigueur formelle, l'intention de Wright était de créer un espace unifié tant visuellement que fonctionnellement.

Frank Lloyd Wright:

Office armchair designed for the Larkin Company Administration Building, 1904

Büro-Armlehnstuhl für das Verwaltungsgebäude der Larkin Company, 1904

Fauteuil de bureau pivotant dessiné pour la Larkin Company, 1904

Frank Lloyd Wright:

Interior of the Larkin Company Administration Building, Buffalo, New York, 1903–05

Das Innere des Verwaltungs-gebäudes der Larkin Company, Buffalo, New York, 1903–05

Intérieur de bureau de la Larkin Company, Buffalo, New York, 1903–05

Josef Hoffmann

1870–1956

Austria . Österreich . Autriche

**Sitzmaschine,
Model No. 670**
c. 1908

**Sitzmaschine,
Modell Nr. 670**
um 1908

**Sitzmaschine,
modèle n° 670**
vers 1908

Stained, laminated wood, bent
solid beechwood, turned wood
and brass fittings

Rahmen Bugholz, Schichtholz und
gedrechselte Buche, gebeizt;
Sitzfläche und Rückenlehne
Schichtholz, Messingbeschläge

Bois lamellé teinté, hêtre massif
cintré, bois tourné et accessoires
en cuivre

Jacob & Josef Kohn, Vienna

Josef Hoffmann:
Sanatorium Purkersdorf,
1904–06

Manufactured by J. & J. Kohn from
about 1908 to 1916, the *Sitzmaschine*, with an adjustable back,
was sold both with and without large
horsehair-filled cushions. The latter
was the more popular option, suggesting that the chair may have been more
often purchased purely for its aesthetic
qualities than for its functionalism. The
Sitzmaschine's stringent geometric
formalism predicts Gerrit Rietveld's
later *Red-and-blue chair* of 1917/18.

Die *Sitzmaschine* mit verstellbarer
Rückenlehne wurde von J. & J. Kohn
von 1908 bis 1916 hergestellt und mit
oder ohne große, roßhaargefüllte Sitzkissen verkauft. Die Käufer zogen im
allgemeinen die letzte Version vor,
vermutlich weil sie den Stuhl eher
wegen seiner ästhetischen Qualitäten
als wegen seiner Funktionalität erwarben. Die *Sitzmaschine* mit ihrem
streng geometrischen Formalismus
nimmt Gerrit Rietvelds *Rot-Blau-Stuhl*
von 1917/18 vorweg.

Fabriqué par J. & J. Kohn de 1908
environ à 1916, cette *Sitzmaschine*
(machine à s'asseoir) à dossier
inclinable, fut commercialisée avec ou
sans grands coussins bourrés de crin
de cheval. Le modèle sans coussin fut
le plus vendu, ce qui laisse à penser
que ce siège était plus acheté pour
ses qualités esthétiques que son fonctionnalisme. Le strict formalisme géométrique annonce le *fauteuil rouge-et-
bleu* de Rietveld de 1917/18.

Josef Hoffmann:
Sitzmaschine, 1905

Josef Hoffmann:

Side chair *Model No. 371*, c. 1906

Stuhl *Modell Nr. 371*, um 1906

Chaise *modèle n° 371*, vers 1906

Gerrit Rietveld

1888–1964

Netherlands . Niederlande . Pays-Bas

Red-and-blue chair
1917/18

Rot-Blau-Stuhl
1917/18

Fauteuil rouge-et-bleu
1917/18

Painted solid beechwood frame with plywood back

Rahmen Buche massiv; Sitzfläche und Rückenlehne Schichtholz, farbig lackiert

Structure de hêtre massif peint, siège et dossier en bois lamellé

G.A. van de Groenekan, De Bilt (reissued by Cassina, Italy, from 1971)

The ancestry of the *Red-and-blue chair*'s essential form can be traced back to the *Morris* chair, via the designs of Josef Hoffmann and Frank Lloyd Wright.[6] The *Red-and-blue chair* is viewed as the first truly modern chair because of the revolutionary philosophical agenda it set. While expressing reductivist aesthetics, the design speculated on standardised mass production through a geometrically abstracted construction of regular and simply joined machined materials.

Die Form des *Rot-Blau-Stuhls* geht im wesentlichen auf den *Morris*-Stuhl und die Entwürfe von Josef Hoffmann und Frank Lloyd Wright zurück.[6] Der *Rot-Blau-Stuhl* gilt als erster wirklich »moderner« Stuhl wegen der radikal neuen Gestaltungsphilosophie, die hinter dem Design steckt. Mit der geometrisch-abstrakten Form strebte Rietveld eine puristische Konstruktion an, die durch ihre einheitlich gestalteten, maschinell bearbeiteten und einfach verzapften Einzelteile eine genormte Massenproduktion erleichtern sollte.

L'hérédité de la forme de base du *fauteuil rouge-et-bleu* peut être retracée jusqu'à la chaise *Morris*, en passant par certains dessins de Hoffmann et de Frank Lloyd Wright.[6] Il est considéré comme le premier siège vraiment moderne du fait des enjeux révolutionnaires qu'il soulève. Tout en exprimant une esthétique de réduction, sa conception laissait entrevoir la possibilité de production en série, grâce à une construction géométrique abstraite en matériaux standard usinés et assemblés avec simplicité.

Gerrit Rietveld, G.A. van der Groenekan, Adriaen van Ostadelaan

Gerrit Rietveld:

Prototype of the *Red-and-blue-chair*, designed in 1918, executed in 1919

Prototyp des *Rot-blau-Stuhls*, entworfen 1918, ausgeführt 1919

Prototype du *fauteuil rouge-et-bleu*, dessiné en 1918 et réalisé en 1919

47

Marcel Breuer

1902–81

Germany . Deutschland .
Allemagne

**Wassily Club chair,
Model No. B3** 1925

**Sessel Wassily,
Modell Nr. B3** 1925

**Fauteuil Wassily,
modèle n° B3** 1925

Bent, nickeled tubular steel frame
(later chrome-plated) with fabric,
canvas or leather

Rahmen: Stahlrohr, vernickelt
(später verchromt); Sitzfläche,
Arm- und Rückenlehnen mit
Eisengarnstoff, Kanvas oder
Leder bespannt

Structure en tubes d'acier cintrés
et nickelés (plus tard chromés),
tissu, toile ou cuir

**Standard-Möbel Lengyel & Co.,
Berlin, and Gebrüder Thonet,
Frankenberg, Germany, from
c.1928 (reissued by Gavina,
Italy from 1962 to 1968 and
Knoll International, Inc., New
York, from 1968 to present)**

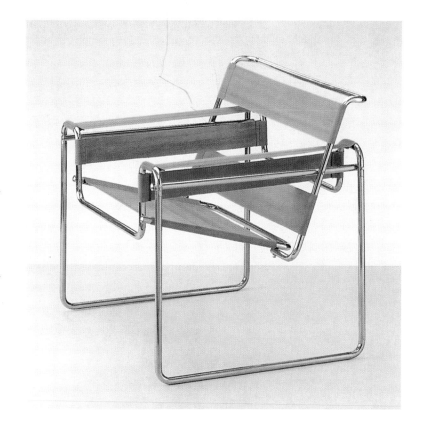

Designed for the painter Wassily
Kandinsky's staff quarters at the
Dessau Bauhaus, the *Model No. B3*
was revolutionary both in materials and
method of manufacture. Breuer's Adler
bicycle is said to have inspired his use
of tubular steel, while Constructivist
sculpture must surely have influenced
the chair's form. The *Wassily* and many
other Modern Movement designs were
first mass-produced in the 1950s and
1960s, when there was a general
reassessment of pre-war Modernist
furniture.

Das *Modell Nr. B3*, ursprünglich für
das Meisterhaus von Wassily Kandinsky in Dessau entworfen, war in
bezug auf Material und Herstellung
revolutionär. Zur Verwendung von
Stahlrohr soll Breuer sein Adler-Fahr-
rad inspiriert haben, während die Form-
gebung des Sessels an konstruktivi-
stische Skulpturen erinnert. Der
Wassily und viele andere Entwürfe
der Klassischen Moderne wurden erst in
den 50er und 60er Jahren, als man das
Vorkriegs-Design wiederentdeckt
hatte, in größeren Stückzahlen
produziert.

Créé pour les bureaux du peintre
Wassily Kandinsky au Bauhaus de
Dessau, ce *modèle n° B3* était révolutionnaire aussi bien au niveau des
matériaux que de la fabrication. On ra-
conte que le vélo Adler que Breuer
venait d'acheter lui avait fait penser aux
tubes d'acier, mais la sculpture cons-
tructiviste a certainement tout autant
influencé les formes de ce siège. Le
Wassily, comme beaucoup d'autres
projets, ne fut réellement produit en
série que dans les années 50 et 60, à
la faveur d'une remise en perspective
de l'importance du siège moderniste.

Marcel Breuer:

Furnishing for a lady gymnastics
teacher, Berlin, 1930

Einrichtung für eine Gymnastik-
lehrerin, Berlin, 1930

Ameublement pour une
professeuse de gymnastique,
Berlin, 1930

Photograph of a woman seated in
a *Wassily* chair wearing a mask
by Oskar Schlemmer, c. 1927

Foto einer Frau mit »Schlemmer«-
Maske in dem Sessel *Wassily*, um
1927

Photo d'une femme avec masque
de Schlemmer dans le fauteuil
Wassily, vers 1927

Eileen Gray

1878–1976

France . Frankreich

Transat chair 1926

Armlehnstuhl Transat 1926

Fauteuil Transat 1926

Upholstered sling seat supported on a solid sycamore frame with chrome-plated metal fittings

Rahmen aus massivem Sykomorenholz, verchromte Beschläge; eingehängtes Sitzpolster, Lederbezug

Structure en sycomore massif avec siège suspendu rembourré, recouvert de cuir, accessoires en métal chromé

Jean Désert, Paris (reissued by Ecart, France from 1978)

Eileen Gray's elegant *Transat* folding chair was based on the traditional steamer chair. The French architect, Jean Badovici, wrote of Gray in the June 1924 issue of "Wendingen", the Dutch design journal: "She is modern in every possible aspect of her style, vision and expression, in her disdain of the old emotional, aesthetic and traditional plastic forms. She has understood that our own times have brought, along with new patterns of life, the necessity of new ways of thinking; that the machine age must transform our sensibilities."[7]

Grays eleganter Armlehnstuhl *Transat* ist den traditionellen Liegestühlen großer Passagierdampfer nachempfunden. Der französische Architekt Jean Badovici schrieb in der niederländischen Zeitschrift »Wendingen« im Juni 1924: »Sie ist modern in ihrem Stil, ihren Visionen und ihrem Ausdruck und in ihrer Verachtung der alten, emotionalen Ästhetik und traditioneller, plastischer Formen. Sie hat verstanden, daß ein neuer Lebensstil und eine neue Denkweise unsere Zeit prägen, daß das Maschinenzeitalter unser Wahrnehmungsvermögen verändern muß.«[7]

L'élégant *Transat* pliant de Gray s'inspirait des chaises longues de paquebot. L'architecte français Jean Badovici écrivit sur Gray dans le numéro de juin 1924 de «Wendingen», le magazine de design néerlandais: «Elle est moderne dans tous les aspects possibles de son style, de sa vision et de son expression... Elle a compris ce que notre époque, avec ses nouveaux modes de vie, nous a apporté: la nécessité de nouvelles manières de ressentir les choses et le fait que l'âge de la machine doit transformer nos sensibilités.»[7]

Eileen Gray:

Transat, reissued by Ecart

Transat, Nachbau von Ecart

Transat, copie d'Ecart

Mart Stam

1899–1986

Netherlands . Niederlande . Pays-Bas

Side chair S33 1926
Reissued by Gebrüder Thonet, Frankenberg

Stuhl S33 1926
Nachbau von Gebrüder Thonet, Frankenberg

Chaise S33 1926
Copie par les Gebrüder Thonet, Frankenberg

L. & C. Arnold GmbH, Schorndorf, Germany (reissued by Gebrüder Thonet, Frankenberg)

Chair, 1926 / Stuhl, 1926 / Chaise, 1926

Lacquered, cast tubular steel frame, internally reinforced with solid metal rods, fabric seat and back

Rahmen aus Gußstahlrohr, lackiert und innen mit Rundstahlstäben verstärkt; Sitzfläche und Rückenlehne aus Stoff

Structure en tubes de fonte d'acier laquée à barres de renfort interne en métal, siège et dossier en tissu

In 1926, Stam made the first prototype chair to incorporate the cantilever principle. Later in the same year, he attended a meeting held in Stuttgart for all the architects taking part in the Deutsche Werkbund exhibition at the Weissenhofsiedlung in 1927. At this conference, Stam presented drawings of the prototype to, among others, Ludwig Mies van der Rohe, who, inspired by Stam's novel concept, designed his own versions of the cantilevered chair.

1926 entwarf Stam den Prototyp des ersten freitragenden Stuhls. Im gleichen Jahr nahm er teil an einem Treffen der Architekten, die sich an der Ausstellung des Deutschen Werkbundes in der Weißenhof-Siedlung im folgenden Jahr beteiligen sollten. Bei dieser Konferenz zeigte er seine Entwurfszeichnungen für den Prototyp auch Mies van der Rohe, der – von Stams neuem Sitzmöbeldesign inspiriert – eine eigene Version des freitragenden Stuhls entwarf.

En 1926, Stam réalisa le premier prototype d'un siège en porte-à-faux. Plus tard, au cours de la même année, il assista à une réunion organisée à Stuttgart pour tous les architectes participant à l'exposition du Deutsche Werkbund, prévue pour 1927 à la Weissenhofsiedlung. A cette conférence, il présenta les dessins de ces prototypes à Mies van der Rohe, entre autres, qui fasciné par la nouveauté de l'idée de Stam dessina sa propre version de chaise en porte-à-faux.

Ludwig Mies van der Rohe

1886–1969

Germany . Deutschland . Allemagne

Weissenhof chair, Model No. MR20 1927

Weißenhof-Stuhl, Modell Nr. MR20 1927

Chaise Weissenhof, modèle n° MR20 1927

Bent, nickel-plated tubular steel, cane seat

Rahmen aus gebogenem Stahlrohr, vernickelt; Sitzfläche aus Rohrgeflecht

Structure en tube d'acier cintré et nickelé, siège canné

Berliner Metallgewerbe Joseph Müller, Berlin from c. 1927–31 and Bamberg Metallwerkstätten, Berlin-Neukölln from 1931

Like Stam's earlier side chair, this more eloquent design of 1927 was first shown publicly at the Weissenhof as part of the Deutscher Werkbund "Die Wohnung" ("The Dwelling") exhibition. Mies' *Model No. MR20* armchair, was received with greater acclaim and later named after this landmark exhibition.

Genau wie ein früherer Stuhl von Stam, so wurde auch dieses gefälligere Design zum erstenmal öffentlich auf der Weißenhof-Ausstellung als Teil der Deutschen Werkbund-Ausstellung »Die Wohnung« gezeigt. Mies' Armlehnstuhl *Modell Nr. MR20* stieß dort auf breite Resonanz und wurde später nach dieser Ausstellung benannt.

Comme le fauteuil de Stam qui l'a précédé, ce design plus éloquent de 1927 a d'abord été présenté au Weissenhof en tant qu'élément de l'exposition du Deutscher Werkbund «Die Wohnung». Le fauteuil *MR20* de Mies fut plus applaudi et a ensuite reçu le nom de cette exposition marquante.

Ludwig Mies van der Rohe:

Pieces from a nine piece dining room suite, c. 1931

Elemente einer neunteiligen Kombination für ein Eßzimmer, um 1931

Elements d'un ensemble de 9 pièces pour salle à manger, vers 1931

Ludwig Mies van der Rohe:

Weissenhof *Model No. MR10* chair, 1927

Weißenhof-Sessel, *Modell Nr. MR10*, 1927

Chaise Weißenhof, *modèle n° MR10*, 1927

Marcel Breuer

1902–81

Germany . Deutschland .
Allemagne

Chair B32 1928
Armchair B64 1928

Stuhl B32 1928
Armlehnstuhl B64 1928

Chaise B32 1928
Fauteuil B64 1928

Chrome-plated, bent tubular steel
frame, bent solid beechwood seat
and back with woven cane

Rahmen Stahlrohr, gebogen und
verchromt; Sitzfläche und Rückenlehne aus Bugholz mit Rohrgeflecht

Structure en tubes d'acier cintrés
et chromés, siège et dossier en
hêtre massif cintré et canné

**Gebrüder Thonet, Frankenberg,
from c.1931 (reissued by
Gavina, Italy, from 1962 to 1968
and Knoll International, Inc.,
New York from 1968 to present)**

Marcel Breuer writes in "das neue
frankfurt" (1927): "One may conclude
that any object properly and practically
designed should "fit" into any room in
which it is used as would any living object, like a flower or a human being."[8]

Marcel Breuer schreibt 1927 in der
Zeitschrift »das neue frankfurt«: »man
darf annehmen, daß jedes objekt mit
einem guten und praktischen design in
jeden raum »paßt«, in dem es gebraucht wird, genau wie jedes leben-
dige objekt, sei es eine blume oder ein
menschliches wesen.«[8]

Marcel Breuer écrivit dans «das neue
frankfurt» en 1927: «On pourrait con-
clure que n'importe quel objet conçu
adéquatement et avec le sens du pratique devrait pouvoir s'adapter à n'importe quelle pièce dans laquelle il est
utilisé, comme tout objet vivant, fleur
ou être humain.»[8]

Thonet brochure, 1930/31,
cover

Thonet-Prospekt, 1930/31,
Einband

Prospectus Thonet, 1930/31,
couverture

The chaises longues described by Le Corbusier as "équipement de l'habitation"[9], are early examples of ergonomic design. The innovative movable seat section with adjustable neckrest affords a great degree of comfort to a wide range of users – a feature that has guaranteed the design's continuing appeal.

Die Chaiselongues, von Le Corbusier, als »Geräte zum Wohnen«[9] bezeichnet, sind frühe Beispiele des ergonomischen Designs. Die innovative Konstruktion der beweglichen Liegefläche und der verstellbaren Kopfstütze bietet den verschiedensten Benutzern ein großes Maß an Komfort – eine Besonderheit, die die noch immer anhaltende Beliebtheit dieses Entwurfs erklärt.

Les chaises longues décrites par Le Corbusier comme un «équipement de l'habitation»[9] sont de précoces exemples de design ergonomique. Le siège réglable en inclinaison, très innovateur, et son repose-tête adaptable assurent un grand degré de confort à toutes sortes d'utilisateurs, caractéristique qui a assuré le succès continu de ce modèle.

Le Corbusier
1887–1965

Pierre Jeanneret
1896–1967

Charlotte Perriand
*1903
France . Frankreich

Chaise longue c. 1928
Chaiselongue um 1928
Chaise longue vers 1928

Le Corbusier:
Model *LC4*, reissued by Cassina, 1965
Modell *LC4*, nachbau von Cassina, 1965
Modèle *LC4*, copie de Cassina, 1965

Le Corbusier:
Chaise longue, Model No. 2072, 1928
Chaiselongue, Modell Nr. 2072, 1928
Chaise longue, modèle n° 2072, 1928

Embru-Werke AG catalogue showing *Model No. 2072*, 1936
Embru-Werke AG, Katalog: *Modell Nr. 2072*, 1936
Embru-Werke AG, catalogue présentant le *modèle n° 2072*, 1936

Black-painted metal, tubular metal framework covered in ponyskin on an elongated H-form base

Schwarz lackiertes Metall, Stahlrohrrahmen, bezogen mit Pferdefell auf einer verlängerten H-förmigen Basis

Métal laqué noir, structure en tube de métal, cuir de poney sur une base en forme de H allongé

Embru-Werke AG, Rüti, Zurich, from 1932. The hide-covered Model No. B306 version of this design was manufactured by Gebrüder Thonet, Frankenberg, from c. 1929 (reissued by Cassina, Italy, from 1965)

Le Corbusier

1887–1965

Pierre Jeanneret

1896–1967

Charlotte Perriand

*1903

France . Frankreich

Le Corbusier collaborated with Charlotte Perriand and his cousin Pierre Jeanneret in the design of this chair, which was initially used in the interior of a villa in Ville-d'Avray and first exhibited at the 1929 Salon d'Automne, Paris. With its undeniable luxury and elegant proportions, the *Grand Confort* is quintessentially of the International Style.

Zusammen mit Charlotte Perriand und seinem Cousin Pierre Jeanneret entwarf Le Corbusier diesen Sessel als Teil der Inneneinrichtung einer Villa in Ville-d'Avray. 1929 wurde er auf dem Salon d'Automne (Paris) der breiten Öffentlichkeit vorgestellt. Der ausgesprochen luxuriöse und elegante Sessel *Grand Confort* ist geradezu eine Verkörperung des Internationalen Stils.

Le Corbusier collabora avec Charlotte Perriand et son cousin Pierre Jeanneret au dessin de ce siège qui fut placé dans une villa de Ville-d'Avray avant d'être exposé pour la première fois au Salon d'Automne (Paris) de 1929. De par son luxe indéniable et ses élégantes proportions, le *Grand Confort* représente la quintessence du style international.

**Grand Confort,
Model No. LC3** 1928

**Sessel Grand Confort,
Modell Nr. LC3** 1928

**Grand Confort,
modèle n° LC3** 1928

Chrome-plated, bent tubular steel frame with loose, leather-covered, upholstered cushions

Rahmen Stahlrohr, gebogen, verchromt; eingelegte Polsterkissen, Lederbezug

Structure en tube d'acier cintré et chromé à coussins mobiles en cuir

Gebrüder Thonet, Vienna & Paris (reissued by Cassina, Italy, from 1965)

Le Corbusier, Pierre Jeanneret, Charlotte Perriand:

LC3 chair, 1928/29 (Cassina)

Sessel *LC3*, 1928/29 (Cassina)

Fauteuil *LC3*, 1928/29 (Cassina)

Le Corbusier, Pierre Jeanneret, Charlotte Perriand:

LC2 chair, 1928/29 (Cassina)

Sessel *LC2*, 1928/29 (Cassina)

Fauteuil *LC2*, 1928/29 (Cassina)

Le Corbusier, Pierre Jeanneret, Charlotte Perriand:

LC2 sofa, 1928/29 (Cassina)

Sofa *LC2*, 1928/29 (Cassina)

Canapé *LC2*, 1928/29 (Cassina)

Ludwig Mies van der Rohe

1886-1969

Germany . Deutschland . Allemagne

Barcelona chair, Model No. MR90 1929

Sessel Barcelona, Modell Nr. MR90 1929

Chauffeuse Barcelona, modèle n° MR90 1929

Bent, chromed flat steel with removable buttoned-leather, upholstered cushions

Rahmen Flachstahl, gebogen, verchromt; abnehmbare Polsterkissen, Lederbezug mit Knöpfen

Acier plat cintré et chromé, acier plat chromé avec coussins amovibles en cuir capitonné

Berliner Metallgewerbe Joseph Müller, Berlin, and, slightly later, Bamberg Metallwerkstätten, Berlin-Neukölln (reissued by Knoll Associates, Inc., New York from 1948)

The *Model No. MR90* was designed for the German pavilion at the 1929 Exposición Internacional in Barcelona and for the specific use of King Alfonso XIII and his queen at the exhibition's opening ceremonies. The form of the chair was based on a folding stool of antiquity known as the "sella curulis". Although the *MR90* appears to be thoroughly modern, the methods used in its manufacture were, ironically, traditional and extremely labour-intensive.

Van der Rohe entwarf das *Modell Nr. MR90* für den Deutschen Pavillon auf der Exposición Internacional von 1929 in Barcelona. Während der Eröffnungsfeier diente es König Alfonso XIII. und der Königin von Spanien als Sitzgelegenheit. Der Sessel mit den lederbezogenen Kissen strahlt Würde und Eleganz aus; seine Form geht zurück auf den zusammenklappbaren Stuhl der Antike, die »sella curulis«. Obwohl das *Modell Nr. MR90* höchst modern wirkt, ist seine Herstellungsweise traditionell und ungewöhnlich arbeitsintensiv.

Ce modèle fut dessiné pour le Pavillon d'Allemagne de l'Exposición Internacional de Barcelone en 1929 et à l'usage exclusif du roi Alphonse XIII et de son épouse lors des cérémonies d'ouverture. De ce siège, dont la forme rappelle les anciennes chaises curules pliantes, émane un sens affirmé du luxe. Bien que le *MR90* apparaisse comme profondément moderne, ses méthodes de fabrication se révélèrent ironiquement très traditionnelles et très longues.

Ludwig Mies van der Rohe:

The German Pavilion, Barcelona International Exhibition, 1929

Der Deutsche Pavillon, Weltausstellung in Barcelona, 1929

Pavillon d'Allemagne, Exposition Internationale de Barcelone, 1929

Reconstruction of the German pavilion at the International Exhibition in Barcelona, 1929

Rekonstruktion des Deutschen Pavillons auf der internationalen Weltausstellung in Barcelona, 1929

Reconstruction du Pavillon d'Allemagne à l'Exposition Internationale de Barcelone en 1929

Alvar Aalto

1898–1976

Finland . Finnland . Finlande

**Paimio chair,
Model No. 41** 1931/32

**Sessel Paimio,
Modell Nr. 41** 1931/32

**Fauteuil Paimio,
modèle n° 41** 1931/32

Bent, laminated birch frame, solid
birch, with painted, bent plywood
seat

Gestell laminiertes, gebogenes
Birkenholz, massiv; Sitz aus
verformtem Schichtholz, lackiert

Structure en bouleau lamellé
cintré, bouleau massif et siège de
contreplaqué cintré et peint

**Oy Huonekalu-ja Rakennust-
yötehdas AB, Turku, Finland
(reissued by Artek, Finland)**

Subsequently known as the *Paimio*
chair, the *Model No. 41* did not figure
in the original interior scheme of
Aalto's Paimio Sanatorium project,
initiated in 1929. The design actually
dates from 1932, when the sanatorium
was completed. Exhibited at the Building Congress for Nordic Countries that
year, the construction of the *Model No.
41* was revolutionary. Where there was
a need for greater pliancy, as in the
scrolls of the seat and back, Aalto
thinned out the laminate by removing
several layers of veneer.

Das *Modell Nr. 41*, das als *Paimio-
Sessel* bekannt wurde, gehörte nicht
zu der Originalausstattung des von
Aalto konzipierten Sanatoriums Paimio,
das 1929 eröffnet wurde. Das Modell
entstand 1932, mit der Fertigstellung
des Sanatoriums, und wurde im selben
Jahr auf dem Baukongreß für Nor-
dische Länder vorgestellt. Die Konstruktion war revolutionär. Um eine
stärkere Krümmung einiger Teile zu er-
reichen, verdünnte Aalto das Schichtholz, indem er einige Lagen Furnierblatt
abtrug.

Ce *modèle n° 41*, le fauteuil *Paimio*, ne
figurait pas à l'origine dans le projet de
décoration d'Aalto pour le Sanatorium
de Paimio en 1929. Son dessin date
en réalité de 1932. Présenté au Congrès de la Construction des Pays
Scandinaves en 1932, il était révolutionnaire dans sa construction. Pour
permettre un meilleur pliage du bois,
en particulier dans les enroulements du
dossier et du siège, Aalto amincit le
lamellé en éliminant plusieurs couches
de placage pour augmenter la souplesse du matériau.

Alvar Aalto:

Model No. 60 stool, 1930–33

Hocker *Modell Nr. 60*, 1930–33

Tabouret *modèle n° 60*,
1930–33

Marcel Breuer:

Chaise longue, 1935/36

Chaiselongue, 1935/36

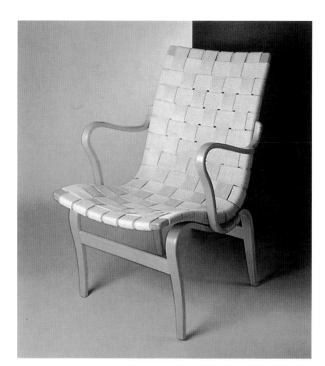

Bruno Mathsson

*1907

Sweden . Schweden . Suède

Eva chair 1934
Stuhl Eva 1934
Chaise Eva 1934

Bent plywood, solid birch and
hemp webbing

Rahmen gebogenes Birken-
Schichtholz; Sitzfläche aus
geflochtenen Hanfgurten

Cadre en bouleau lamellé,
sangles de chanvre tressées

**Firma Karl Mathsson, Varnamo,
Sweden (reissued by Dux,
Sweden from 1966)**

Bruno Mathsson's own summer
house in Frösakull, 1961

Bruno Mathssons eigenes
Sommerhaus in Frösakull, 1961

Maison de vacances de Bruno
Mathsson à Frösakull, 1961

Mathsson designed the *Eva* chair as
well as the later *Pernilla* chaise longue,
a lounge chair and an ottoman as a
functional and aesthetically pleasing
furniture group. Mathsson has declared: "the business of sitting never
ceases to amaze me."[10]

Mathsson entwarf den Stuhl *Eva*, die
Chaiselongue *Pernilla*, einen
Liegestuhl und eine Ottomane als Teile
einer funktionalen und ästhetisch
ansprechenden Möbelgruppe.
Mathsson sagte einmal: »Das Problem
des Sitzens gibt mir immer wieder
Rätsel auf.«[10]

Mathsson créa cette chaise *Eva* ainsi
que plus tard la chaise longue *Pernilla*
et une autre chaise longue et une ottomane avec le double souci de la fonction et de l'esthétique. Il déclara un jour
que «s'asseoir est un sujet qui n'a
jamais cessé d'éveiller ma curiosité.»[10]

Gerrit Rietveld

1888–1964

Netherlands . Niederlande .
Pays-Bas

Zig-Zag chair 1934
Stuhl Zig-Zag 1934
Chaise Zig-Zag 1934

Solid elm construction

Konstruktion aus massivem
Ulmenholz

Construction en orme massif

**G.A. van de Groenekan, De Bilt,
Netherlands (reissued by
Cassina, Italy, from 1971)**

Using only four elements joined with a system of dovetailing secured with brass nuts and bolts, the *Zig-Zag* chair's visual simplicity belies a relatively complex construction. Examples of this design were also manufactured by Metz & Co. and in 1935 the company produced several variations, including a high-backed version and an armchair. This painted *Zig-Zag* chair was made by Gerard A. van de Groenekan in 1938 for his personal use.

Der *Zig-Zag*-Stuhl, der aus nur vier Elementen besteht, wird mit Hilfe von Schwalbenschwanzverbindungen – verstärkt durch Muttern und Schrauben – zusammengebaut. Trotz der einfachen Form ist seine Konstruktion überaus komplex. Außer bei der oben genannten Firma wurde dieses Modell auch von Metz & Co. produziert, die 1935 diverse Varianten herstellten, u.a. eine Version mit hoher Lehne und einen Armlehnstuhl. Der abgebildete *Zig-Zag*-Stuhl wurde von Gerard A. van de Groenekan 1938 zum persönlichen Gebrauch angefertigt.

Avec seulement quatre éléments montés en queue d'aronde et maintenus par un boulonnage de cuivre, l'apparente simplicité de la chaise *Zig-Zag* cache en réalité une construction assez complexe. Des modèles en furent également fabriqués par Metz & Co.(Amsterdam) et, en 1935, la société produisit plusieurs variations dont une version à haut dossier et un fauteuil. Cette chaise *Zig-Zag* a été réalisée par Gerard A. van de Groenekan en 1938 pour son usage personnel.

Gerrit Rietveld:

Interior in Stoop Family House,
Velp, photographed in 1950

Inneneinrichtung, Haus der
Familie Stoop, Velp,
1950 fotografiert

Vue de l'intérieur de la maison
Stoop, Velp, photographiée
en 1950

Reissued *Zig-Zag* chairs
manufactured by Cassina

Nachgebaute *Zig-Zag*-Stühle,
produziert von Cassina

Réédition des chaises *Zig-Zag*
par Cassina

Giuseppe Terragni

1904 – 43

Italy . Italien . Italie

Follia chair 1934 – 36
Stuhl Follia 1934 – 36
Chaise Follia 1934 – 36

Solid wood seat and back, painted black, connected with a stainless steel backrest-support spring

Sitzfläche und Rückenlehne aus massivem Holz, schwarz lackiert; Verbindung zwischen Sitzfläche und Rückenlehne durch Edelstahlfedern

Siège et dossier en bois massif peint en noir, réunis par un support de dossier en acier inoxydable souple

Reissued under licence by Zanotta, Italy, from 1971

The *Follia* chair was designed for the Casa del Fascio, the Italian Fascist party headquarters in Como. Modernist architecture and designs such as the *Follia*, the *Lariana* and the *Sant'Elia* chairs were viewed favourably by the Italian Fascists until the late 1930s, when the prevailing Rationalism was generally superseded by the state-promoted neo-Classical Novecento style.

Der *Follia*-Stuhl wurde speziell für die Casa del Fascio, das Hauptquartier der Italienischen Faschistischen Partei in Como, entworfen. Die zeitgenössische, moderne Architektur und das moderne Design, z.B. der Stühle *Follia*, *Lariana* und *Sant'Elia*, wurden von den italienischen Faschisten bis gegen Ende der dreißiger Jahre favorisiert; dann wurde der vorherrschende Rationalismus europaweit vom Neoklassizismus des 20. Jahrhunderts verdrängt, dem nun auch die staatlichen Organe Italiens den Vorzug gaben.

La chaise *Follia* a été spécialement créée pour la Casa del Fascio, siège du parti fasciste à Côme. Il est intéressant de noter que l'architecture moderniste et des modèles comme, par exemple, les chaises *Follia*, *Lariana* et *Sant'Elia* furent appréciées par les fascistes italiens jusqu'à la fin des années 30 quand le rationalisme prévalant fut généralement remplacé par un style néo-classique approuvé par l'Etat.

Giuseppe Terragni:
Casa del Fascio, Como, 1932 – 36

Giuseppe Terragni:
Lariana chair, 1935/36
Stuhl *Lariana*, 1935/36
Chaise *Lariana*, 1935/36

Giuseppe Terragni:
Sant'Elia chair, 1936
Stuhl *Sant'Elia*, 1936
Chaise *Sant'Elia*, 1936

59

Jorge Ferrari-Hardoy

1913–75

Juan Kurchan

unknown

Antonio Bonet

unknown

Argentina . Argentinien . Argentine

Butterfly chair,
Model No. 198 1938

Stuhl Butterfly,
Modell Nr. 198 1938

Chaise Butterfly,
modèle n° 198 1938

Tubular steel frame with leather
sling seat

Rahmen aus gebogenem Stahlrohr, lackiert; eingehängter Bezug
aus Leder

Structure tubulaire en acier, siège
de cuir suspendu

Knoll Associates, Inc., New York
from c.1950 to c.1975 (reissued
by Stöhr Import-Export GmbH,
Germany, from 1982 to present)

"Hardoy characterised this chair as 'an improvement on previous designs' which he and his colleagues had made for their own offices, little dreaming it would ever become so popular."[11] The *Butterfly* chair was initially produced by Artek-Pascoe and approximately 1,500 were sold. After the Second World War, Knoll took over production. A lawsuit later ensued regarding copyright infringement, which Knoll eventually lost. Consequently, the *Model No. 198* became one of the most copied chair designs in recent history.

»Hardoy beschrieb den Sessel als »Verbesserung früherer Entwürfe«, die er und seine Kollegen ausgeführt hatten, wobei sie nicht im Traum daran gedacht hatten, daß dieses Modell einmal so beliebt werden würde.«[11] Der *Butterfly*-Sessel wurde zunächst von Artek-Pascoe produziert; verkauft wurden etwa 1.500 Stück. Nach dem Zweiten Weltkrieg übernahm Knoll die Produktion. Einen Rechtsstreit wegen Verletzung des Copyrights verlor Knoll. In der Folge wurde das *Modell Nr. 198* zum meistkopierten Stuhl der jüngeren Designgeschichte.

«Hardoy considérait cette chaise comme «une amélioration de projets antérieurs» que lui et ses collègues avaient réalisés pour leurs propres bureaux, n'imaginant pas qu'ils puisssent connaître le succès.»[11] La chaise *Butterfly* fut initialement produite par Artek-Pascoe qui en vendit environ 1.500 exemplaires. Après la Seconde Guerre mondiale, Knoll reprit la production. Plus tard, un procès eut lieu sur le non-respect de ces droits que Knoll perdit. Ce modèle devint l'un des sièges les plus copiés de l'histoire récente du design.

Interior designed by Knoll International showing *Butterfly Model No. 198* chair, c.1960

Inneneinrichtung von Knoll International, zu sehen ist der *Butterfly*-Sessel, *Modell Nr. 198*, um 1960

Intérieur conçu par Knoll International, chaise *Butterfly*, modèle n° *198*, vers 1960

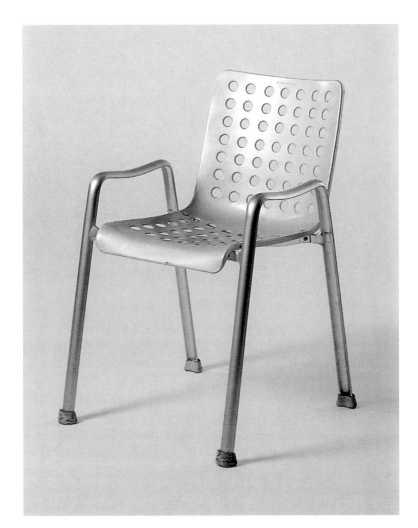

Hans Coray

*1906

Switzerland . Schweiz . Suisse

Landi stacking chair
1939

Stapelstuhl Landi
1939

Chaise empilable Landi
1939

Bent and pressed aluminium

Aluminium, gestanzt und geformt

Aluminium embouti et cintré

**Blattmann Metallwarenfabrik
AG, Wädenswil, Switzerland
(reissued by Zanotta, Italy,
from 1970)**

This 'proto-High Tech' design was commissioned by Hans Fischli for the grounds of the "Landesausstellung" (Swiss National Exhibition) held in Zurich in 1939. Weighing just over three kg, the Landi stacking chair was designed for both interior and exterior use. It was not marketed internationally until the 1950s, when it was widely acclaimed for its strength and durability.

Dieses »Proto-High-Tech«-Design wurde von Hans Fischli für das Gelände der Landesausstellung in Zürich 1939 in Auftrag gegeben. Der Landi-Stuhl wog gut drei Kilogramm und war für den Gebrauch in Innen- und Außenräumen konzipiert. International wurde er erst in den 50er Jahren vermarktet, nachdem man in weiten Kreisen seine Stärke und Haltbarkeit erkannt hatte.

Ce modèle proto-High-Tech fut commandé par Hans Fischli pour les abords de la «Landesausstellung» (Exposition Nationale Suisse) de Zurich, en 1939. Ne pesant qu'un peu plus de trois kilos, cette chaise empilable était conçue aussi bien pour un usage extérieur qu'intérieur. Elle ne fut pas commercialisée internationalement avant les années 50 et fut alors saluée pour sa solidité et sa durabilité.

"Landesausstellung" (Swiss National Exhibition), Zurich, 1939

»Landesausstellung« (Schweizer Nationalausstellung), Zürich, 1939

»Landesausstellung« (Exposition Nationale Suisse), Zurich, 1939

Carlo Mollino

1905 – 73

Italy . Italien . Italie

Side Chair designed for Lisa and Gio Ponti 1940

Stuhl, entworfen für Lisa und Gio Ponti 1940

Chaise dessinée pour Lisa et Gio Ponti 1940

Polished brass frame with Resin-flex upholstered bifurcated seat and back

Rahmen aus poliertem Messing; zweigeteilte, gepolsterte Sitz-fläche und Rückenlehne, Resin-flexbezug

Structure de cuivre poli, siège et dossier rembourrés, recouverts de Resinflex

Probably Apelli & Varesio, Turin, Italy

Carlo Mollino:

Bent wood and laminated *10-ply Ash* Side chair, 1949

10-ply Ash-Stuhl (lamierte und geformte Esche), 1949

Chaise *10-ply Ash* (Frène lamellé et moulé), 1949

Mollino's life and work were dictated by his firm belief that everything was "permissible as long as it is fantastic". Certainly, his life-long interest in occultism is reflected in the form of this chair, which is clearly based on a cloven hoof. The chair was designed for Lisa and Gio Ponti.

Mollinos Leben und Arbeit standen unter dem Motto »alles ist erlaubt, vorausgesetzt, es ist phantastisch«. Vorbild für die Form des Stuhls, die zweifellos sein lebenslanges Interesse am Okkultismus reflektiert, war offen-sichtlich ein gespaltener Huf. Der Stuhl war ein Entwurf für Lisa und Gio Ponti.

La vie et l'œuvre de Mollino furent dictées par sa croyance définitive que tout était «autorisé à condition d'être fantastique». L'intérêt qu'il témoigna sa vie durant à l'occultisme se retrouve dans la forme de cette chaise qui évoque à l'évidence un pied fourchu. Cette chaise a été dessinée pour Lisa et Gio Ponti.

Carlo Mollino:

Armchair with curved armrest, 1952

Sessel mit gebogener Armlehne, 1952

Chaise avec accoudoir incurvé, 1952

Carlo Mollino:

Chair for the Casa di Agra, 1955

Stuhl für die Casa di Agra, 1955

Chaise pour Casa di Agra, 1955

Carlo Mollino

1905–73

Italy . Italien . Italie

Armchair for Minola House
1944

Sessel für das Minola-Haus
1944

**Fauteuil pour la maison
Minola** 1944

Ebonised wood frame with velvet-
covered upholstery

Holzrahmen, schwarz gebeizt;
Polsterung mit Samt bezogen

Structure de bois noirci, rembourrage recouvert de velours

**Probably Apelli & Varesio, Turin,
Italy**

Carlo Mollino: "The best explanation
of one's work is contained in its silent
ostentation."[12] This armchair was designed for the house of Ada and Cesare Minola in Turin, Italy.

Carlo Mollino: »Die beste Erklärung
für die Arbeit, die man tut, gibt ihre
stumme Prahlerei.«[12] Der Sessel wurde für das Haus von Ada und Cesare
Minola in Turin, Italien, entworfen.

Carlo Mollino: «La meilleure explication
du travail de quelqu'un est toute en-
tière contenue dans sa présence silen-
cieuse.»[12] Ce fauteuil a été dessiné
pour la maison de Ada et Cesare
Minola à Turin, Italie.

Living room in the house of Ada
and Cesare Minola in Turin, 1944

Wohnraum im Haus von Ada und
Cesare Minola in Turin, 1944

Salle de séjour de la villa de Ada
et Cesare Minola à Turin, 1944

63

Charles &
Ray Eames

1907–78 & 1913–88
USA . Etats-Unis

LCM (Lounge Chair Metal)
1945/46
Sessel, Modell LCM
1945/46
Chaise LCM 1945/46

Slunkskin (animal hide) covered,
moulded plywood seat and back,
attached with rubber shock-
mounts to a chrome-plated bent
tubular steel frame with self-
levelling feet

Sitzschale und Rückenlehne aus
mit Fell bezogenem geformtem
Schichtholz, mit elastischen
Gummischeiben am Rahmen
befestigt; Rahmen aus gezogenem, verchromtem Stahlrohr
mit selbsttätig höhenausgleich-
enden Beinen

Siège et dossier en contreplaqué
moulé recouverts de veau mort-
né, reliés par des blocs de caoutchouc à un cadre de tube d'acier
cintré et chromé avec piètement à
hauteur réglable

**Evans Products Company,
Venice, California from 1946 to
1949 and Herman Miller Inc.,
Zeeland, Michigan, from 1949
(Slunkskin version manufac-
tured 1948–53)**

The *LCM* forms part of the moulded
plywood group of chairs, the prototypes of which were first shown in New
York in December 1945. Impressed by
what he saw there, Eliot Noyes, director of Industrial Design at the Museum of Modern Art, gave Charles
Eames the museum's first one-man
show in 1946. As a result, George
Nelson introduced the Eameses to D.J.
De Pree, the managing director of
Herman Miller, Inc., – and so began
one of the most fruitful collaborations
between manufacturer and designer
ever recorded.

Der Sessel *LCM* ist Teil einer Kollektion von Sitzmöbeln aus verformtem,
schichtverleimtem Sperrholz, die
Ende1945 in New York vorgestellt
wurde. Den Direktor der Abteilung Industrial Design des Museum of Modern Art, Eliot Noyes, beeindruckte die
Präsentation, und er ermöglichte
Charles Eames 1946 die erste One-
man-show des Museums. George
Nelson war begeistert und stellte die
Eames dem Generaldirektor von Herman Miller, Inc., D.J. De Pree, vor. So
begann eine äußerst fruchtbare
Zusammenarbeit.

La *LCM* fait partie du groupe de
sièges en «contreplaqué moulé» dont
les prototypes furent à l'origine présentés à New York en 1945. Eliot
Noyes, directeur du Design Industriel
au Museum of Modern Art, offrit à
Eames la première exposition personnelle jamais consacrée par le musée à
un designer (1946). A la suite de cette
exposition, George Nelson présenta
les Eames à D.J. De Pree, directeur-
gérant d'Herman Miller, Inc. C'est ainsi
que commença l'une des collaborations les plus fructueuses qui aient jamais existé entre fabricant et créateur.

Charles & Ray Eames:
LCW, 1946

Charles & Ray Eames:
DCM, 1946

Charles & Ray Eames:
LCW, 1946

In his pursuit of a unified and organic form of design, Saarinen's principal concern was with human anatomy and its relationship to furniture. He said that the design of the *Womb* chair represented an "attempt to achieve psychological comfort by providing a great big cup-like shell into which you can curl up and pull up your legs (something that women seem especially to like to do)".[13]

Saarinen strebte ein ganzheitliches, organisches Design an und orientierte sich dabei vor allem an der menschlichen Anatomie und ihrer Relation zum Möbel. Er sagte, der Sessel *Womb* sei ein »Versuch, das Gefühl von Behaglichkeit zu erzeugen – und zwar indem man eine große schalenförmige Muschel wählte, in die man sich mit angezogenen Beinen schmiegen kann (was Frauen anscheinend besonders gern tun).«[13]

Le principal souci de Saarinen, dans sa recherche d'une forme de design organique et unifié, était l'anatomie et ses relations avec le mobilier. Il déclara que le dessin de ce siège représentait «une tentative de parvenir à un confort psychologique en offrant une sorte de grande coque dans laquelle vous pouvez vous blottir et ramener vos jambes (ce que les femmes aiment particulièrement faire).»[13]

Eero Saarinen

1910–61

USA . Etats-Unis

**Womb chair,
Model No. 70** 1946

**Sessel Womb,
Modell Nr. 70** 1946

**Fauteuil Womb,
modèle n° 70** 1946

Fabric-covered, upholstered, moulded fibreglass seat shell, with loose latex-foam cushions, supported on a bent tubular steel frame with nylon swivel glides

Rahmen aus gebogenem Stahlrohr, Sitzschale aus geformtem Fiberglas; Polsterung mit Stoff bezogen, lose eingelegte Kissen mit Latexschaumstoff-Füllung; höhenausgleichende Gleitfüße aus Nylon mit Kugelgelenk

Coque de siège en fibre de verre moulée, rembourrée et recouverte de tissu avec coussins amovibles en mousse de latex sur cadre en tubes d'acier cintrés et glissières de pivotement en nylon sur rotules

Knoll Associates, Inc., New York, from 1948 to present

Herbert Matter:

Knoll advertisement for *Womb* chair, c.1950

Knoll-Werbung für den Sessel *Womb*, um 1950

Publicité de Knoll pour le fauteuil *Womb*, vers 1950

Eero Saarinen:

Three models from a 1948 collection

Drei Modelle aus einer Kollektion von 1948

Trois modèles d'une collection de 1948

65

Hans Wegner

*1914

Denmark . Dänemark . Danemark

Classic armchair 1949
Armlehnstuhl Classic 1949
Fauteuil Classic 1949

Solid teak construction with
woven cane seat

Rahmen Teakholz massiv;
Sitzfläche aus Rohrgeflecht

Teak massif et siège canné

Johannes Hansen, Denmark
(reissued by PP Møbler,
Allerørd, Denmark from 1992)

"Wegner's original title for the *Classic* chair was the *Round* chair... but the name *Classic* chair soon caught on and was advocated by its admirers, who often referred to it as *The Chair*. Wegner designed this classic when he was only thirty-five years old and tended to be a little reticent in accepting the honour of having designed The Chair, believing that he had not at that point reached the height of his creative powers and was therefore not deserving of such an honour."[14]

»Wegners ursprünglicher Name für diesen Stuhl war *Round Chair* ..., aber die Bezeichnung *Classic* bürgerte sich schnell ein und wurde auch von seinen Bewunderern befürwortet, die ihn oft als *den Stuhl* bezeichneten. Wegner entwarf den Stuhl *Classic* schon im Alter von 35 Jahren und reagierte immer ein wenig zurückhaltend, wenn man ihn aufgrund dieses Stuhldesigns verehrte, denn er glaubte, den Höhepunkt seines Schaffens noch nicht erreicht zu haben und daher eine solche Ehre nicht verdient zu haben.«[14]

«Le nom donné originellement par Wegner à ce fauteuil *Classic* était *Round Chair*, mais le terme de *Classic* fut préféré et défendu par ses admirateurs qui souvent l'appelaient *La Chaise*. Wegner dessina ce modèle alors qu'il n'avait que vingt-cinq ans et montrait quelques réticences à accepter l'honneur de l'avoir dessiné, pensant qu'il était encore loin d'avoir atteint la puissance créative et qu'il ne méritait donc pas un tel honneur.»[14]

Hans Wegner:
Chinese chair, 1944
Chinesischer Stuhl, 1944
Chaise chinoise, 1944

Hans Wegner:
Peacock chair, 1947
Stuhl *Peacock*, 1947
Chaise *Peacock*, 1947

Hans Wegner:
Stacking chairs, 1949
Stapelstühle, 1949
Chaises empilables, 1949

In 1948, Marco Zanuso was commissioned by the Pirelli Company to investigate the potential of latex foam as a material suitable for upholstery. Later, in March 1950, the company established the Arflex firm to manufacture Zanuso's and other designers' foam-upholstered furniture. The *Antropus* was the first chair produced by Arflex and it is a tribute to Zanuso's unquestionable genius that it remains in production today.

1948 wurde Marco Zanuso von der Pirelli Company beauftragt, die Möglichkeiten von Latexschaumstoff als Polstermaterial zu untersuchen. Im März 1950 gründete Pirelli die Firma Arflex, um die schaumstoffgepolsterten Sitzmöbel von Zanuso und anderen Designern zu produzieren. *Antropus* war der erste Stuhl, den Arflex herstellte, und es ist Zanusos großem Können zuzuschreiben, daß sein Stuhl noch heute produziert wird.

En 1948, Pirelli demanda à Marco Zanuso d'explorer les possibilités de la mousse de latex dans le domaine du garnissage. Plus tard, en mars 1950, Pirelli créa Arflex pour réaliser les projets de Zanuso et d'autres designers de meubles recouverts de mousse de latex. L'*Antropus* fut le premier siège produit par Arflex et le fait qu'il soit toujours en production aujourd'hui est en soi un hommage au génie incontesté de Zanuso.

Marco Zanuso

*1916

Italy . Italien . Italie

Antropus chair 1949
Sessel Antropus 1949
Fauteuil Antropus 1949

Fabric-covered, latex foam upholstered, moulded plywood

Rahmen geformtes Schichtholz; Polsterung aus Latexschaumstoff, mit Stoff bezogen

Cadre en bois lamellé moulé garni de mousse de latex et recouvert de tissu

Arflex, Italy, from 1950 to present

Marco Zanuso:

Lady armchair, 1951

Sessel *Lady*, 1951

Fauteuil *Lady*, 1951

Franco Albini:

Fiorenza chair, 1952

Sessel *Fiorenza*, 1952

Fauteuil *Fiorenza*, 1952

Ernest Race

1913–64

Great Britain . Großbritannien .
Grande-Bretagne

**Antelope chair with
matching table** 1950

**Armlehnstuhl Antelope mit
dazugehörigem Tisch** 1950

**Chaise Antelope avec table
assortie** 1950

Painted, bent steel rod frame with
painted, moulded plywood seat

Rahmen und Rückenlehne
gebogener Rundstahl, lackiert;
Sitzfläche aus geformtem Schichtholz

Structure en acier cintré peint
et siège en contreplaqué moulé
peint

**Ernest Race Ltd., UK, from
1950 to present (table 1950
to c. 1955)**

The *Antelope* chair was designed for
the Royal Festival Hall's outdoor
terraces at the year-long Festival of
Britain exhibition of 1951. Designed to
comply with the constraints of national
rationing, the *Antelope* chair's spindly
legs terminating on ball feet echoed
the new imagery of nuclear physics
and molecular chemistry.

Der *Antelope*-Stuhl war anläßlich der
Ausstellung Festival of Britain von
1951, die ein Jahr lang dauerte, speziell für die Außenterrassen der Royal
Festival Hall entworfen worden; er
entsprach den restriktiven Bedingungen der nationalen Rationierungs-
maßnahmen. Seine staksigen Beine
endeten in kugelförmigen Füßen – ein
Motiv, das das zunehmende Publi-
kumsinteresse an Nuklearphysik und
Molekularbiologie widerspiegelte.

La chaise *Antelope* fut créée pour les
terrasses en plein air du Royal Festival
Hall à l'occasion de l'exposition du
Festival de Grande-Bretagne qui dura
toute l'année 1951. Dessinés en pensant aux contraintes du rationnement
d'après-guerre, ses maigres pieds se
terminant par des boules reflétaient
l'intérêt grandissant du public pour la
physique nucléaire et la chimie
moléculaire.

Antelope chairs and tables in the
Café of the Homes and Gardens
Pavilion, Festival of Britain, 1951

Stühle und Tische aus der
Antelope-Serie im Café des
Homes and Gardens Pavillon,
Festival of Britain, 1951

Chaises et tables *Antelope* dans
le Café du Pavillon Homes and
Gardens, Festival of Britain, 1951

Antelope chairs outside the Lion
and Unicorn Pavilion, Festival of
Britain, 1951

Antelope-Stühle vor dem Lion and
Unicorn Pavillon, Festival of
Britain, 1951

Chaises *Antelope* devant le Lion
and Unicorn pavillon, Festival of
Britain, 1951

Advertising leaflet showing
designs by Jean Prouvé, Steph
Simon, Paris, 1950s

Werbebroschüre mit Entwürfen
von Jean Prouvé, Steph Simon,
Paris, 50er Jahre

Pospectus montrant des créations
de Jean Prouvé, Steph Simon,
années 50

Jean Prouvé

1901–84
France . Frankreich

Antony chair 1950
Stuhl Antony 1950
Chaise Antony 1950

Bent and painted tubular steel
and flat steel frame, with moulded
plywood seat

Rahmen Stahlrohr und Flachstahl,
gebogen, lackiert; Sitzschale
geformtes Schichtholz

Structure en tube d'acier cintré
peint et acier plat, siège en
contreplaqué moulé

**Les Ateliers Jean Prouvé S.A.,
Maxéville, France, from 1950
to 1954**   69

Originally designed for use at the University of Strasbourg, the *Antony* chair was manufactured by Prouvé's own company, founded in 1931, and was distributed by Steph Simon, Paris. Prouvé gave up furniture design when he left his company in 1953.

Der *Antony*-Sessel war ein Entwurf für die Ausstattung der Universität von Straßburg. Er wurde in Prouvés eigener, 1931 gegründeter Firma hergestellt und von Steph Simon, Paris, vertrieben. Prouvé gab seine Tätigkeit als Möbeldesigner auf, nachdem er seine Firma 1953 verlassen hatte.

Conçue à l'origine pour l'Université de Strasbourg, cette chaise fut fabriquée par l'usine que Prouvé avait ouverte en 1931 et distribuée par Steph Simon, Paris. Prouvé abandonna la création de mobilier lorsqu'il quitta sa société en 1953.

Harry Bertoia

1915–78

USA . Etats-Unis

Diamond chair 1950–52

Sessel Diamond 1950–52

Fauteuil Diamond 1950–52

Bent and welded steel rod construction, either chrome-plated or
vinyl-coated finish

Konstruktion aus gebogenem
Rundstahl, geschweißt und
verchromt oder vinylbeschichtet

Construction en tiges de fer cin-
trées et soudées, chromées ou
gainées de vinyl

**Knoll International, Inc., New
York, from c.1953 to present**

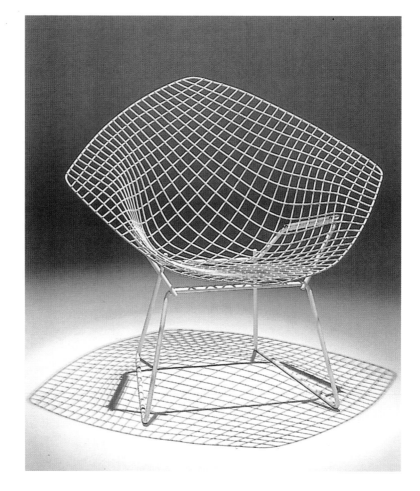

Harry Bertoia:

The Bertoia Collection, 1951

"In sculpture, I am concerned primarily with space, form and the character-istics of metal. In the chairs, many functional problems have to be satisfied first... but when you get right down to it, the chairs are studies in space, form and metal too. If you will look at them, you will find they are mostly made of air, just like sculpture. Space passes right through them."[15]

»Bei der Skulptur interessiert mich vor allem das Verhältnis von Form und Raum und die Eigenschaften des Metalls. Bei den Stühlen muß man zuerst viele funktionale Probleme lösen... aber genaugenommen sind Stühle auch Studien in Raum, Form und Metall. Wenn man genau hinschaut, wird einem klar, daß sie hauptsächlich aus Luft bestehen, genau wie die Skulptur. Der Raum geht direkt durch sie hindurch.«[15]

«En sculpture, je m'intéresse essen-tiellement à la forme spatiale et aux caractéristiques du métal. En matière de sièges, de nombreux problèmes fonctionnels doivent d'abord être ré-solus… mais lorsque vous allez au fond des choses, vous vous apercevez qu'un siège est une étude de l'espace, de la forme et également du métal. Si vous le regardez, vous constaterez qu'il est surtout fait d'air, comme une sculp-ture. L'espace circule à travers lui.»[15]

Charles & Ray Eames:
Rocking-chair *RAR 1*, 1950
Schaukelstuhl *RAR 1*, 1950
Chaise à bascule *RAR 1*, 1950

Charles &
Ray Eames

1907–78 & 1913–88
USA . Etats-Unis

DAR (Dining Armchair Rod)
1950–53

**DAR (Eßzimmer-
Armlehnstuhl Rod)**
1950–53

**DAR (Chaise de salle à
manger Rod)** 1950–53

Moulded, fibreglass-reinforced,
polyester seat shell connected to
a metal rod base with rubber
shock-mounts

Sitzschale aus fiberglas-
verstärktem Polyester, am
Untergestell aus Metallstangen
mit Gummipuffern befestigt

Coque de siège en fibre de verre
moulée et polyester renforcé,
réunie au piètement de métal par
des blocs de caoutchouc

**Zenith Plastics, Gardena, Cali-
fornia, for Herman Miller, Inc.
from 1950 to c. 1953 and Herman Miller, Inc., Zeeland, Michigan, from c. 1953 to c. 1972**

Charles & Ray Eames:
La Chaise, 1948

The *DAR* forms part of the Eameses'
revolutionary *Plastic Shell* group of
chairs. This was the culmination of
ideas explored by Charles Eames and
Eero Saarinen in prototype chairs for
the Museum of Modern Art's "Organic
Design in Home Furnishings" competition in 1940. Having submitted a number of designs with stamped metal
seat shells to MoMA's "International
Competition for Low Cost Furniture" in
1948, the Eameses developed the
chairs in fibreglass in collaboration
with Herman Miller, Inc., UCLA and
Zenith Plastics.

Der Stuhl *DAR* gehört zu der *Plastic-
Shell*-Stuhlkollektion von Charles und
Ray Eames. Diese Stuhlkollektion re-
sultierte aus den Ideen, die 1940 von
Charles Eames und Eero Saarinen an-
hand von Stuhl-Prototypen für den »Or-
ganic Design in Home Furnishings«-
Wettbewerb des Museum of Modern
Art entwickelt worden waren.
Nachdem die Brüder Eames bereits
1948 mit einer Reihe von Stuhl-Ent-
würfen mit gepreßten Sitzschalen aus
Metall am »International Competition
for Low Cost Furniture« des MoMA
teilgenommen hatten, entwickelten sie
in Zusammenarbeit mit den Firmen
Herman Miller, Inc., UCLA und Zenith
Plastics Stühle aus Fiberglas.

Ce *DAR* fait partie du groupe de
sièges révolutionnaires *Plastic Shell*
des Eames. Il peut être considéré
comme le point d'aboutissement lo-
gique des idées explorées antérieure-
ment par Charles Eames et Eero Saarinen dans leur série de sièges prototypes. Après le MoMA «International
Competition for Low Cost Furniture»
de 1948, les Eames reçurent une
bourse et furent parrainés par Herman
Miller, Inc. pour mettre au point leurs
sièges plastiques (fibre de verre) en
collaboration avec l'Université UCLA et
Zenith Plastics.

71

William Katavolos
*1924

Ross Littell
*1924

Douglas Kelley
*1928

USA . Etats-Unis

T chair, Model No. 3LC
1952

T-Stuhl, Modell Nr. 3LC
1952

Chaise T, modèle n° 3LC
1952

Chrome-plated tubular steel and
enamelled steel frame with leather
sling

Rahmen aus verchromtem Stahlrohr und emailliertem Stahl;
eingehängte Lederbespannung

Structure en tube d'acier chromé
et acier émaillé, siège suspendu
en cuir

**Laverne Originals, New York
(reissued by Cadsana, Italy,
from c. 1988)**

Continuing the tradition of Modern
Movement geometric formalism, Katavolos, Littell & Kelley aimed "to work
through to a way of beauty usefully
conceived in essential structure,
intrinsically materialized and appro-
priately performed".[16] The *3LC* uses a
system of concealed screws to secure
the sling seat onto the frame, pre-
dating by six years a solution utilised
by Charles Eames on his Aluminium
Group of chairs. The *3LC* was later
dubbed "the T chair" by the art critic
Clement Greenberg.

Katavolos, Littell und Kelley setzten
den geometrischen Formalismus der
Moderne fort, sie sahen »die Schönheit
in der aufs Wesentliche beschränkten
Form, in der angemessenen, material-
gerechten Gestaltung und in der sau-
beren Verarbeitung«.[16] Beim Modell
3LC verwandte man verdeckte Schrauben, um die Lederbespannung am
Rahmen zu befestigen – damit hatte
man eine Lösung vorweggenommen,
ähnlich derjenigen, die Charles Eames
für seine Aluminiumstühle fand. Modell
3LC wurde vom Kunstkritiker Clement
Greenberg später »T-Stuhl« getauft.

Poursuivant la tradition du formalisme
géométrique du Mouvement moderniste, Katavolos, Littell & Kelley avaient
pour but «d'aboutir à une forme de
beauté conçue, pour sa structure es-
sentielle, dans un esprit d'utilité, faisant
appel à des matériaux évidents et mis
en œuvre avec à-propos.»[16] La *3LC*
utilise un système d'écrous dissimulés
pour fixer le siège suspendu au cadre,
devançant de six ans la solution que
retiendra Charles Eames pour ses
sièges en aluminium. Elle fut surnom-
mée «chaise T» par le critique d'art
Clement Greenberg.

**William Katavolos, Ross Littell &
Douglas Kelley:**

New York sofas, 1952

Sofas *New York*, 1952

Canapés *New York*, 1952

"A machine for sitting, of the greatest sophistication, it has a retractable foot rest, and its elements can be adjusted to take up to *486* positions. The rubber arms, lined with a steel spring, and forming a parabolic curve, are a particularly notable feature."[17]

»Der Liegesessel ist eine Sitzmaschine von größter Einfachheit und Eleganz; er ist mit einer einklappbarer Fußstütze ausgerüstet, und die diversen Bestandteile können in *486* Positionen gebracht werden. Die parabolisch gekrümmten Armstützen sind durch eine Stahlfeder verstärkt und mit Gummi überzogen; sie sind ein besonders interessantes Konstruktionselement.«[17]

«Machine pour s'asseoir, de la plus grande sophistication, elle possède un repose-pieds rétractable et ses éléments peuvent prendre jusqu'à *486* positions différentes. Les accoudoirs de caoutchouc, armés d'une ressort d'acier plat, forment une courbe parabolique et sont particulièrement originaux.»[17]

Osvaldo Borsani

*1911

Italy . Italien . Italie

**Chaise-longue,
Model No. P40** 1954

**Chaiselongue,
Modell Nr. P40** 1954

**Chaise longue,
modèle n° P40** 1954

Pressed steel frame with latex foam upholstery and rubber-covered steel spring arms

Rahmen aus gestanztem Stahl; Latexschaum-Polsterung, mit Gummi überzogene Stahlfeder-Armlehnen

Structure en acier embouti avec rembourrage en mousse de latex et accoudoirs en acier souple recouvert de caoutchouc

**Tecno, Italy, from 1954
to present**

Tecno promotional photograph of the *Model No. P40*

Tecno-Werbung für den Sessel *Modell Nr. P40*

Tecno-Publicité de Tecno pour le fauteuil *modèle n° P40*

Arne Jacobsen

1902–71

Denmark . Dänemark . Danemark

3107 chair 1955

Stuhl 3107 1955

Chaise 3107 1955

Teak veneer, moulded plywood
seat with chrome-plated, bent
tubular steel base

Sitzschale geformtes Schichtholz
mit Teakholz furniert; Untergestell
aus gebogenem Stahlrohr

Siège en contreplaqué plaqué de
teak sur piètement en tube d'acier
cintré et chromé

**Fritz Hansen, Denmark, from
1955 to present**

Arne Jacobsen:

3107 & 3207, 1955

Arne Jacobsen:

3100 Ant chairs with
B413 table, 1952

3100-Ant-Stühle mit
B413-Tisch, 1952

Chaises *3100 Ant*
avec table *B413*, 1952

The *Series* 7 group of chairs, which
includes the *3107*, was awarded a
Grand Prix at the 1957 Milan Triennale. Initially available only in wood-
veneer finishes, coloured versions
were later introduced. Jacobsen's
approach to the complex moulding of
the seat and back out of one piece of
plywood was clearly influenced by the
earlier work of Charles and Ray Eames.

Die *Serie* 7, zu der auch der Stuhl Nr.
3107 gehört, gewann 1957 auf der
Mailänder Triennale einen Grand Prix.
Anfangs war die Serie nur furniert zu
haben, später wurden farbige Versionen hergestellt. Zweifellos war Jacobsen durch die frühen Arbeiten von
Charles und Ray Eames zu der kompli-
zierten Verformung von Sitzschale und
Rückenlehne aus einem einzigen Stück
Schichtholz angeregt worden.

Les chaises de la Série 7, qui com-
prend la *3107*, reçurent un Grand Prix
à la Triennale de Milan de 1957. Uni-
quement disponibles à l'origine en
placage de bois, ses versions en couleur furent introduites un peu plus tard.
L'approche de Jacobsen des problèmes complexes de moulage de
cette chaise réalisée en un seul morceau de contreplaqué fut clairement
influencée par les travaux antérieurs de
Charles et Ray Eames.

Arne Jacobsen:

Variants of the *3100 &
3107* chairs, 1952–55

Varianten der Stühle
3100 & 3107, 1952–55

Variantes des chaises
3100 & 3107, 1952–55

Eero Saarinen

1910–61

USA . Etats-Unis

Tulip chair 1955–57
Stuhl Tulip 1955–57
Chaise Tulipe 1955–57

Plastic-coated, cast-aluminium base supporting a moulded fibreglass seat shell with loose, fabric-covered, foam-filled cushion

Sitzschale aus fiberglasverstärktem Kunststoff; Untergestell aus kunststoffbeschichtetem Aluminium; loses Sitzkissen aus Schaumstoff, mit Stoff bezogen

Coque de siège en fibre de verre sur piètement en aluminium moulé, avec coussin amovible en mousse, recouvert de tissu

Knoll International, Inc., New York, from 1957 to present

Eero Saarinen:

Pedestal Group, 1957

Saarinen strove for an organic unity of design. The *Pedestal* group, though visually unified, was a disappointment to Saarinen, as he was unable to achieve material unity – plastics technology did not allow for a single-moulded pedestal chair form. Instead, a cast-aluminium base had to be integrated with the fibreglass seat-shell. The use of a pedestal base, however, did fulfil one of Saarinen's intentions – to clean up the "slum of legs". He later said, "Modern chairs, with shell shapes and cages of little sticks below… became a sort of metal plumbing".[18]

In seinem Design hat Saarinen stets die Einheit von Form und Material angestrebt. Die *Pedestal*-Gruppe war eine Enttäuschung für ihn, weil es ihm wegen der Unzulänglichkeit der Kunststoffindustrie nicht gelungen war, die Stühle aus einem einzigen Material herzustellen. Statt dessen verband man die Sitzschale aus fiberglasverstärktem Kunststoff mit einem Fuß aus Gußaluminium. Später sagte er: »Diese Stühle mit ihren schalenförmigen Sitzen und den käfigartigen Gestellen aus Metallstäben darunter... glichen immer eher Klempnerarbeiten.«[18]

Tout au long de sa carrière, Saarinen s'efforça d'atteindre une unité organique de conception. Ce groupe de sièges sur piètement, bien que d'une grande homogénéité visuelle, fut une déception pour lui car la technologie des plastiques n'était pas encore assez avancée pour permettre de réaliser en une seule pièce ce type de forme. Il fallut ajouter à la coque de fibre de verre une base d'aluminium moulé. Il déclara: «Ces sièges, avec leurs formes en coque et leurs cages de petits bâtons par dessous, devenaient une sorte d'exercice de plomberie.»[18]

Knoll International advertising shot showing *Pedestal* Group in outside setting, c. 1960

Werbespot der Firma Knoll International, auf der die *Pedestal*-Gruppe im Freien zu sehen ist, um 1960

Publicité de Knoll International montrant le groupe de sièges *Pedestal* à l'air libre, vers 1960

75

Gio Ponti

1891–1979

Italy . Italien . Italie

**Superleggera chair,
Model No. 699** 1955–57

**Stuhl Superleggera,
Modell Nr. 699** 1955–57

**Chaise Superleggera,
modèle n° 699** 1955–57

Solid ash frame with ebonised or
natural finish, rush seat

Rahmen Esche massiv, natur-
farben oder schwarz gebeizt;
Sitzfläche aus Binsengeflecht

Structure de frêne massif, finition
naturelle ou noire, siège paillé

**Cassina, Italy, from 1957
to present**

Extremely light in weight, the *Super-leggera* was based on a traditional
chair produced in the fishing village of
Chiavari, Italy. The evolution of this
vernacular precedent would have appealed to Ponti, who attempted to design furniture (in his words) "without
adjectives".

Der extrem leichte Stuhl *Superleggera*
ging auf einen traditionellen Stuhl zurück, der in dem italienischen Fischer-
dorf Chiavari hergestellt wurde. Dieser
bodenständige Vorläufer mußte Ponti,
der (nach seinen eigenen Worten) Möbel »ohne Eigenschaften« entwerfen
wollte, allein schon aus diesem Grund
gefallen.

D'un poids extrêmement léger, la
Superleggera s'inspire des chaises
traditionnelles du village de pêcheurs
de Chiavari, en Italie. Ce précédent
régional attira l'attention de Ponti qui
s'efforçait de créer des meubles –
selon ses propres mots – «sans
adjectifs».

Alessandro Mendini:

Gio Ponti's *Superleggera*,
redesigned 1978

Gio Pontis *Superleggera*,
Redesign von 1978

Chaise *Superleggera* de Gio
Ponti, redessinée en 1978

Sori Yanagi

*1915
Japan . Japon

Butterfly stool 1956
Stuhl Butterfly 1956
Tabouret Butterfly 1956

Moulded plywood with metal
stretcher

Geformtes Schichtholz mit
Metallsteg

Contreplaqué moulé et traverse
de métal

Tendo Mokko, Japan

The *Butterfly* stool can be seen as a delicate and harmonious synthesis of Eastern and Western culture. Highly favoured in America during the 1950s, it was easy to dismantle and transport.

Den *Butterfly*-Stuhl kann man als gefällige, ausgewogene Synthese östlicher und westlicher Kultur betrachten. Er war in den 50er Jahren in den Vereinigten Staaten sehr beliebt; man konnte ihn leicht zerlegen und transportieren.

Le tabouret *Butterfly* peut être vu comme une synthèse délicate et harmonieuse des cultures occidentale et orientale. Très apprécié aux Etats-Unis pendant les années 50, il était facile à démonter et à transporter.

Poul Kjaerholm

*1929

Denmark . Dänemark . Danemark

Chair, Model No. PK22 1956

Stuhl, Modell Nr. PK22 1956

Chaise basse, modèle n° PK22 1956

Chrome-plated steel frame with leather seat and back

Rahmen aus Stahl, verchromt; Sitzfläche und Rückenlehne mit Leder bespannt

Structure en acier chromé, siège et dossier en cuir

E. Kold Christensen A/S, Denmark, from c. 1956 to c. 1970 and Fritz Hansen, Denmark, from c. 1970 to present

Kjaerholm's elegant designs owe much to the designers of the Modern Movement. The *PK22* chair is reminiscent of Mies van der Rohe's *Barcelona* chair of 1929 and the ancestry of Kjaerholm's remarkable *Hammock* chaise longue, Model No. *PK24*, can be traced to Le Corbusier's chaise longue of 1928.

Kjaerholms elegante Entwürfe sind dem Design der Klassischen Moderne sehr verpflichtet. Der Stuhl *PK22* erinnert an Mies van der Rohes *Barcelona*-Sessel von 1929, und die elegante Chaiselongue *Hammock*, Modell Nr. *PK24*, geht auf Le Corbusiers Chaiselongue von 1928 zurück.

Les élégantes créations de Kjaerholm doivent beaucoup aux dessinateurs du Mouvement moderniste. La chaise *PK22* rappelle la *Barcelona* chair de Mies van der Rohe (1929) et l'ancêtre de la remarquable chaise longue *Hammock* de Kjaerholm, le modèle n° *PK24*, n'est pas sans évoquer la chaise longue de 1928 de Le Corbusier.

Poul Kjaerholm:

PK22 chairs, *PK31* sofa and *PK24* chaise longue, c. 1956, 1958 & 1965

Stühle *PK22*, Sofa *PK31* und Chaiselongue *PK24*, um 1956, 1958 & 1965

Chaises *PK22*, sofa *PK31* et chaise longue *PK24*, vers 1956, 1958 & 1965

Poul Kjaerholm:

Hammock chaise longue PK24, 1965

Chaiselongue *Hammock* PK24, 1965

Chaise longue *Hammock* PK24, 1965

Although visually light in weight, with its wedge-like form seemingly hovering in space, the *Coconut* chair is in fact extremely heavy, owing to the considerable amount of steel used in its construction. The chair's unique shape, as its name suggests, was inspired by a cracked section of coconut.

Der Sessel *Coconut* scheint mit seiner keilartigen Sitzschale geradezu zu schweben, aber in Wirklichkeit macht ihn die große Menge Stahl, die die Konstruktion des Untergestells erfordert, ungewöhnlich schwer. Wie der Name suggeriert, ähnelt der Stuhl einem Stück einer Kokosnuß.

Bien qu'apparemment légère, avec sa forme d'aile flottant dans l'espace, cette chauffeuse est en fait extrêmement lourde du fait de l'énorme quantité d'acier utilisée pour sa fabrication. Sa forme unique, comme son nom le suggère, fut inspirée par un morceau de noix de coco brisée.

George Nelson

1907–86

USA . Etats-Unis

Coconut chair 1956
Sessel Coconut 1956
Chauffeuse Coconut 1956

Fabric-covered, foam-upholstered, steel shell, supported on chrome plated steel legs

Sitzschale aus Stahl, Polsterung aus Schaumstoff, mit Stoff bezogen; Untergestell aus Rundstahl, verchromt

Coque d'acier rembourrée de mousse recouverte de tissu sur piétement d'acier chromé

Herman Miller, Inc., USA, from 1956 to c. 1975 (reissued by Vitra GmbH, Germany, from 1988)

George Nelson:
Marshmallow sofa, 1952
Sofa *Marshmallow*, 1952
Canapé *Marshmallow*, 1952

George Nelson:
Kangaroo chair, 1956
Sessel *Kangaroo*, 1956
Fauteuil *Kangaroo*, 1956

79

Charles &
Ray Eames

1907–78 & 1913–88

USA . Etats-Unis

**Lounge chair and footstool,
Model Nos. 670 & 671**
1956/57

**Sessel mit Hocker,
Modell Nr. 670 & Nr. 671**
1956/57

**Chaise longue et
repose-pieds,
modèles n° 670 & 671**
1956/57

Rosewood veneer, moulded
plywood seat-shells with leather-
covered, foam-and-down-filled
cushions, on swivelling cast-
aluminium base

Sitzschale geformtes Schichtholz
mit Rosenholzfurnier, Schaumstoffpolster und Daunenkissen mit
Lederbezug; drehbarer Säulenfuß
aus Gußaluminium

Plaqué de bois de rose, coques
de sièges en contreplaqué moulé
avec coussins rembourrés de
mousse et de plume recouverts
de cuir, sur socle pivotant d'aluminium moulé

Herman Miller Inc., Zeeland,
Michigan, from 1957 to present

The *Model No. 670* was the Eameses
first design for the luxury end of the
furniture market, retailing at $634 in
1957. Originally conceived as a
birthday gift for the film director Billy
Wilder, the Lounge chair is unasham-
edly masculine, exuding a sense of
executive power and comfort through
its generous proportions and use of
high-quality materials.

Mit dem *Modell Nr. 670* hatten
Charles und Ray Eames ihr erstes
Möbelstück der Luxusklasse entworfen, 1957 betrug der Einzelhandels-
preis 634 Dollar. Der Sessel, als Ge-
burtstagsgeschenk für Filmregisseur
Billy Wilder entworfen, war unverhoh-
len maskulin in seiner Ausstrahlung
und signalisierte durch seine großzügi-
gen Abmessungen und die erstklas-
sige Qualität des Materials Macht und
Reichtum.

Ce *modèle n° 670* fut le premier dessin des Eames pour le haut du marché.
Il était vendu 634 $ en 1957. Conçue
au départ comme un cadeau d'anniver-
saire pour le metteur en scène Billy
Wilder, cette chaise longue affirme sa
masculinité et, à travers ses géné-
reuses proportions et l'utilisation de
matériaux de haute qualité, affiche
aussi bien son grand confort qu'un
certain sens du pouvoir.

Charles Kratka:

Exploded drawings of
Model No. 670, showing
components

Skizzen des *Modells Nr. 670*, auf
denen die Einzelkomponenten des
Stuhls zu erkennen sind

Dessins explosés du
modèle n° 670 montrant
la composition du siège

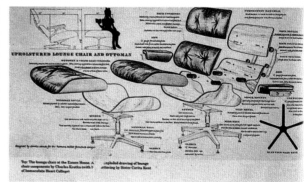

George Nelson Associates:

Laminated wood chair, known as *Pretzel* chair, 1952

Schichtholz-Sessel, bekannt unter der Bezeichnung *Pretzel*-Sessel, 1952

Fauteuil en bois lamellé, connu sous le nom *Pretzel*, 1952

Paul Goldman

*1912
USA . Etats-Unis

Cherner chair 1957
Armlehnstuhl Cherner 1957
Fauteuil Cherner 1957

Walnut veneer moulded plywood

Geformtes Schichtholz mit Nußbaumfurnier

Contreplaqué moulé plaqué de noyer

Plycraft, Inc., Massachusetts, from 1957 to present

This extremely elegant chair evolved from the earlier *Pretzel* armchair of 1952 by George Nelson Associates, the latter's design in turn having been inspired by Gebrüder Thonet's *Model No. 9* chair of c.1904. The design of the *Cherner* chair, with its sinuous armrest and single moulded seat and back, was originally ascribed to Norman Cherner and, on other occasions, to George Mulhauser. This was a marketing ploy conceived by Paul Goldman, the designer of the chair and owner of the manufacturing company.

Dieser elegante Stuhl ging auf den älteren *Pretzel*-Sessel von 1952 von George Nelson Associates zurück, dessen Form wiederum vom *Modell Nr. 9* der Gebrüder Thonet von 1904 inspiriert worden war. Der Entwurf des *Cherner*-Armlehnstuhls mit seinen geschwungenen Armstützen und der aus einem Stück geformten Sitz- und Rückenschale wurde Norman Cherner zugeschrieben und ein andermal George Mulhauser – ein Marketingmanöver, das sich Paul Goldman, der Designer des Stuhls und Inhaber der Herstellerfirma, ausgedacht hatte.

Ce très élégant fauteuil est inspiré d'un précédent modèle *Pretzel* de George Nelson Associates (1952) dont le dessin rappelait à son tour le *modèle n° 9* des Gebrüder Thonet (1904). Avec ses accoudoirs sinueux et son siège et son dossier en une seule pièce, il fut à l'origine attribué à Norman Cherner et même à George Mulhauser. C'était une sorte d'astuce de marketing de Paul Goldman, son créateur et en même temps propriétaire de l'usine de fabrication.

Paul Goldman:
Cherner side chair, 1957
Stuhl *Cherner*, 1957
Chaise *Cherner*, 1957

Achille &
Pier Giacomo
Castiglioni

*1918 & 1913–68

Italy . Italien . Italie

Mezzadro stool 1957

Hocker Mezzadro 1957

Tabouret Mezzadro 1957

Tractor seat on chrome plated, bent flat steel stem with wing-nut, solid beech footrest

Traktorsitz auf einer Stütze aus gebogenem, verchromtem Flachstahl, mit einer Flügelmutter befestigt; Fußstütze Buche massiv

Siège de tracteur sur support d'acier plat cintré avec écrou papillon, repose-pied en hêtre massif

Zanotta, Italy, from 1970 to present

Exploiting Marcel Duchamp's concept of the "ready-made" in furniture design, the *Mezzadro* (Sharecropper) stool was deemed too radical to be put into production until thirteen years after its original date of design. Interestingly, a similar design incorporating a tractor seat in its construction, by Baldwin and Machado, is illustrated in George Nelson's book "Chairs" of 1953.

Der Hocker *Mezzadro*, mit dem sich Achille und Pier Castiglioni Marcel Duchamps Konzept des »Ready-made« für das Möbeldesign zunutze machten, wurde für so avantgardistisch gehalten, daß er erst dreizehn Jahre nach Erscheinen des Entwurfs in Serie ging. Ein ähnlicher Entwurf von Baldwin und Machado, ebenfalls mit einem Traktorsitz, ist in George Nelsons Buch »Chairs« von 1953 abgebildet.

Appliquant le concept des «ready-made» de Marcel Duchamp à la conception du meuble, ce tabouret *Mezzadro* (Métayer) fut jugé tellement radical qu'il ne fut produit que treize ans après sa date de conception. Il est intéressant de noter qu'un modèle similaire à un siège de tracteur, de Baldwin et Machado, est illustré dans le livre de George Nelson «Chairs» de 1953.

Achille Castiglioni:

Primate, 1970

Achille &
Pier Giacomo
Castiglioni:

Sella, 1957

Achille &
Pier Giacomo
Castiglioni:

Allunaggio, 1965

These highly organic and materially unified designs formed part of the *Invisible Group*, which also included the *Buttercup* and *Lily* chairs as well as the better-known *Champagne* dining chair. The Lavernes later licensed to other manufacturers their innovative process of moulding perspex which had been developed for the production of these chairs.

Diese durch und durch organischen, aus einem einzigen Material gestalteten Entwürfe gehören zu der *Invisible Group*, zu der auch die Stühle *Buttercup* und *Lily* so wie der noch bekanntere Speisezimmerstuhl *Champagne* zählen. Später vergaben Erwine und Estelle Laverne die Lizenz für ihre innovative Technologie, die speziell für die Herstellung dieser Plexiglasstühle entwickelt worden war, an andere Firmen.

Ces modèles très organiques et réalisés avec un seul matériau font partie du *Invisible Group* qui comprenait également les fauteuils *Buttercup* et *Lily* ainsi que la chaise *Champagne* encore plus connue. Les Laverne cédèrent ensuite les licences de fabrication du procédé de moulage du perspex qu'ils avaient mis au point.

Erwine & Estelle Laverne

*1909 & *1915

USA . Etats-Unis

Daffodil and Jonquil chairs
1957

Sessel Daffodil und Jonquil
1957

Fauteuils Daffodil et Jonquil
1957

Moulded perspex seat shell and base with loose fabric-covered foam-filled cushion

Sitzschale und Sockel aus geformtem Perspex-Kunststoff; loses Sitzkissen aus Schaumstoff, mit Stoff bezogen

Coque et pied de siège en perspex moulé avec coussin amovible en mousse recouvert de tissu

Laverne Originals, New York
from 1957 to c. 1972

Erwine & Estelle Laverne:

Lotus Chair, 1958

Stuhl *Lotus*, 1958

Chaise *Lotus*, 1958

Arne Jacobsen

1902–71

Denmark . Dänemark . Danemark

Egg chair,
Model No. 3316 1957

Sessel Egg,
Modell Nr. 3316 1957

Fauteuil Egg,
modèle n° 3316 1957

Fabric covered, foam-upholstered, moulded fibreglass seat shell on a swivelling cast-aluminium base, with loose seat cushion

Sitzschale aus glasfaserverstärktem Kunststoff, Schaumstoff-Polsterung, mit Stoff bezogen, loses Sitzkissen; drehbarer Säulenfuß aus Gußaluminium

Coque de fibre de verre rembourrée de mousse et recouverte de tissu, sur socle d'aluminium pivotant, avec coussin de siège amovible

Fritz Hansen, Denmark, from 1958 to present

The *Egg* chair was originally designed for one of Jacobsen's major architectural projects, the Royal SAS Hotel in Copenhagen. He designed not only the building, its interior and furniture, but also the light fixtures, carpets, cutlery and even the ashtrays – effecting a meticulously detailed and refined unity of design.

Den *Egg*-Sessel hat Jacobsen ursprünglich für eines seiner wichtigsten Architekturprojekte, das Royal SAS Hotel in Kopenhagen, konzipiert. Er entwarf nicht nur das Gebäude, die Innenausstattung und die Möbel, sondern auch die Beleuchtungskörper, die Teppiche, das Besteck und sogar die Aschenbecher – wobei ihm eine subtile, bis ins kleinste Detail gehende Einheitlichkeit seines Designs gelang.

Ce fauteuil fut conçu au départ pour l'un des plus importants chantiers architecturaux de Jacobsen, le Royal SAS Hotel, à Copenhague. Il réalisa non seulement le bâtiment, sa décoration intérieure et son mobilier, mais également les luminaires, les tapis, la coutellerie et même les cendriers, atteignant une unité de conception méticuleusement raffinée et détaillée.

Arne Jacobsen:

Swan chair, 1957

Sessel *Swan*, 1957

Fauteuil *Swan*, 1957

Interior of Fritz Hansen Showroom showing *Egg* chairs

Inneneinrichtung des Fritz-Hansen-Ausstellungsraums, in dem die *Egg*-Stühle zu sehen sind

Salle d'exposition de Fritz Hansen, vue intérieure avec fauteuils *Egg*

George Nelson

1907 – 86
USA . Etats-Unis

MAA chair 1958
Stuhl MAA 1958
Chaise MAA 1958

Moulded fibreglass seat and back
with stainless steel fittings and
rubber sockets, on a bent tubular
steel base

Sitz- und Rückenschale fiberglasverstärkter Kunststoff; Kugelgelenk aus rostfreiem Stahl und
Hartgummischeiben; Untergestell
gezogenes Stahlrohr

Siège et dossier en fibre de verre
moulée avec accessoires en acier
inoxydable et emboîtements de
caoutchouc, sur base en tube
d'acier cintré

**Herman Miller, Inc., Zeeland,
Michigan**

Part of the *Swagged-leg* group of
chairs, the *MAA* was only produced for
one year before it was withdrawn,
owing to an inherent design flaw. The
rubber sockets, which are welded to
the back of the chair and connect with
a system of pivoting ball pins allowing
the back section to articulate through
90°, degrade under stress. Once the
critical ball-and-socket joint is weak-
ened, the back disconnects from the
rest of the chair. Despite this, the concept of an independently articulating
moulded-plastic back element was
exceptionally innovative.

Der zur *Swagged-leg*-Gruppe gehö-
rende *MAA*-Stuhl wurde nur ein Jahr
hergestellt, bevor man die Produktion
einstellte. Bei starker Beanspruchung
nutzten sich die an die Rückenlehne
geschweißten Kugelgelenke ab, die mit
drehbaren Kugelgelenkstiften verbunden waren, wodurch sich die Rückenlehne um 90° schwenken ließ. Ist das
Gelenk erst einmal geschwächt, löst
sich die Rückenlehne vom Stuhl. Trotz-
dem war die Idee einer vom Untergestell unabhängig beweglichen
Rückenlehne aus Kunststoff innovativ.

Faisant partie de la série *Swagged-leg*,
la *MAA* ne fut produite qu'une année
seulement avant d'être retirée pour
défaut de conception. Après un certain
temps, le dossier se décrochait car
les emboîtements de caoutchouc
s'abîmaient. Ils étaient électronique-
ment soudés au dos du siège et con-
nectés par un double système de
roulements à bille pivotant permettant
au dossier de pivoter sur 90°. Malgré
ce défaut essentiellement technique, le
concept d'un dossier articulé indépendant en plastique apportait une
innovation majeure.

George Nelson:
DAF chair, 1958
DAF-Stuhl, 1958
Chaise *DAF*, 1958

Charles & Ray Eames

1907–78 & 1913–88

USA . Etats-Unis

Aluminium Group side chair, Model No. EA105 1958

Stuhl aus der Aluminium Group, Modell Nr. EA105 1958

Chaise du groupe Aluminium, modèle n° EA105 1958

Aluminium frame with leather or vinyl upholstered sling seat

Rahmen aus Aluminium, eingehängtes Sitzpolster mit Leder- oder Vinylbezug

Cadre en aluminium, siège suspendu rembourré, recouvert de cuir ou de vinyle

Herman Miller, Inc, Zeeland, Michigan, from 1958 to present

The *Aluminium Group* of chairs and tables was first produced as a special project for Alessandro Girard and Eero Saarinen's Irwin Miller House in Columbus, Indiana. The brief submitted to the Eameses described a series of chairs that could be used indoors or outdoors. During the development stage, this furniture was often referred to as the "leisure group". Ironically, it is now almost exclusively used within the office environment.

Die Stuhl- und Tischserie *Aluminium Group* wurde ursprünglich als Sonderanfertigung für das von Alessandro Girad und Eero Saarinen entworfene Irwin Miller House in Columbus, Indiana, entwickelt. Im Auftragsschreiben an die Brüder Eames war von einer Stuhlserie die Rede, die sowohl für Innen- als auch für Außenräume verwendbar sein sollte. In der Entwicklungsphase wurden diese Stühle häufig als »Freizeitmöbel« bezeichnet. Paradoxerweise werden sie jedoch heute fast ausschließlich als Büromöbel benutzt.

Le groupe de sièges et de tables *Aluminium* fut au départ un projet spécialement conçu par Alessandro Girard et Eero Saarinen pour la maison d'Irwin Miller à Colombus, Indiana. Le cahier des charges soumis aux Eames décrivait principalement une série de sièges à utiliser aussi bien à l'intérieur qu'à l'extérieur. Pendant la phase de mise au point, cet ensemble fut souvent baptisé le groupe loisirs ce qui me manque pas d'ironie quand on sait que ces sièges sont aujourd'hui presque toujours utilisés dans des bureaux.

Charles & Ray Eames:

Lounge armchairs, *Model No. 682*, shown in outside setting, 1958

Armlehnsessel, *Modell Nr. 682*, im Freien, 1958

Chaises longues *modèle n° 682*, à l'air libre, 1958

Charles & Ray Eames:
Aluminium Group, 1958

Highly futuristic, Panton's upholstered *Cone* chair and slightly later wire *Cone* and *Heart* chairs were the result of a conscious decision to divorce himself from any preconceived notions of how a chair should be designed. When conceptualising a design, Panton concerned himself primarily with the inherent potential of new materials and their application in generating new forms.

Pantons ausgesprochen avantgardistischer *Cone*-Stuhl und seine späteren *Cone*- und *Heart*-Stühle sind Resultate seiner bewußten Abkehr von bestehenden Vorstellungen, wie ein Stuhl auszusehen habe. Wenn Panton einen neuen Entwurf konzipierte, befaßte er sich vor allem mit dem Potential neuer Materialien und deren Verwendbarkeit für die Gestaltung neuer Formen.

Très futuriste, cette chaise *Cone* rembourrée est légèrement postérieure aux modèles en fil d'acier *Cone* et *Heart*, qui avaient pour point de départ l'abandon de toute idée préconçue sur les principes de construction d'un siège. En conceptualisant son idée, Panton s'intéressa principalement au potentiel de nouveaux matériaux et de leur application dans la génération de formes nouvelles.

Verner Panton

*1926

Denmark . Dänemark . Danemark

Upholstered Cone chair
1958

Stuhl Cone, gepolstert
1958

Chaise Cone rembourrée
1958

Fabric-covered, foam upholstered, bent sheet metal construction on a chrome-plated base

Rahmen aus geformten Metallblechen, Schaumstoffpolsterung mit Stoff bezogen; verchromter Metallfuß

Construction en tôle de métal cintrée, rembourrage de mousse recouverte de tissu, sur piètement chromé

Plus-linje, Denmark, from 1959 to c. 1966

Verner Panton sitting in *Heart* chair, 1959

Verner Panton in seinem *Heart*-Stuhl, 1959

Verner Panton assis sur la chaise *Heart*, 1959

Verner Panton:
Wire *Cone* chair, 1959
Wire-*Cone*-Stuhl, 1959
Chaise *Wire Cone*, 1959

Advertisement for the Wire *Cone* chair

Werbefoto für den Stuhl Wire *Cone*

Publicité pour la chaise Wire *Cone*

Achille & Pier Giacomo Castiglioni

*1918 & 1913–68

Italy . Italien . Italie

Sanluca armchair 1959
Sessel Sanluca 1959
Fauteuil Sanluca 1959

Leather-covered, polyurethane foam-upholstered frame on rosewood legs

Rahmen mit Leder bezogen und mit Polyurethanschaum gepolstert; Beine aus Rosenholz

Structure rembourrée de mousse de polyuréthane, recouverte de cuir, sur piètement en bois de rose

Gavina, Italy (later Simon International, Italy), from 1960 to 1990, and Bernini, Italy, from 1990 to present

Dino Gavina, Achille & Pier Giacomo Castiglioni photographed with the *Sanluca* armchair in the San Luca portico, Bologna, 1960

Dino Gavina, Achille & Pier Giacomo Castiglioni, fotografiert mit dem Armlehnsessel *Sanluca* vor dem Torbogen von San Luca, Bologna, 1960

Dino Gavina, Achille & Pier Giacomo Castiglioni photographiés avec *Sanluca* sous le portique de San Luca, Bologne, 1960

Although designed for industrial production, the *Sanluca* chair was manufactured by hand. "In (this) chair the convergence of the architect's brilliance and the commercial indifference of the manufacturer (who is first and foremost an aesthetic operator) is the basis for the remarkable construction of a figurative language, with powerful architectural intonations, which have nothing to do with stylistic conventions." Carlo Scarpa said of this design: "this is an armchair for which a formalist like myself would gladly take credit."[19]

Der *Sanluca* war zwar für die Massenproduktion konzipiert, wurde aber in Handarbeit hergestellt. »Hier ist die Verschmelzung der Ideen des Designers mit der kommerziellen Gleichgültigkeit des Herstellers (der in erster Linie vom ästhetischen Standpunkt her operiert) Voraussetzung für das Zustandekommen einer figurativen Sprache mit architektonischen Anklängen, die nichts mit stilistischen Konventionen zu tun hat.« Carlo Scarpa bemerkte: »Das Verdienst, einen solchen Sessel geschaffen zu haben, würde ich mir, als Formalist, gern anrechnen lassen.«[19]

Bien que destiné à la production industrielle, ce fauteuil fut fabriqué à la main. «Dans ce fauteuil, la convergence du brio de l'architecte et de l'indifférence aux contingences commerciales du fabricant (qui est d'abord et avant tout un opérateur esthétique) est à la base de cette remarquable construction d'un langage figuratif, aux puissantes intonations architecturales, étranger au concept et à la pratique de style.» Carlo Scarpa déclara de cette création: «Voici un fauteuil dont un formaliste comme moi aimerait à être crédité.»[19]

Studio Simon:

Sforzesca chair, 1986 (designed as a homage to the Castiglioni brothers)

Sessel *Sforzesca*, 1986 (entworfen als Hommage an die Brüder Castiglioni)

Fauteuil *Sforzesca*, 1986 (dessinée en hommage aux frères Castiglioni)

The first single-form, materially unified chair design in plastic, the *Stacking* chair was not put into full-scale manufacture until 1968. Originally prototyped in GFK Polyester (fibreglass-reinforced plastic), early production models were produced in moulded "Baydur" (PU-hardfoam) and then lacquered. In 1970 the material was changed to "Luran-S", an injection-moulded non-reinforced thermoplastic.[20] Panton writes, "I attempt to make good designs with new materials. My pieces try to be versatile and accessible to all classes of buyer."[21]

Als erster aus einem einzigen Material und in einem einzigen Guß hergestellter Stuhl gelangte der *Stapelstuhl* erst 1968 zur Serienreife. Der Prototyp wurde aus GFK-Polyester (fiberglasverstärkter Kunststoff), die ersten in Serie produzierten Exemplare aus verformtem, später lackiertem »Baydur« (PU-Hartschaumstoff) hergestellt. Seit 1970 verwendet man »Luran-S«, einen nicht fiberglasverstärkten, durch Erwärmung im Spritzgußverfahren formbaren Kunststoff.[20] Panton schreibt: »Ich versuche mit neuen Materialien gutes Design zu machen. Meine Stücke sollen vielseitig verwendbar und erschwinglich sein.«[21]

Premier siège réalisé avec un seul matériau plastique, cette chaise ne fut pas réellement produite en série avant 1968. Le premier prototype fut réalisé en polyester GFK (plastique renforcé de fibre de verre) et les premiers modèles produits en «Baydur» moulé (Mousse dure PU) puis laqués. En 1970, ce matériau fut abandonné pour le «Luran-S», un thermoplastique moulé par injection et non renforcé.[20] Panton écrivit: «Je tente de faire de bons projets avec des matériaux nouveaux. Mes œuvres essayent d'être polyvalentes et accessibles.»[21]

Verner Panton

*1926

Denmark . Dänemark . Danemark

Stacking chair
c. 1960 – 67

Stapelstuhl
um 1960 – 67

Chaise empilable
vers 1960 – 67

Injection-moulded Luran-S thermoplastic

Im Spritzgußverfahren hergestellte Konstruktion aus Luran-S-Thermokunststoff

Thermoplastique Luran-S moulé par injection

Vitra GmbH, Germany, for Herman Miller, Inc., New York, from 1968 to 1979, and Herman Miller, Inc., New York, from 1973 to 1975

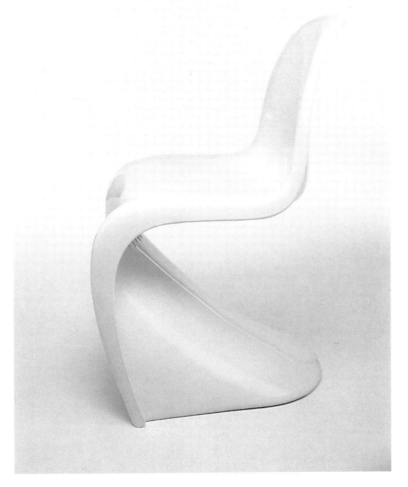

Verner Panton:

Living Tower, 1969

Wohnturm, 1969

Tour d'habitation, 1969

89

Cesare Leonardi & Franca Stagi

*1935 & *1937

Italy . Italien . Italie

**Ribbon chair,
Model No. CL9** 1961

**Stuhl Ribbon,
Modell Nr. CL9** 1961

**Chaise Ribbon,
modèle n° CL9** 1961

Chrome-plated, bent tubular steel base with moulded fibreglass seat section

Formgepreßte Sitzschale aus glasfaserverstärktem Kunststoff auf verchromten Gestell aus gezogenem Stahlrohr

Piètement en tube d'acier cintré et chromé, siège en fibre de verre moulée

Bernini, Italy, from 1961 to 1969, and Elco, Italy, from 1969

The continuous band of moulded fibreglass forming the sculptural seat section of this remarkable design is attached to the tubular steel base by means of rubber shock-mounts. This construction allows the cantilevered CL9 an inherent degree of springiness.

Die skulptural gestaltete Sitzfläche, ein durchgehendes Band aus fiberglasverstärktem Kunststoff, ist durch elastische Gummipuffer mit dem Stahlrohrgestell verbunden. Diese Konstruktion verleiht dem freitragenden Stuhl CL9 seine federnde Elastizität.

La bande continue en fibre de verre moulée qui forme le siège de ce modèle très sculptural est fixée au piètement tubulaire au moyen de blocs de caoutchouc. Cette construction confère à ce siège en porte-à-faux un certain degré de flexibilité.

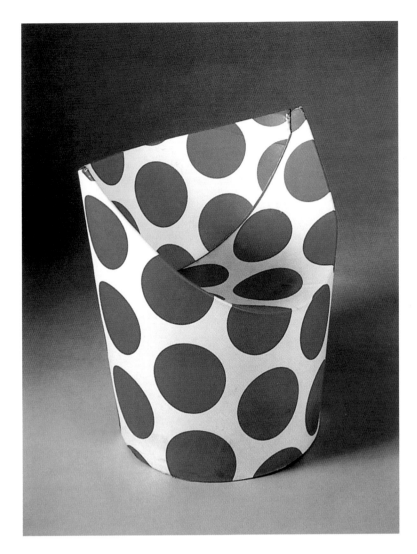

Peter Murdoch

*1940

Great Britain . Großbritannien .
Grande-Bretagne

Child's chair 1963
Kinderstuhl 1963
Chaise d'enfant 1963

Polyethylene-coated, laminated
paperboard

Mit Polyäthylen überzogener,
schichtverleimter Karton

Carton lamellé enduit de
polyéthylène

**International Paper, USA, from
1964 to 1965**

Peter Murdoch:

Those Things table, 1967
Tisch *Those Things*, 1967
Table *Those Things*, 1967

Designed while Murdoch was studying
at the Royal College of Art in London,
the polka-dotted *Child's chair* is an
icon of the Pop era. Its low production
costs and inherent disposability were
ideally suited to the demands of the
mass consumer market in the 1960s.
Later, in 1967, Murdoch designed the
similarly constructed *Those Things*
chair, table and stool, for which he
received a Council of Industrial
Design award.

Der *Kinderstuhl* mit dem auffallenden
Punktmuster ist eine Ikone der Popära.
Murdoch entwarf ihn während seiner
Studienzeit am Royal College of Art in
London. Seine niedrigen Herstellungs-
kosten und seine materialbedingte
Kurzlebigkeit machten den Stuhl zu
einem idealen Produkt des Massen-
konsums der 60er Jahre. 1967 entwarf
Murdoch die ähnlich konstruierte Grup-
pe *Those Things*, bestehend aus Stuhl,
Tisch und Hocker, für die er mit dem
Preis des Council of Industrial Design
ausgezeichnet wurde.

Conçue alors que Murdoch étudiait
encore au Royal College of Art, Londres, cette *Chaise d'enfant* à pois est
devenue une véritable icône de la
période Pop. Ses faibles coûts de
production et son caractère jetable,
par nature, correspondaient idéalement
aux attentes du marché de la grande
consommation des années 60. En
1967, Murdoch dessina une chaise,
une table et un tabouret *Those Things*,
de principe similaire, pour lesquels il
reçut une distinction du Council of
Industrial Design.

Robin Day

*1915

Great Britain . Großbritannien .
Grande-Bretagne

Polyprop chair 1962/63
Stuhl Polyprop 1962/63
Chaise Polyprop 1962/63

Injection-moulded, polypropylene
seat shell on chrome-plated or
painted bent tubular steel base

Sitzschale aus Polypropylen, im
Spritzgußverfahren hergestellt;
Untergestell gebogenes Stahlrohr,
verchromt oder lackiert

Coque de siège en polypropylène
moulé par injection sur piètement
de tube d'acier cintré, chromé ou
laqué

S. Hille & Co. Ltd, UK (later to
become Hille International, UK),
from 1963 to present

Polyprop chair under test at FIRA
Polyprop-Stuhl im Test, bei FIRA
Chaise *Polyprop* testée chez FIRA

The *Polyprop* is one of the most successful contract chairs ever produced.
A single tool can produce 4,000 seat
shells per week and from 1963 to the
present over 14 million chairs have
been sold in twenty-three countries.
Day writes: "Designers have respon-
sibilities other than the profit motive,
and must be increasingly concerned
with conservation and the sensible use
of the planet's resources... I am less
interested in fashion than in a synthesis
of good construction, good function
and aesthetics."[22]

Der *Polyprop* ist einer der erfolgreich-
sten, jemals industriell produzierten
Stühle. Eine einzige Maschine kann
4.000 Sitzschalen pro Woche produzieren. Von 1963 bis heute sind über
14 Millionen Stück in 23 Ländern verkauft worden. Day schreibt: »Designer
haben andere Verantwortlichkeiten als
die Gewinnmaximierung, sie sind im
zunehmenden Maße für die Erhaltung
und die vernünftige Verwendung der
Ressourcen dieses Planeten verantwortlich... Ich bin weniger am Modi-
schen interessiert, als an der Synthese
von guter Konstruktion, guter Funktion
und Ästhetik.«[22]

Le *Polyprop* est l'un des sièges les
plus vendus au monde. De 1963 à nos
jours, plus de 14 millions d'exemplaires
ont été commercialisés dans vingt-trois
pays. Day écrit: «Les designers ont des
responsabilités qui ne se limitent pas à
la seule recherche du profit et doivent
se sentir de plus en plus concernés
par la protection et l'utilisation intelli-
gente des ressources de la planète...
Je suis moins intéressé à la mode qu'à
une synthèse de bonne construction,
de bonne fonction et d'esthétique.»[22]

Robin Day:
Stacked *Polyprops*
Polyprops gestapelt
Polyprops empilées

Robin Day:
Polyprop chairs, 1963–67
Polyprop-Stühle, 1963–67
Chaises *Polyprop*, 1963–67

Eero Aarnio

*1932
Finland . Finnland . Finlande

Ball or Globe chair
1963–65

Ball- oder Globe-Sessel
1963–65

Fauteuil Ball ou Globe
1963–65

Fabric-covered, foam-upholstered, moulded, glass-reinforced polyester seat shell with painted aluminium base

Kugelförmige Sitzschale aus fiberglasverstärktem Polyester, Schaumstoffpolster, mit Stoff bezogen; Sockel aus Aluminium, lackiert

Coque de siège en polyester moulé renforcé de fibre de verre, rembourrée de mousse recouverte de tissu, sur base d'aluminium peint

Asko Oy, Finland, from 1966 to c. 1980 and from c. 1983 to 1987 (reissued by Adelta Finland from 1992)

Eero Aarnio designed the *Ball*, *Pastille* (*Gyro*), *Tomato* and *Bubble* series of chairs as a complete departure from traditional forms of seating. Employing state-of-the-art manufacturing technology, Aarnio's designs express the iconoclasm of the 1960s. Both materially and in terms of their production, however, these chairs were of a high quality and did not embrace Pop culture's aesthetic of disposability.

Zu Eero Aarnios Entwürfen zählen die Stuhlserien *Ball*, *Pastille* (*Gyro*), *Tomato* und *Bubble*, mit denen er eine vollkommene Abkehr von der herkömmlichen Sitzmöbelform vollzog. Aarnio machte sich die neuesten Erkenntnisse moderner Herstellungstechnologien zunutze; seine Entwürfe waren Ausdruck der bilderstürmerischen Ideen der sechziger Jahre. Was Material und Produktionstechnik betrifft, waren die Stühle von bester Qualität und entsprachen nicht der Wegwerfmentalität der Popkultur.

Eero Aarnio conçut les gammes de sièges *Ball*, *Pastille* ou *Gyro*, *Tomato* et *Bubble* en rupture complète avec les formes traditionnelles de sièges. Faisant appel à une technologie de fabrication d'avant-garde, ses dessins expriment l'esprit iconoclaste des années 60. Cependant, que ce soit en termes de matériaux ou de fabrication, il s'agissait de sièges de haute qualité qui ne participaient ni de l'esthétique ni de la recherche du "jetable" de la culture Pop.

Eero Aarnio:

Mustangs, c. 1970

Mustangs, um 1970

Mustangs, vers 1970

Eero Aarnio:

Bubble chair, c. 1967

Stuhl *Bubble*, um 1967

Chaise *Bubble*, vers 1967

Joe Colombo

1930–71

Italy . Italien . Italie

**Universale chair,
Model No. 4867** 1965

**Stuhl Universale,
Modell Nr. 4867** 1965

**Chaise Universale,
modèle n° 4867** 1965

Injection-moulded "Cycolac"
ABS plastic (1974 to 75 PA6
nylon and 1975 to present polypropylene)

Stuhlkörper im Spritzgußverfahren
aus »Cycolac«-ABS-Kunststoff
hergestellt (von 1974 bis 1975
aus PA6-Nylon, von 1975 bis
heute aus Polypropylen)

Chaise en plastique ABS
«Cycolac», moulé par injection (de
1974 à 1975, nylon PA6 et de
1975 à ce jour, polypropylène)

**Kartell, Italy, from 1967
to present**

Joe Colombo:
Armchair *4801/5*, 1964/65
Armlehnstuhl *4801/5*, 1964/65
Fauteuil *4801/5*, 1964/65

"Visiona" exhibition at Bayer AG,
Leverkusen, 1969

Ausstellung »Visiona« bei der
Bayer AG, Leverkusen, 1969

Exposition «Visiona», Bayer AG,
Leverkusen, 1969

The first full-scale chair to be injection-
moulded, the *4867* had interchangeable legs of two heights and could be
stacked into sets of three. Originally
known as the *4860*, the model number
changed in 1974 when the materials
used and the shape of the seat profile
were altered. Colombo said: "All the
objects needed in a house should be
integrated with the usable spaces;
hence they no longer ought to be
called furnishings but equipment."[23]

Der Universale *Nr. 4867* war der erste
im Spritzgußverfahren hergestellte
Stuhl; er hatte auswechselbare Beine
in zwei verschiedenen Höhen und ließ
sich bis zu drei Exemplaren stapeln.
Die ursprüngliche Bezeichnung
Nr. 4860 wurde 1974 geändert; man
wählte damals ein anderes Material
und veränderte die Form der Sitzfläche. Colombo: »Alle in einem Haus-
halt benötigten Gegenstände sollten in
die entsprechenden Räume integriert
werden; man sollte sie daher nicht
mehr als Möbel, sondern als Ausstattung bezeichnen.«[23]

Première chaise à être moulée par injection, la *4867* possédait des pieds
interchangeables de deux hauteurs différentes et pouvait s'empiler par trois
unités. Identifiée à l'origine comme la
4860, son numéro changea en 1974
lorsque d'autres matériaux furent utilisés et que la forme du siège fut mo-
difiée. Colombo écrivit: «Tous les
objets dont a besoin une maison devraient être intégrés dans les espaces
utilitaires; ils ne devraient donc plus
être appelés meubles mais
équipements.»[23]

Used in Stanley Kubrick's film "2001: A Space Odyssey", the *Djinn* series derived its title from a spirit in Islamic mythology that can assume human or animal form and control men with its supernatural powers. During the 1960s, the emerging popular interest in Eastern mysticism influenced the decorative arts in Europe and America.

Die *Djinn*-Serie, die in Stanley Kubricks Film »2001: Odyssee im Weltraum« zu sehen war, ist nach einer Gestalt aus der islamischen Mythologie benannt. Sie erscheint als Mensch oder Tier und kann den Menschen mit ihren übernatürlichen Kräften beherrschen. Während der 60er Jahre beeinflußte das allgemein wachsende Interesse am Mystizismus östlicher Kulturen die angewandte Kunst in Europa und den USA.

Utilisée dans le film de Stanley Kubrick «2001: Odyssée de l'espace», la série *Djinn* doit son nom à un esprit qui, en pays musulman, peut prendre forme humaine ou animale et dominer l'homme grâce à des pouvoirs surnaturels. Pendant les années 60, l'intérêt de plus en plus grand pour le mysticisme oriental influença les arts décoratifs en Europe et en Amérique. Les couleurs franches des jerseys utilisés au départ pour cette série étaient safran, écarlate, vert olive, tous coloris de sensibilité orientale.

Olivier Mourgue

*1939

France . Frankreich . France

Djinn chair and stool
1965

Stuhl und Hocker Djinn
1965

Siège et tabouret Djinn
1965

Stretch fabric-covered, polyurethane foam-upholstered, bent tubular steel frame

Rahmen gebogenes Stahlrohr; Polsterung aus Polyurethanschaumstoff, mit Stretchstoff bezogen

Structure en tube d'acier cintré rembourrée de mousse de polyuréthane, recouverte de jersey extensible

Airborne International, France, from 1963 to 1976

Still from Stanley Kubrick's Film "2001: A Space Odyssey", showing Space Station

Standfoto aus Stanley Kubricks Film »2001: Odyssee im Weltraum«, auf dem die Raumstation zu sehen ist

Image du Film de Stanley Kubrick «2001 : Odyssée de l'espace» montrant une station spatiale

Olivier Mourgue:

Djinn chaise longue, 1963

Djinn-Chaiselongue, 1963

Chaise longue *Djinn*, 1963

Kazuhide
Takahama

*1930

Japan . Japon

Suzanne seat 1965

Sitzmöbel Suzanne 1965

Siège Suzanne 1965

Fabric-covered, polyurethane foam-upholstered, tubular steel frame with chrome-plated steel fittings

Rahmen Stahlrohr; Polsterung aus Polyurethanschaumstoff, mit Stoff bezogen; Beschläge aus verchromtem Stahl

Structure en tube d'acier rembourrée de mousse de polyuréthane et recouverte de tissu, accessoires en acier chromé

Gavina, Italy, from 1965 to 1968, and Knoll International, Inc., New York, from 1968 to 1989

Utilising large block constructions of polyurethane foam, Takahama designed the *Marcel, Raymond* and *Suzanne* modular seating units for Dino Gavina in 1965. "All three were ideas generated in the laboratory of manufacturing and aesthetic experimentation, specific to the culture in question."[24]

Bei Takahamas aus Modulen zusammengesetzten Sitzmöbel *Marcel, Raymond* und *Suzanne,* die er 1965 für Dino Gavina entwarf, handelt es sich um blockartige Konstruktionen aus Polyurethanschaum. »Alle drei waren Ideen, die im Versuchslabor für Produktionsmethoden und ästhetische Gestaltung geboren wurden und für die betreffende Kultur charakteristisch sind.«[24]

A partir de gros blocs de mousse polyuréthane, Takahama créa les sièges modulaires *Marcel, Raymond* et *Suzanne* pour Dino Gavina en 1965. «Tous trois étaient nés d'idées issues du laboratoire du fabricant et d'expérimentations esthétiques, spécifiques à la culture en question.»[24]

Warren Platner explains: "I felt there was room for the kind of decorative, gentle, graceful kind of design that appeared in a period style like Louis XV… It is important that if you design a chair you produce something that enhances the person in it."[25]

Warren Platner sagt über seine Entwürfe: »Ich fand, daß es an der Zeit war für ein dekoratives, weich fließendes, elegantes Design von der Art des Louis-XV-Stils… Wenn man einen Stuhl entwirft, ist es wichtig, daß man etwas kreiert, das die Person, die darin Platz nimmt, aufwertet.«[25]

«Je sentais qu'il y avait une place pour le type de dessin décoratif, agréable et gracieux qui apparut dans une période stylistique comme celle de Louis XV… Il est important, lorsque vous dessinez un siège, de produire quelque chose qui mette en valeur la personne qui s'y asseoit.» Warren Platner.[25]

Warren Platner

*1919

USA . Etats-Unis

**Platner chair,
Model No. 1725A** 1966

**Platner-Stuhl,
Modell Nr. 1725A** 1966

**Fauteuil Platner,
modèle n° 1725A** 1966

Nickel-plated steel construction with fabric-covered, foam-rubber upholstery

Rahmen Stahl vernickelt; Schaumstoffpolsterung, mit Stoff bezogen

Construction en acier nickelé, rembourrage en mousse de caoutchouc recouverte de tissu

Knoll International, Inc., New York, from 1966 to present

Warren Platner:

Platner Collection, 1966

Warren Platner:

Platner Collection, 1966

Archizoom
Associati

1966–74

Italy . Italien . Italie

Superonda 1966

Wohnlandschaft Superonda
1966

Siège-sculpture Superonda
1966

Vinyl-covered polyurethane foam

Polyurethanschaum, mit Vinyl
bezogen

Mousse de polyuréthane recouverte de vinyl

**Poltronova, Italy, from 1966
to present**

Cut from a single block of polyurethane foam, the *Superonda* is exceptionally lightweight and easy to move. It can be configured in several ways – either as a chaise longue, sofa or divan – and is a highly interactive design, functioning more as a plaything than as a serious seating solution.

Die Wohnlandschaft *Superonda* ist aus einem einzigen Block Polyurethanschaumstoff geschnitten. Sie ist extrem leicht und bequem zu transportieren. Je nachdem wie man sie aufstellt, kann man sie als Sofa oder Chaiselongue benutzen – ein Design, das zu Verwandlungen auffordert, aber eher eine Spielerei als ein ernstzunehmender Entwurf ist.

Taillée dans un bloc de mousse de polyuréthane, la *Superonda* est extrêmement légère et se déplace donc facilement. Elle peut servir à plusieurs usages, chaise longue, sofa ou divan. C'est un concept hautement convivial, plus ludique que réellement fonctionnel.

Archizoom Associati:

Mies chair, 1969

Mies-Stuhl, 1969

Chaise *Mies*, 1969

Archizoom Associati:

Superonda sofa (detail), 1966

Wohnlandschaft *Superonda*
(Detail), 1966

Siège-sculpture *Superonda*
(détail), 1966

Roberto Matta

*1911

Chile . Chili

Malitte seating system
1966

Wohnlandschaft Malitte
1966

Système Malitte
1966

Fabric-covered polyurethane foam

Polyurethanschaumstoff, mit Stoff
bezogen

Mousse de polyuréthane recouverte de tissu

Gavina, Italy, from 1966 to 1968,
and Knoll International, Inc.,
New York, from 1968 to 1974

Roberto Matta, best known as a Sur-realist painter, confidently exploited the potential of polyurethane foam in creating this sculptural seating system. Although seen at the time as highly whimsical, the *Malitte* was an extremely innovative and functional design, rationally conceived for high-volume production. It was particularly well suited to the less formal and minimalist interiors that were becoming increasingly popular in the late 1960s.

Roberto Matta, der vor allem als sur-realistischer Maler bekannt ist, schöpf-te mit dem Entwurf seiner skulpturalen Wohnlandschaft sehr kühn die Mög-lichkeiten von Polyurethanschaum aus. Obwohl das Design damals als schrul-lig galt, war es ungewöhnlich innovativ und funktional. Nicht zuletzt handelte es sich um einen rationalen Entwurf, der auf die Produktion von großen Stückzahlen abzielte. Besonders gut eignete sich der Entwurf für unkonven-tionelle, minimalistische Interieurs, die in den 60er Jahren immer beliebter wurden.

Roberto Matta, plus connu comme peintre surréaliste, exploita sans hési-tation le potentiel de la mousse de polyuréthane pour créer ce concept de siège-sculpture. Bien que considéré à l'époque comme un objet hautement bizarre, le *Malitte* était une création extrêmement innovatrice et fonction-nelle, conçue pour une production en série. Elle correspondait particulière-ment bien aux intérieurs moins forma-listes et moins minimalistes devenant à la mode à la fin des années 60.

99

Günter Belzig

*1941

Germany . Deutschland .
Allemagne

Floris chair 1967

Stuhl Floris 1967

Chaise Floris 1967

Moulded, fibreglass-reinforced
polyester

Geformter, fiberglasverstärkter
Polyester

Polyester moulé renforcé de fibre
de verre

Brüder Belzig Design, Germany,
from 1968 (reissued limited
edition by Galerie Objekte,
Munich, from 1992)

This extraordinary anthropomorphic chair, produced by Günter, Berthold and Ernst Belzig, was first shown at the Cologne Furniture Fair in 1968. Intended as a totally weather-resistant stacking chair, only fifty examples were originally manufactured, as its hand laid-up, two-part construction proved too complicated for efficient industrial production.

Dieser außergewöhnlich anthropomorphe Stuhl, den die Brüder Günter, Berthold und Ernst Belzig herstellten, wurde auf der Kölner Möbelmesse von 1968 vorgestellt. Er wurde als wetterbeständiger Stapelstuhl konzipiert, dennoch wurden anfangs nur fünfzig Exemplare hergestellt, denn die zweiteilige Konstruktion, die teilweise Handarbeit erforderte, war für eine effiziente Massenproduktion zu kompliziert.

Cet extraordinaire siège anthropomorphique produit par Günter, Berthold et Ernst Belzig fut tout d'abord présenté au Salon du Meuble de Cologne en 1968. Modèles empilables résistant aux intempéries, seuls cinquante exemplaires en furent fabriqués au départ, car la construction en deux parties se révéla trop complexe pour une production industrielle rentable.

Günter Belzig with his range
of children's furniture

Günter Belzig mit seinen
Kindermöbeln

Günter Belzig et ses
meubles pour enfants

Pierre Paulin:

Ribbon chair, *Model No. 582*, 1965

Sessel *Ribbon, Modell Nr. 582*, 1965

Fauteuil *Ribbon, modèle n° 582*, 1965

Pierre Paulin

*1927

France . Frankreich

Chair, Model No. 577
1967

Sessel, Modell Nr. 577
1967

Chauffeuse, modèle n° 577
1967

Fabric-covered, foam-upholstered, tubular steel frame

Stahlrohrgestell; Schaumstoffpolsterung, mit Jersey bezogen

Structure en tube d'acier rembourrée de mousse et recouverte de tissu

Artifort, Netherlands, from 1967 to present

Pierre Paulin:

Chair, *Model No. 560*, 1963

Sessel, *Modell Nr. 560*, 1963

Fauteuil, *modèle n° 560*, 1963

The *577* chair, which rests directly on the floor, allows the user to assume a relaxed and informal posture. Through his use of visually unified, abstracted sculptural forms, combined with an understanding of ergonomics and the degree to which his designs afford the sitter freedom of movement, Paulin's chairs are not only beautiful to look at but also extremely comfortable to use.

Der Sessel *Nr. 577* hat weder Beine noch Untergestell; er liegt direkt auf dem Boden. So kann der Benutzer eine entspannte, unkonventionelle Haltung einnehmen, die dem saloppen Lebensstil der Zeit entsprach. Paulin verbindet ganzheitliche, ungegenständlich-skulpturale Formen mit einer individuellen Auslegung ergonomischer Prinzipien und gestattet dem Benutzer seiner Sitzmöbel viel Bewegungsfreiheit. Daher sind sie nicht nur schön anzusehen, sondern auch äußerst bequem.

La chauffeuse *n° 577*, qui repose directement sur le sol, permet à son utilisateur de trouver une position détendue et informelle, ce qui était tout à fait dans l'air du temps de cette période. A travers leurs formes sculpturales abstraites, simples et lisses, combinant une sensibilité réelle à l'ergonomie et à la recherche de liberté de mouvement, les sièges de Paulin ne sont pas seulement beaux mais extrêmement confortables.

Pierre Paulin:

Chair, *Model No. 598*, 1972

Sessel, *Modell Nr. 598*, 1972

Fauteuil, *modèle n° 598*, 1972

Jonathan De Pas
Donato D'Urbino
Paolo Lomazzi
Carla Scolari

all born in the 1930s

alle in den dreißiger Jahren
geboren

nés au cours des années 30

Italy . Italien . Italie

Blow chair 1967

Blow-Sessel 1967

Fauteuil Blow 1967

High-frequency welded PVC
(Polyvinylchloride)

PVC-Folie (Polyvinylchlorid),
hochfrequenzverschweißt

Feuille de PVC (chlorule de
polyvinyle) soudée électronique-
ment

Zanotta, Italy, from 1967
to 1991

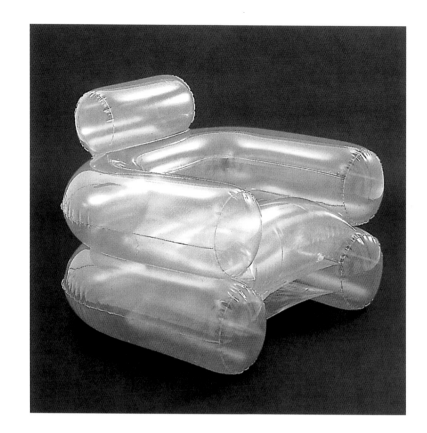

The *Blow* chair, the first inflatable chair successfully mass-produced in Italy, is an icon of 1960s popular culture. Inexpensive to manufacture, it possessed an intrinsic expendability that dismissed the traditional associations of high cost and permanence with chair design. Only recently taken out of production, the *Blow* chair could be used in an interior or exterior context and was even suitable for use in swimming pools.

Der *Blow*-Sessel, das erste aufblasbare Sitzmöbel, in Italien mit großem Erfolg in Serie produziert, ist eine Ikone der Popkultur der Sechziger. Seine geringen Herstellungskosten machten ihn zu einer Art Konsumgegenstand und veränderten grundlegend die bisherigen Vorstellungen von hohen Produktionskosten und Haltbarkeit. Der *Blow*-Sessel konnte in Innen- und Außenräumen verwendet werden; er eignete sich sogar für die Benutzung im Swimmingpool. Seine Produktion wurde erst vor kurzem eingestellt.

Le fauteuil *Blow*, premier siège gonflable produit avec succès en Italie, est devenu une icône de la culture populaire des années 60. Economique à fabriquer, il présentait des caractères intrinsèques de produit «consommable» qui niaient les idées reçues traditionnelles sur le coût élevé et la permanence. Retiré de la production récemment seulement, il pouvait servir aussi bien à l'extérieur qu'à l'intérieur, et même au bord d'une piscine.

**De Pas, D'Urbino, Lomazzi &
Scolari:**

Zanotta stand at Eurodomus 3,
Turin

Stand der Firma Zanotta auf der
Eurodomus 3, Turin

Stand de la firme Zanotta à
l'Eurodomus 3, Turin

**De Pas, D'Urbino,
Lomazzi & Scolari:**

Blow chairs

Blow-Sessel

Chaises *Blow*

From a range of cardboard furniture pieces that included modular seating, storage units and tables, the *Papp* chair was one of the first designs to explore the possibilities of cardboard seating and as such can be seen as an important precursor of Frank Gehry's *Easy Edges* series of 1972. The *Papp* chair's form, however, is reminiscent of a plywood cut-out chaise-longue designed in 1953 by Vittorio Gregotti, Lodovico Meneghetti and Giotto Stoppino.

Der *Papp*-Stuhl war Teil einer Gruppe von Möbeln aus Karton: Sitzmodule, Anbauschränke und Tische. Er gehörte zu den ersten Entwürfen, die Einsatzmöglichkeiten von Pappmöbeln erprobte und daher als wichtiger Vorläufer von Frank Gehrys Entwurf *Easy Edges* von 1972 angesehen werden kann. Die Form des *Papp*-Stuhls erinnert an die Chaiselongue aus schichtverleimtem Sperrholz, die Vittorio Gregotti, Lodovico Meneghetti und Giotto Stoppino 1953 entworfen hatten.

Faisant partie d'une gamme de mobilier comprenant des sièges modulaires, des rangements et des tables, la chaise *Papp* fut l'une des premières chaises à explorer les possibilités du carton et peut être considérée à ce titre comme un important précurseur de la gamme *Easy Edges* de Frank Gehry (1972). Sa forme rappelle néanmoins une chaise longue en contreplaqué découpé dessinée en 1953 par Vittorio Gregotti, Lodovico Meneghetti et Giotto Stoppino.

Peter Raacke

*1928

Germany . Deutschland . Allemagne

Papp chair 1967
Papp-Stuhl 1967
Chaise Papp 1967

Cardboard

Karton

Carton

Faltmöbel Ellen Raacke, Germany, from 1967 to present

Joe Colombo

1930 – 71

Italy . Italien . Italie

Additional Living System
1967/68

Tubular iron frame upholstered in fabric-covered polyurethane foam, with metal clamps

Stahlrohrrahmen mit stoffüberzogener Polyurethanschaum-Polsterung und Metallklammern

Cadre en tube de fer garni de mousse polyuréthane recouverte de tissu, pinces métalliques

Sormani, Italy, from 1968 to 1971

This extraordinary seating system is convertible into several combinations. Equally ingenious and innovative was Colombo's *Visiona* habitat, a space-age living cell, designed in 1969 for Bayer. Colombo explained: "Today the problem lies in offering furnishing which is purely autonomous, independent of architectural considerations and flexible and programmable enough that it suits every present and future room set-up."

Dieses außergewöhnliche Sitzmöbelsystem läßt sich zu verschiedenen Einheiten zusammensetzen. Genauso ausgefallen und innovativ war Colombos 1969 für die Bayer AG entworfene *Visiona*-Ausstattung, eine Wohnzelle wie in einer Raumstation. Colombo erklärte sein Design wie folgt: »Heutzutage muß man eine Einrichtung anbieten können, die von architektonischen Vorgaben unabhängig ist. Sie muß so flexibel und integrationsfähig sein, daß sie sowohl gegenwärtigen als auch zukünftigen Raumkonzepten genügt.«

Ce système de fauteuils tout à fait extraordinaire peut être combiné de diverses façons. L'ensemble *Visiona* que Colombo avait réalisé en 1969 pour Bayer était lui aussi étonnant et innovatif. Il s'agissait d'une cellule habitable ressemblant à une station spatiale. Colombo fournissait l'explication suivante: «Aujourd'hui, nous devons proposer des meubles autonomes, ne se rattachant en rien à des considérations architectoniques. Ils doivent être flexibles et programmables afin de pouvoir s'adapter à toute installation intérieure, présente et future.»

Joe Colombo:

Additional Living System, 1967/68

Joe Colombo:

Elda chair, 1965

Sessel *Elda*, 1965

Fauteuil *Elda*, 1965

Joe Colombo:

Roto Living Unit, 1969

The *Pastille*, or as it is sometimes known, the *Gyro*, is a novel approach to the traditional rocking-chair format. A singular chair design intended for interior and exterior use, it won an AID award in 1968. "Aarnio is always ahead of his time. Although perhaps the most international of Finnish designers of furniture, he is nevertheless intensely individual. Not a follower of any school, but conceivably the founder of one."[26]

Der *Pastille*- oder *Gyro*-Sessel, wie er auch genannt wird, ist Ausdruck einer völlig neuen Auffassung von der Konstruktion eines Schaukelstuhls, wie man ihn bisher kannte. Dieser einzigartige Stuhl, der für die Verwendung drinnen und draußen konzipiert wurde, gewann 1968 den AID-Award. »Aarnio ist seiner Zeit immer voraus. Er ist vielleicht der internationalste aller finnischen Designer, ist aber dennoch durch und durch Individualist. Er gehört keiner Schule an, ist aber offensichtlich Gründer einer Schule.«[26]

Le *Pastille*, connu aussi sous le nom de *Gyro*, marque une approche très nouvelle du siège à bascule. Conçu pour l'intérieur ou l'extérieur, ce modèle remporta un prix AID en 1968. «Aarnio est toujours en avance sur son temps. Bien qu'il soit peut-être le plus international des créateurs de meubles finlandais, il possède néanmoins une très forte personnalité. Ce n'est pas un suiveur d'une quelconque école, mais sans doute le fondateur d'un nouveau mouvement.»[26]

Eero Aarnio

*1932

Finland . Finnland . Finlande

Pastille or Gyro chair
1968

Sessel Pastille oder Gyro
1968

Fauteuil Pastille ou Gyro
1968

Moulded, glass-reinforced polyester

Fiberglasverstärkter, geformter Polyester

Polyester moulé, renforcé de fibre de verre

Asko Oy, Finland, from 1968 to c. 1980 (reissued from 1991 to present)

Stendig promotional photograph of *Gyro* chairs, c. 1970

Werbefoto von Stendig: *Gyro*-Stühle, um 1970

Photographie publicitaire de Stendig montrant les chaises *Gyro*, vers 1970

Piero Gatti

*1940

Cesare Paolini

1937–83

Franco Teodoro

*1939

Italy . Italien . Italie

Sacco chair 1968

Sitzsack 1968

Siège Sacco 1968

Vinyl bag containing semi-
expanded polystyrene pellets

Vinylsack, gefüllt mit halbauf-
geschäumten Styroporkugeln

Sac de vinyl rempli de billes de
polystyrène semi-expansé

**Zanotta, Italy, from 1968
to present**

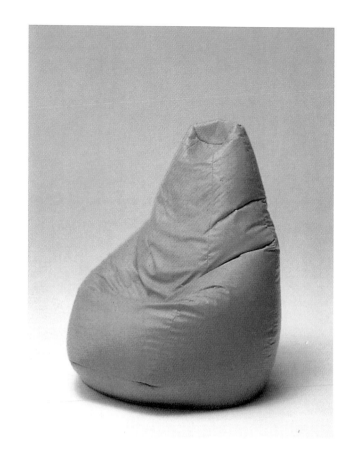

The first commercially produced bean-bag seat, the *Sacco* easily adapts to whatever position the sitter assumes. The designers originally proposed a fluid-filled transparent envelope but the excessive weight and complications of filling it eventually led to the inspired choice of semi-expanded polystyrene beads. It was claimed by Zanotta to be "The Chair of 1001 Nights (1000 positions by day, one position by night, marvellously comfortable)."[27]

Der erste kommerziell hergestellte Sitzsack, der *Sacco*, verändert seine Form, je nachdem welche Position man einnimmt. Die Designer hatten ursprünglich eine mit Flüssigkeit gefüllte, transparente Hülle vorgeschlagen, sich aber wegen des ungeheuren Gewichts und der Schwierigkeiten beim Einfüllen schließlich für halbaufgeschäumte Styroporkügelchen entschieden. Zanotta meinte, es sei »der Stuhl von 1001 Nacht (1000 Positionen am Tag, eine bei Nacht, herrlich bequem)«.[27]

Premier siège-sac commercialisé, le *Sacco* s'adapte immédiatement à n'importe quelle position. Ses designers avaient au départ proposé une enveloppe transparente emplie de liquide, mais le poids et les complications du remplissage conduisirent à ce choix inspiré de petites billes de polystyrène semi-expansé. Zanotta le présenta comme «le siège des mille et une nuits – 1000 positions pour le jour, une pour la nuit, merveilleusement confortable».[27]

Piero Gatti photographed with a
prototype of the *Sacco*

Piero Gatti, fotografiert mit einem
Sacco-Prototyp

Photographie de Piero Gatti avec
un prototype du *Sacco*

Gatti, Paolini & Teodoro:

Capitello chair, 1971

Stuhl *Capitello*, 1971

Siège *Capitello*, 1971

Compressed and vacuum-packed in a PVC wrapper, the *Up 5* chair literally bounced into life when unwrapped. Pesce described his *Up Series* as "transformation" furniture, intended to turn the act of purchasing into a "happening". With specific reference to *Up 5*, Pesce declared: "In that design I was expressing my own view of women: they have always been, against their own wills, prisoners of themselves. So I felt like giving this armchair the shape of a woman with a ball on her feet, which is indeed the traditional image of the prisoner."[28]

Der *Up-5*-Sessel, der vakuumverpackt in PVC-Folie geliefert wurde, sprang buchstäblich ins Leben. Pesce nannte seine exzentrischen *Up*-Serien »Verwandlungsmöbel«. Der Akt des Kaufens wurde zum Happening. In bezug auf die *Up-5*-Serie erklärte Pesce: »In diesem Design habe ich meine persönliche Sicht der Frauen ausgedrückt: sie sind stets Gefangene ihres Wesens. Deshalb wollte ich diesem Sessel die Gestalt einer Frau mit einer Kugel an den Füßen geben – einer Gestalt, die dem traditionellen Bild eines Strafgefangenen entspricht.«[28]

Comprimé et livré sous emballage sous vide, le fauteuil *Up 5* éclosait littéralement à la vie lorsque l'enveloppe de plastique était déchirée. Gaetano Pesce décrivit cette gamme *Up* comme un mobilier «à transformation». Se référant spécifiquement au *Up 5*, Pesce déclara: «A travers ce fauteuil, j'exprimais mes vues personnelles sur les femmes. C'est pourquoi j'ai eu envie de donner à ce fauteuil la forme d'une femme avec une boule attachée à ses pieds, ce qui est en fait l'image traditionnelle du prisonnier.»[28]

Gaetano Pesce

*1939

Italy . Italien . Italie

Up 5 (Donna) 1969
Sessel Up 5 (Donna) 1969
Fauteuil Up 5 (Donna) 1969

Stretch fabric-covered, moulded polyurethane foam

Geformter Polyurethanschaumstoff, mit Stretchstoff bezogen

Mousse de polyuréthane moulée, recouverte de tissu élastique

C&B Italia (later to become known as B&B Italia), Italy, from 1969 to 1976

A photo by Zaugg for a C&B Italia advertising campaign for the *Up* series, c. 1970

Ein Foto von Zaugg für die C&B-Italia-Werbekampagne der *Up*-Serien, um 1970

Une photographie de Zaugg pour une campagne publicitaire de C&B Italia pour les séries *Up*, vers 1970

Gaetano Pesce:
Up Series, 1969

Up 5 Donna bouncing into life
Up 5 Donna springt ins Leben
Up 5 Donna en pleine éclosion

Giancarlo Piretti:

Plia chairs with *Plano* table, 1969
Plia-Stühle mit *Plano*-Tisch, 1969
Chaises *Plia* et table *Plano*, 1969

Giancarlo Piretti

*1940

Italy . Italien . Italie

Plia chair 1969
Stuhl Plia 1969
Chaise Plia 1969

Chrome-plated steel frame with
moulded perspex seat and back

Rahmen aus Stahl, verchromt;
Sitz- und Rückenschale aus geformtem Perspex-Kunststoff

Structure d'acier chromé, siège et
dossier en perspex moulé

**Castelli, Italy, from 1969
to present**

The *Plia* chair is an efficient modern reworking of the traditional wooden folding chair. When collapsed, the *Plia* is only an inch in depth, excluding the central hub. Piretti also designed a similar folding armchair, the *Plona*, in 1970, followed in 1971 by a matching desk, the *Plano*. The *Plia* has won several prizes, including the Bundespreis "Gute Form" in 1973.

Der Stuhl *Plia* ist eine effiziente, moderne Überarbeitung des traditionellen Klappstuhls aus Holz. Zusammengefaltet ist er etwa 2,5 cm dick (ohne die Nabe in der Mitte). 1970 entwarf Piretti einen ähnlichen zusammenklappbaren Armlehnstuhl, das Modell *Plona*, und 1971 den dazugehörigen *Plano*-Schreibtisch. Der *Plia* wurde mit mehreren Preisen ausgezeichnet, u. a. 1973 mit dem Bundespreis »Gute Form«.

Le siège *Plia* est une réinterprétation moderne convaincante de la traditionnelle chaise pliante en bois. Repliée, la *Plia* ne mesure que 4 cm d'épaisseur, hors moyeu central. Piretti dessina également un fauteuil pliant similaire, le *Plona*, en 1970 et un bureau assorti, le *Plano* en 1971. La *Plia* a remporté plusieurs distinctions dont le prix fédéral «Gute Form», en 1973.

Vico Magistretti:

Gaudí chair, 1970

Stuhl *Gaudí*, 1970

Chaise *Gaudí*, 1970

Aiming to create a single-piece chair in compression-moulded plastic with a traditional four-legged form, Magistretti brilliantly resolved the technical difficulties associated with the strength of the legs by configuring them in an "S" shape. He based this solution on the leg design of his earlier injection-moulded *Stadio* table of 1966. The *Gaudí* and *Vicario* armchairs, both designed in 1970, are similarly constructed and equally restrained.

Magistretti löste die technischen Probleme, die sich bei der Konstruktion eines klassischen, vierbeinigen Stuhls aus hochdruckgeformtem Kunststoff in bezug auf die Tragfähigkeit der Füße ergeben, indem er sie S-förmig profilierte. Diese Idee basierte auf den Erfahrungen, die er bei einem früheren Möbel aus hochdruckgeformtem Kunststoff, dem Tisch *Stadio* aus dem Jahr 1966, gemacht hatte. Auch die Armlehnstühle *Gaudí* und *Vicario* von 1970 unterliegen den gleichen Konstruktionsprinzipien und sind ebenso unaufdringlich in ihrer Gestaltung.

Afin de réaliser une chaise à quatre pieds en un seul élément de plastique moulé par compression, Magistretti résolut brillamment les difficultés techniques posées par la solidité des pieds en leur donnant une forme en S. Cette solution venait de sa table *Stadio*, créée en 1966. De même que la *Selene*, les fauteuils *Gaudí* et *Vicario*, tous deux dessinés en 1970 et de construction similaire et tout aussi sobre, traduisent le classicisme de la philosophie de Magistretti.

Vico Magistretti

*1920

Italy . Italien . Italie

Selene chair 1969

Stuhl Selene 1969

Chaise Selene 1969

Compression-moulded 'Reglar' fibreglass-reinforced polyester

Hochdruckgeformter, fiberglasverstärkter ›Reglar‹-Polyester

Résine renforcée moulée par injection

Artemide, Italy, from 1969 to present

Wendell Castle

*1932
USA . Etats-Unis

Molar sofa 1969/70
Sofa Molar 1969/70
Canapé Molar 1969/70

Moulded glass-reinforced
polyester

Geformter, fiberglasverstärkter
Polyester

Polyester moule renforce de fibre
de verre

Beylerian Limited, USA, from
1970 to c. 1975

Best known for his superbly crafted wooden furniture, Castle translated his highly organic forms into plastic. The surrealistic *Molar* sofa and matching *Molar* chair were based on the shape of large back teeth. Not intended for high-volume production, the *Molar* group and the similar *Castle* series of chairs were exclusively distributed by Stendig, New York.

Castle, der in erster Linie für seine hervorragend gearbeiteten Holzmöbel bekannt ist, übersetzte seine organischen Formen in Kunststoff. Das surrealistisch anmutende Sofa *Molar* und der dazugehörige Stuhl hatten die Form von riesigen Backenzähnen. Die Gruppe *Molar* und die ähnliche Sitzmöbelgruppe *Castle* waren nicht für die Massenproduktion vorgesehen; sie wurden exklusiv von der Firma Stendig, New York, vertrieben.

Plus connu pour ses meubles en bois superbement exécutés, Castle traduisit ses formes organiques en plastique. Ce canapé surréaliste et son fauteuil assorti s'inspiraient de la forme d'une molaire. Non conçues pour être produites en grande série, la gamme *Molar* et celle de sièges similaires de Castle étaient distribuées en exclusivité par Stendig, New York.

Wendell Castle:
Castle Chair, 1970
Stuhl *Castle*, 1970
Chaise *Castle*, 1970

Jonathan De Pas
Donato D'Urbino
Paolo Lomazzi

all born in the 1930s

alle in den dreißiger Jahren
geboren

nés au cours des années 30

Italy . Italien . Italie

Joe chair 1970
Sessel Joe 1970
Fauteuil Joe 1970

Leather-covered, moulded
polyurethane foam

Geformter Polyurethanschaumstoff, mit Leder bezogen

Mousse de polyuréthane moulée,
recouverte de cuir

**Poltronova, Italy, from 1971
to present**

Named after the baseball legend Joe
DiMaggio, the design of this gigantic
glove was inspired by the oversized
and out-of-context sculptures of Claes
Oldenburg. The form of the *Joe* chair
can also be seen as an ironic comment
on the proliferation of reissued Bauhaus furniture covered with high-priced
glove leather.

Dieser Entwurf, der nach dem legen-
dären Baseballspieler Joe DiMaggio
benannt war und einen riesigen Hand-
schuh darstellte, war inspiriert von
Claes Oldenburgs überlebensgroßen
Skulpturen verfremdeter Alltagsgegen-
stände. Der Sessel *Joe* kann auch als
ironischer Kommentar zur verschwen-
derischen Gestaltung neu aufgelegter
Bauhaus-Möbel verstanden werden,
die mit teurem Handschuhleder bezogen waren.

Nommé d'après le célèbre joueur de
base-ball, Joe DiMaggio, cet énorme
gant doit son inspiration aux sculptures
surdimensionnées d'objets sortis de
leur contexte, de Claes Oldenburg. La
forme de ce fauteuil peut également
être vue comme un commentaire ironique sur la prolifération des rééditions
de meubles du Bauhaus recouverts de
coûteuses pausseries de gant.

Rodney Kinsman

*1943

Great Britain . Großbritannien .
Grande-Bretagne

Omkstak chair 1971

Stuhl Omkstak 1971

Chaise Omkstak 1971

Tubular steel frame with epoxy-
coated pressed sheet-steel seat
and back

Rahmen aus Stahlrohr; Sitz und
Rückenlehne aus gestanztem und
geformtem Stahlblech, mit Epoxyharz (emailleähnliches Kunstharz)
überzogen

Cadre en tube d'acier, siège et
dossier en tôle d'acier emboutie
traitée époxy

**Bieffeplast, Italy, from 1972
to present**

The *Omkstak* chair epitomises the
High-Tech style of the mid-1970s. It is
a highly rational design that was intended for interior and exterior use. Kinsman notes: "It is irresponsible to design things that don't last visually. I
don't believe that products should
have such an ephemeral form that they
will be out of date long before they
should be."[29]

Der *Omkstak*-Stuhl, ein Höhepunkt des
rationalen High-Tech-Designs der 70er
Jahre, war für die Verwendung für drinnen und draußen gedacht. Kinsman
sagte dazu: »Es ist unverantwortlich,
Dinge zu entwerfen, an denen man
sich schnell satt sieht. Ich bin nicht der
Meinung, Produkte sollten eine so kurz-
lebige Gestalt haben, daß sie aus der
Mode kommen, lange bevor es an der
Zeit wäre.«[29]

La chaise *Omkstak* représente le
sommet du style High-Tech du milieu
des années 70. C'est un modèle
rationnel conçu aussi bien pour l'intérieur que l'extérieur. Kinsman note:
«C'est faire preuve d'irresponsabilité
que de dessiner des objets qui ne
possèdent pas une certaine durée de
vie visuelle. Je ne crois pas que les
produits doivent avoir une forme
tellement éphémère qu'ils se trouvent
dépassés avant la date à laquelle ils
devraient normalement l'être.»[29]

This chair and table form part of the *Easy Edges* series, which comprised seventeen pieces in cardboard. To increase the strength and resilience of the construction, the layers of cardboard were laminated at right angles to one another. Originally conceived as low-cost furniture, *Easy Edges* was so immediately successful that Gehry withdrew the series from production after only three months, fearing that his ascendancy as a popular furniture designer would distract him from realising his potential as an architect.

Der Stuhl und der Tisch sind Teile der Serie *Easy Edges*, die siebzehn Stücke aus Pappe umfaßte. Um die Festigkeit und die Elastizität zu steigern, wurden die einzelnen Schichten jeweils in einem Winkel von 90° übereinandergelegt. Die Stücke der Kollektion *Easy Edges* wurden als Niedrigpreismöbel konzipiert und waren derart erfolgreich, daß Gehry die Produktion nach drei Monaten stoppte, weil er befürchtete, daß sein Aufstieg als populärer Möbeldesigner ihn daran hindern würde, sein Können als Architekt zu beweisen.

Cette chaise et cette table font partie de la gamme *Easy Edges* qui comprenait dix-sept éléments en carton. Pour accroître la solidité et la résistance du montage, les couches de carton étaient lamellées selon un angle de 90°. Conçu à l'origine comme un mobilier économique, *Easy Edges* connut immédiatement un tel succès que Gehry retira sa gamme de production après trois mois seulement, craignant que cette réussite de dessinateur de meubles bon marché ne l'empêche de poursuivre ses ambitions d'architecte.

Frank O. Gehry

*1929
USA . Etats-Unis

Easy Edges collection 1972
Kollektion Easy Edges 1972
Gamme Easy Edges 1972

Laminated corrugated cardboard
Schichtverleimte Wellpappe
Carton ondulé laqué

Jack Brogan, USA (some models reissued by Vitra GmbH, Germany, from 1992)

Frank O. Gehry:
Experimental Edges: *Little Beaver, Carumba & Bubbles*, 1987

Mario Bellini

*1935

Italy . Italien . Italie

Cab chair 1977
Stuhl Cab 1977
Chaise Cab 1977

Enamelled steel frame with zip-fastened saddle-stitched leather covering

Rahmen aus emailliertem Stahl, vernähter Lederbezug mit Reißverschluß

Structure d'acier émaillé recouverte de cuir cousu point sellier et zippé

Cassina, Italy, from 1977 to present

This elegant chair helped maintain Italy's reputation in the 1970s for high-quality, innovative design. The leather upholstery of the *Cab* chair zips directly onto the skeletal steel frame and functions as a supporting material. Bellini also designed the similarly constructed *Cab* armchair and sofa. All remain in production and are available with either white, tan or black leather covers.

Dieser elegante Stuhl trug in den 70er Jahren dazu bei, Italiens Ruf als ein Land für hochwertiges, innovatives Design zu festigen. Der Lederbezug schmiegt sich durch das Reißverschlußsystem wie eine Haut an den skelettartigen Stuhlrahmen aus Stahl und erhält so eine tragende Funktion. Neben diesem Stuhl entwarf Bellini den ähnlich konstruierten *Cab*-Armlehnstuhl und das *Cab*-Sofa. Alle Modelle sind noch in Produktion und mit weißem, braunem oder schwarzem Lederbezug erhältlich.

Cette chaise élégante contribua à maintenir, au cours des années 70, la réputation italienne de créations innovatrices de haute qualité. Le cuir est directement fixé sur la structure par une fermeture à glissière et fonctionne comme un matériau de soutien. Dans cette série, Bellini dessina également un fauteuil *Cab* et un sofa, proposés en cuir blanc, marron clair ou noir, et toujours fabriqués aujourd'hui.

Mario Bellini:

Cab sofa, 1987
Sofa *Cab*, 1987
Canapé *Cab*, 1987

Believing "good design" (Modernism) to be dead, Mendini "redesigned" furniture in an attempt to demonstrate, among other things, that the intellectual content of a design can be derived solely from decorative embellishment. Andrea Branzi further explained: "Operations of redesign consisted of touching-up found objects or famous products of design to illustrate the impossibility of designing something new in respect to what has already been designed."[30]

Mendini war der Meinung, »gutes Design« sei tot, und begnügte sich mit dem »Re-Design« von Möbeln. Damit wollte er unter anderem demonstrieren, daß man den geistigen Gehalt eines Designs allein an der dekorativen Verzierung ablesen könne. Andrea Branzi bemerkte dazu: »Redesign besteht darin, daß man Fundstücke oder Entwürfe berühmter Designer aufpeppt, um zu zeigen, daß es absolut unmöglich ist, etwas Neues zu entwerfen, was nicht schon entworfen worden ist.«[30]

Croyant à la mort du «bon design», Mendini repensait le mobilier pour tenter de montrer, entre autres, que le contenu intellectuel d'une création peut ne venir que d'embellissements décoratifs. Andrea Branzi expliqua plus tard que: «Les opérations de re-design consistent à retoucher des objets trouvés ou des créations célèbres du design pour illustrer l'impossibilité de dessiner quelque chose de nouveau.»[30]

Alessandro Mendini

*1931
Italy . Italien . Italie

Proust's armchair 1978
Prousts Sessel 1978
Le fauteuil de Proust 1978

Existing chair with hand-painted decoration

Bereits existierender Sessel mit handgemalter Verzierung

Fauteuil existant peint à la main

Studio Alchimia, Italy (out of production)

Alessandro Mendini:

Joe Colombo's 4860, "Re-Design" 1978

Joe Colombos 4860, »Re-Design« von 1978

Joe Colombo's 4860, »Re-Design« de 1978

Alessandro Mendini:

Dorifora chair, "Re-Design" 1984

Dorifora-Stuhl, »Re-Design« von 1984

Chaise *Dorifora*, «Re-Design» de 1984

115

Ron Arad

*1951

Great Britain . Großbritannien .
Grande-Bretagne

Rover chair 1981
Sessel Rover 1981
Chauffeuse Rover 1981

Tubular steel frame supporting a
salvaged Rover 2000 car seat

Stahlrohrrahmen, darauf ein
ausgeschlachteter Autositz aus
einem Rover 2000

Cadre de tube d'acier, siège de
Rover 2000

**One Off Ltd, UK, from 1981
to 1991**

During the early 1980s, the work of the
British avant-garde was characterised
by the inclusion of found objects in
their furniture designs. These rough
and ready pieces gave way to more
materially sophisticated work in the
mid-1980s, such as Arad's *Well
Tempered* chair. Also available as a
two-seater, the *Rover* chair, born out of
the High-Tech style, bears a striking
yet unintentional similarity to Jean
Prouvé's adjustable armchair prototype
of 1924.

Die Verwendung gebrauchter Gegenstände für ihr Design charakterisierte
die Arbeiten der britischen Avantgarde.
Die ersten, recht groben Ready-mades
wurden Mitte der 80er Jahre in bezug
auf Material und Ausführung von an-
spruchsvolleren Arbeiten abgelöst –
ein Beispiel dafür war Arads Sessel
Well Tempered. Der Sessel *Rover* war
auch als Zweisitzer erhältlich. Das Modell, das seinen Ursprung im High-
Tech-Design hatte, war dem Prototyp
des verstellbaren Sessels von Jean
Prouvé von 1924 sehr ähnlich – wenn
auch unbeabsichtigt.

Au début des années 80, les travaux
de l'avant-garde britannique se carac-
térisaient par l'inclusion d'objets trouvés dans ses créations de meubles.
Vers le milieu des années 80, ces éléments bruts ouvrirent la voie, dans certains cas, à des créations mieux finies
et plus sophistiquées, comme, par
exemple, le fauteuil *Well Tempered*
d'Arad. Egalement proposée en version deux places, la chauffeuse *Rover*,
enfant du High-Tech, présente une
similarité frappante, bien que non
voulue, avec le prototype de fauteuil
réglable de Jean Prouvé (1924).

Ron Arad:
Well Tempered chair, 1986/87
Sessel *Well-Tempered*, 1986/87
Fauteuil *Well Tempered*, 1986/87

Mario Botta

*1943
Switzerland . Schweiz . Suisse

Seconda chair 1982
Stuhl Seconda 1982
Chaise Seconda 1982

Steel frame with epoxy-coated, perforated sheet steel seat and expanded polyurethane back rest

Rahmen aus Stahl, Sitzfläche aus perforiertem Stahlblech, mit Epoxyharz (emailleähnliches Kunstharz) beschichtet; Rücken-lehne aus aufgeschäumtem Poly-urethanschaumstoff

Structure d'acier, siège en acier perforé laqué époxy (résine synthétique façon émail), dossier en polyuréthane expansé

**Alias, Italy, from 1982
to present**

Mario Botta:

Quinta chairs, 1985
Stühle Quinta, 1985
Chaises Quinta, 1985

Evolving stylistically from 1970s High-Tech, the Seconda chair epitomises the "Matt Black" style of the 1980s. Arising in part as a rejection of the decorative excesses of design movements such as Memphis, "Matt Black" seat furniture is frequently uncomfortable and uncompromising in expressing its hard-edged "rational" aesthetic. For this reason, designs such as the Seconda chair are best described as Post-Modern rather than Modern.

Der Stuhl Seconda, Höhepunkt des »Matt-Black«-Stils der 80er Jahre, hatte sich aus dem High-Tech-Design der 70er Jahre entwickelt. Die »Matt-Black«-Sitzmöbel, die man zum Teil als Gegenbewegung zu den dekorativen Exzessen von Designbewegungen wie z.B. Memphis deuten kann, sind meist unbequem und stellen kompromißlos ihre rationale, kantige Ästhetik zur Schau. Daher gehören Entwürfe wie der Seconda eher zur Moderne als zur Postmoderne.

Venue du style High-Tech des années 70, la chaise Seconda incarne le style «Matt Black» (noir mat) des années 80. Nés du rejet des excès décoratifs de mouvements comme Memphis, les meubles «Matt Black» sont souvent in-confortables et sans concessions dans l'expression de leur rigueur esthétique «rationnelle». Pour cette raison, des créations comme la Seconda peuvent davantage être qualifiées de post-modernes que de modernes.

Mario Botta:

Seconda chairs, 1982
Seconda-Stühle, 1982
Chaises Seconda, 1982

Philippe Starck

*1949
France . Frankreich

Costes chair 1982
Sessel Costes 1982
Fauteuil Costes 1982

Painted tubular steel frame with
bent mahogany plywood back and
leather-covered, foam-upholstered
seat

Rahmen aus Stahlrohr, lackiert;
Rückenlehne aus gebogenem
Mahagoni-Schichtholz; Sitzfläche
mit Schaumstoffpolsterung,
Lederbezug

Cadre de tube d'acier peint avec
dossier en contreplaqué d'acajou
cintré, siège garni de mousse et
recouvert de cuir

**Driade, Italy, from 1985
to present**

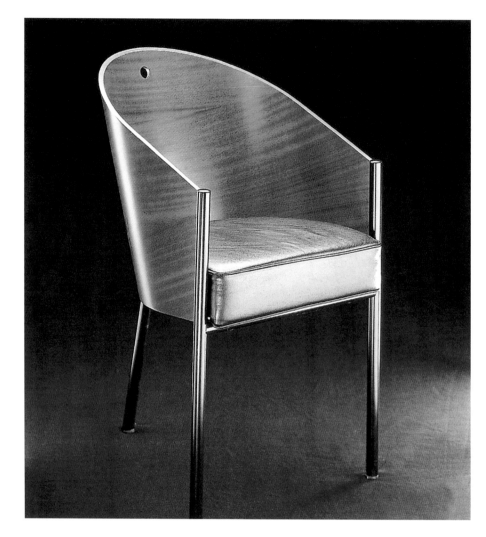

Perhaps Philippe Starck's best-known
chair design, the *Costes* was originally
designed for the Café Costes in Paris.
He has explained that the chair was
designed with three legs so that the
waiters at the café would trip up only
half as much as is usual. The *Pratfall*,
a lower lounge-chair version of the
Costes, was designed the same year.

Der *Costes*-Sessel ist Starcks bekann-
tester Stuhl, er hat ihn ursprünglich für
das Café Costes in Paris entworfen.
Starck erklärte, daß er dem Sessel drei
Beine gegeben habe, damit die Kellner
des Cafés nur halb soviel stolperten
wie gewöhnlich. Der *Pratfall*, eine nie-
drige Liegesesselversion des *Costes*-
Sessels, entstand im gleichen Jahr.

Le siège sans doute le plus célèbre de
Starck, ce modèle *Costes*, fut spécialement dessiné pour le Café
Costes, à Paris. Starck expliqua que le
fauteuil n'avait que trois pieds pour
que les serveurs aient moins de pas à
faire en tournant autour. Le modèle
Pratfall, version chauffeuse du *Costes*,
fut dessiné la même année.

Philippe Starck:
Café Costes, 1982

At the launch of the first Memphis Collection, Ettore Sottsass wrote: "All that walking through realms of uncertainty... all that talking with metaphors and utopia... all that getting away from it all... has given us a certain experience; we've become good explorers. Maybe we can navigate dangerous rivers, penetrate jungles where no-one has ever been. There's no reason for getting worked up. We can finally make our way with ease; the worst is over."[31]

Die erste öffentliche Präsentation der Memphis-Kollektion kommentierte Ettore Sottsass: »Dieser endlose Marsch durch Sphären der Ungewißheit... dieses endlose Gerede voller Seifenblasen... diese endlosen Versuche, davon wegzukommen... all das hat uns ein gewisses Maß an Erfahrung gebracht. Vielleicht können wir in gefährlichen Gewässern navigieren, den unentdeckten Dschungel durchdringen. Es gibt keinen Grund, sich aufzuregen. Wir können unseren Weg ganz gelassen zu Ende gehen; das Schlimmste ist vorbei.«[31]

Lors du lancement de la première collection Memphis, Ettore Sottsass écrivit: « Tout ces mouvements dans l'univers de l'incertitude... tout ces discours de métaphores et d'utopie... tous ces rejets de tout... nous ont donné une certaine expérience; nous sommes devenus de bons explorateurs. Peut-être voguerons-nous sur des rivières dangereuses, pénétrerons-nous des jungles où personne n'a jamais mis le pied. Il n'y a aucune raison d'avoir peur. Nous pourrons finalement trouver notre voie sans trop de peine; le pire est derrière nous.»[31]

Michele De Lucchi

*1951

Italy . Italien . Italie

First chair 1983

Stuhl First 1983

Chaise First 1983

Epoxy-coated, tubular metal frame with painted wood elements

Metallrohrrahmen, mit Epoxy (emailleähnliches Kunstharz) überzogen; farbig lackierte Holzelemente

Cadre de tubes métalliques traités époxy, éléments de bois peint

Memphis, Italy, from 1983 to c. 1987

119

Stiletto Studios

*1959

Germany . Deutschland .
Allemagne

Consumer's Rest 1983

Zinc-plated, cut and bent super-
market trolley

Supermarkt-Einkaufswagen, ver-
zinkt, geschnitten und gebogen

Chariot de supermarché coupé
et cintré, zingué

**Brüder Siegel GmbH & Co. KG,
Berlin, from 1983**

The *Consumer's Rest* is a "ready-
made" design which has been produced as an edition of 100. There is a
smaller version for children, *Short Rest*,
available in a colour choice of red, yellow and blue. The first example of the
Consumer's Rest was presented in
1983 by Christian Borngräber to Dr.
Wolfgang Schepers for the design
collection at The Museum of Art,
Düsseldorf.

Der Einkaufswagen *Consumer's Rest*
ist ein Ready-made, das in einer Auflage von 100 Stück produziert wurde.
Die kleinere Version für Kinder, *Short
Rest*, ist in Rot, Gelb und Blau erhältlich. Das erste Exemplar des *Consumer's Rest* übergab Christian Borngräber 1983 an Dr. Wolfgang Schepers für die Designkollektion des
Kunstmuseums der Stadt Düsseldorf.

Ce *Consumer's Rest* est un «ready-
made» produit en 100 exemplaires. Il
en existe une version plus petite pour
enfants, *Short Rest*, disponible en
rouge, bleu et jaune. Le premier exemplaire fut offert par Christian Borngräber au Dr. Wolfgang Schepers pour
la collection de design du Musée d'Art
de Düsseldorf.

Stiletto Studios:

Consumer's Rest & Short Rest,
1983

Lane's *Etruscan* chair is perhaps one of his more rational designs, yet it is still highly expressive, appearing spontaneously composed. Lane does not attempt to turn design into art but enjoys working on the murky edges of both disciplines. Only one of his designs is industrially produced, the *Atlas* table by the Italian company, Fiam, from 1988. More recently, Lane has been devoting his attentions to large-scale sculpture commissions.

Lanes *Etruscan*-Stuhl gehört zu seinen eher rationalen Entwürfen, dennoch wirkt er äußerst expressiv und spontan. Lane will Design nicht zur Kunst machen, fischt aber gern in den trüben Wassern am äußersten Rand beider Disziplinen. Nur einer seiner Entwürfe ging in die Massenproduktion; es war der *Atlas*-Tisch, den die italienische Firma Fiam seit 1988 produziert. In der letzten Zeit hat Lane sich auf Auftragsarbeiten für großformatige Skulpturen konzentriert.

Cette chaise *Etruscan* est sans doute l'un des projets les plus rationalistes de Lane, tout en restant extrêmement expressive dans sa composition faussement spontanée. Lane ne confond pas art et design, mais aime travailler aux limites des deux disciplines. Une seule de ses créations, la table *Atlas*, a été produite industriellement par la société italienne Fiam, à partir de 1988. Plus récemment, il s'est consacré à des commandes de sculptures de grandes dimensions.

Danny Lane

*1955

Great Britain . Großbritannien . Grande-Bretagne

Etruscan chair 1984
Stuhl Etruscan 1984
Chaise Etruscan 1984

Glass, forged mild steel and carved marble

Glas, geschmiedeter Flußstahl und behauener Marmor

Verre, acier doux et marbre taillé

Danny Lane, UK

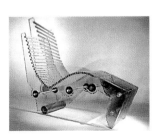

Shiro Kuramata

1934 – 91

Japan . Japon

How High the Moon
1986/87

Sessel How High the Moon
1986/87

**Fauteuil How High
the Moon** 1986/87

Nickel-plated, wire-mesh construction

Konstruktion aus vernickeltem Stahlgitter

Construction en grillage nickelé

**Vitra GmbH, Germany, from
1986 to present**

Shiro Kuramata:

*Begin the Beguine – Homage to
Josef Hoffmann*, 1985

Hommage an Hoffmann, 1985

Hommage à Hoffmann, 1985

Through his intriguing choice of materials and graceful use of proportions, Kuramata's *How High the Moon* expresses a highly refined sense of lightness and space. Peter Dormer writes, "His art lies in the ease with which his materials do his work. There is no stress in Kuramata's imagery – hence they present themselves gently."[32]

In der provokativen Wahl des Materials und der Ausgewogenheit der Proportionen des Sessels *How High the Moon* erkennt man Kuramatas feines Gespür für Leichtigkeit und Raumaufteilung. Peter Dormer schreibt: »Seine Kunst liegt in der Ungezwungenheit, mit der seine Materialien für ihn arbeiten. In Kuramatas Erfindungen gibt es nichts Angespanntes – sie präsentieren sich mit natürlicher Anmut.«[32]

A travers le choix d'un matériau étrange et des proportions pleines de grâce, ce fauteuil de Kuramata exprime un sens très raffiné de la légèreté et de l'espace. Peter Dormer écrit: «Son art (de Kuramata) réside dans l'aisance avec lesquels ses matériaux font leur travail. Il n'y a pas de tension dans l'imagerie de Kuramata – ces matériaux peuvent donc s'offrir au regard en toute sérénité.»[32]

Jasper Morrison

*1959

Great Britain . Großbritannien .
Grande-Bretagne

Thinking Man's chair 1987
Thinking-Man's-Stuhl 1987
Chaise Thinking Man's 1987

Painted, bent tubular steel and flat
steel bars

Gebogenes Stahlrohr und Flachstahl, farbig lackiert

Tube d'acier cintré peint et barres
d'acier plat

**Cappellini, Italy, from 1988
to present**

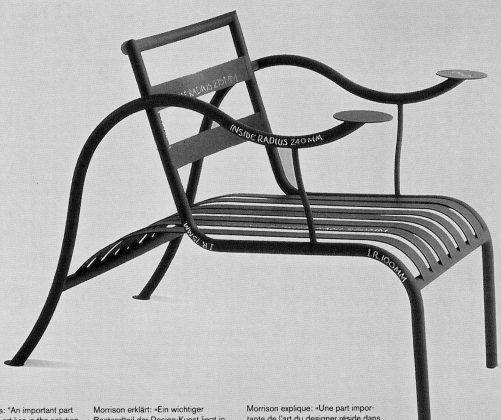

Morrison explains: "An important part of the designer's art lies in the solution of (the design's) manufacture: the quantity needed for the size of the intended market, and the costs involved. The balance of these variables is every bit as important to the art of design as its sculptural content. Indeed, the two aspects are interwoven, and to ignore either in pursuit of the other is to miss the point of designing."[33]

Morrison erklärt: »Ein wichtiger Bestandteil der Design-Kunst liegt in der Lösung von Produktionsproblemen: der Produktions-Auflage, die für den angepeilten Markt erforderlich ist, in Relation zu den anfallenden Kosten. Das Gleichgewicht dieser beiden Variablen ist für die Design-Kunst genauso wichtig wie ihr plastischer Gehalt. Diese beiden Aspekte gehören eng zusammen, und einen von beiden zugunsten des anderen zu vernachlässigen bedeutet, daß man das Wesen des Designs verfehlt.«[33]

Morrison explique: «Une part importante de l'art du designer réside dans la solution d'un problème de fabrication: la quantité nécessaire pour la taille du marché visé et les coûts. L'équilibre de ces variables est tout aussi important pour l'art du design que le contenu sculptural. En fait, ces deux aspects sont liés et ignorer l'un pour atteindre l'autre serait passer à côté de l'essence même du design.»[33]

123

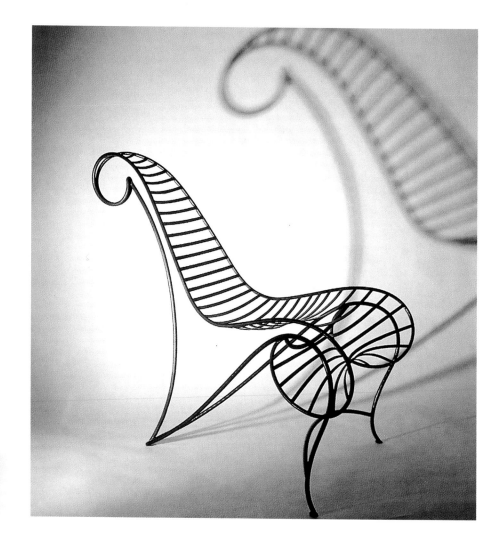

André Dubreuil:
Paris chair, 1988
Stuhl *Paris*, 1988
Chaise *Paris*, 1988

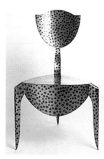

André Dubreuil

*1951
France . Frankreich

Spine chair 1988
Stuhl Spine 1988
Chaise Spine 1988

Bent and welded mild steel
Weichstahl, gebogen und
geschweißt
Acier doux, cintré et soudé

**A.D. Decorative Arts Ltd.,
France (originally UK), from
1988 to present**

Alluding to previous decorative styles, the *Spine* chair is hand-forged by a blacksmith in the Dordogne region of France. Because Dubreuil's designs depend on such labour-intensive production methods, his furniture is produced only in small quantities. Like many avant-garde designers, Dubreuil prefers the flexibility and scope for personal creativity that exclusive and small-scale methods of operation provide.

Der *Spine*-Stuhl orientiert sich an Stilarten vergangener Epochen; er wird von einem Schmied in der Dordogne, Frankreich, von Hand gefertigt. Da Dubreuils Entwürfe diese und ähnliche arbeitsintensive Produktionsmethoden erfordern, werden seine Möbel nur in geringen Mengen hergestellt. Wie viele Avantgarde-Designer legt er Wert auf die Flexibilität und die größeren Entfaltungsmöglichkeiten seiner Kreativität, die ihm exklusive Herstellungsmethoden mit kleinen Stückzahlen bieten.

Faisant allusion à des styles décoratifs historiques, cette chaise est forgée à la main par un forgeron traditionnel en Dordogne. Parce que les créations de Dubreuil dépendent de méthodes de production coûteuses en heures de travail, ses meubles ne sont produits qu'en petites quantités. Comme de nombreux designers d'avant-garde, Dubreuil attache beaucoup de prix à la souplesse et à la liberté créative que permet une production exclusive et à petite échelle.

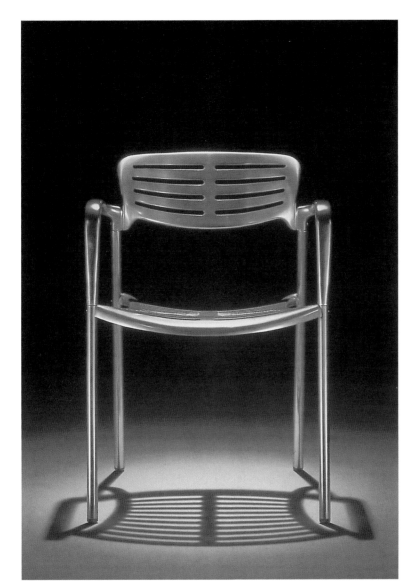

Jorge Pensi

*1946

Spain . Spanien . Espagne

**Toledo chair,
Model No. 2604** 1988

**Stuhl Toledo,
Modell No. 2604** 1988

**Siège Toledo,
modèle n° 2604** 1988

Cast aluminium

Gußaluminium

Fonte d'aluminium

**Amat s.a., Spain, from 1988
to present**

The *Toledo* is a reworking of earlier chair designs intended for use in Spanish open-air cafés. This highly functional chair recalls Gio Ponti's appeal for "furniture without adjectives".

Der *Toledo*-Stuhl ist eine Neubearbeitung älterer Stuhlentwürfe, die für die Terrassen in spanischen Straßencafés gedacht waren. Dieser ausgesprochen funktionale Stuhl läßt an Gio Pontis Forderung nach »Möbeln ohne Eigenschaften« denken.

Le *Toledo* est une réinterprétation d'un précédent modèle conçu pour les terrasses de café. Ce siège très fonctionnel rappelle le goût de Gio Ponti pour un «mobilier sans adjectifs».

Ron Arad

*1951

Great Britain . Großbritannien .
Grande-Bretagne

Big Easy Volume 2
1988
Sessel Big Easy Volume 2
1988
Siège Big Easy Volume 2
1988

Blackened sheet steel with
welded and polished stainless
steel

Geschwärztes Stahlblech und
polierter, geschweißter Edelstahl

Tôle d'acier noirci, soudures en
acier inoxydable poli

**One Off Ltd., UK, from 1988
to present**

The individual elements of Arad's *Volume* series chairs are cut from a pattern and then welded together. Each chair, therefore, varies slightly as a result of the welding process and can be seen as unique. The polished stainless steel welds stand out against the blackened steel construction and are intended to be read as a freehand line drawing. An upholstered version of this chair is currently produced by Moroso, Italy.

Die einzelnen Elemente von Arads *Volume*-Serie werden nach Vorlagen ausgeschnitten und zusammengeschweißt. Durch das Schweißen weicht jeder Stuhl ein wenig von der Norm ab und kann als Unikat bezeichnet werden. Die polierten Schweißnähte des Edelstahls heben sich von der Konstruktion aus geschwärztem Stahlblech ab und sollen als freihändig gezogene Linien gelesen werden. Zur Zeit wird in Moroso, Italien, eine gepolsterte Version dieses Sessels hergestellt.

Les divers éléments des sièges de la série *Volume* d'Arad sont coupés d'après un modèle, puis soudés ensemble. Du fait du procédé de soudure, aucun siège n'est donc strictement identique à l'autre et peut être considéré comme une pièce unique. Les soudures en acier inoxydable poli ressortent sur le fond noir et se lisent comme un dessin à main levée. Une version rembourrée de ce siège est actuellement produite par Moroso, Italie.

Ron Arad:
A.Y.O.R., 1990

Tom Dixon:

Upholstered *Bird*
chaise longue, 1992

Gepolsterter
Bird-Liegesessel, 1992

Chaise longue *Bird*
rembourrée, 1992

Tom Dixon

*1959

Great Britain . Großbritannien .
Grande-Bretagne

S chair 1988

Stuhl S 1988

Chaise S 1988

Welded mild steel frame with
woven wicker, raffia or latex
rubber

Rahmen aus Weichstahl,
geschweißt, Bast- und Binsengeflecht oder Latexüberzug

Cadre en acier doux soudé, siège
tissé en raphia ou en caoutchouc

Cappellini, Italy, from 1992

Tom Dixon:

S chair, 1988

Stuhl *S*, 1988

Chaise *S*, 1988

Tom Dixon's woven wicker and raffia *S* chairs of 1988 have recently been adapted for production in full upholstery. Celebrated throughout the 1980s by the international design press, the poetic and emotionally charged work of the British avantgarde is now being taken seriously by established manufacturers. Firms such as Vitra, Cappellini and Moroso have all begun either limited or full-scale production of this expressive furniture aimed primarily at the domestic market.

Dixons *S*-Stühle von 1988 mit Raffia-oder Binsengeflecht werden seit kurzem mit Polsterung hergestellt. Das poetische und emotional aufgeladene Design der britischen Avantgarde, das internationale Designpublikationen in 80ern priesen, wird heute von etablierten Herstellern ernst genommen. Firmen wie Vitra, Cappellini und Moroso haben entweder mit limitierten Auflagen begonnen oder die Produktion dieser ausdrucksvollen – hauptsächlich für den jeweiligen heimischen Markt bestimmten – Möbel voll anlaufen lassen.

Les chaises *S* de jonc et de raffia tressé de 1988 ont récemment été adaptées pour être produites en version rembourrée. Célébrée tout au long des années 80 par la presse internationale du design, l'œuvre poétique et émotionnellement chargée de l'avant-garde britannique est maintenant prise au sérieux par les grands fabricants. Des firmes comme Vitra, Cappellini et Moroso ont toutes commencé à produire en série limitée ou à grande échelle ces meubles expressifs qui étaient à l'origine destinés au seul marché domestique.

Shiro Kuramata

1934–91

Japan . Japon

Miss Blanche chair 1989
Stuhl Miss Blanche 1989
Fauteuil Miss Blanche 1989

Paper flowers cast in acrylic resin
with tubular aluminium legs

Papierblumen, in Acryl gegossen;
Beine aus Aluminiumrohr

Fleurs de papier incluses dans
une rèsine acrylique, pièterment
en tube d'aluminium

Kokuyo Co., Japan

Conceived for limited production, *Miss Blanche* is a visually delicate chair with its fall of red paper roses suggesting, perhaps, the frailty of love. Kuramata combines unusual forms and materials in a masterly fashion to produce minimalistic designs that run counter to preconceived notions of what furniture can look like or be made from.

Der Stuhl *Miss Blanche*, ein graziles Möbel, das mit seinen fallenden roten Papierrosen die Zerbrechlichkeit der Liebe anzudeuten scheint, wurde für eine limitierte Auflage konzipiert. Kuramata kombiniert auf meisterliche Art und Weise ungewöhnliche Formen und Materialien zu einem minimalistischen Design, das den herkömmlichen Vorstellungen, wie Möbel aussehen und aus welchen Materialien sie sein sollten, zuwiderläuft.

Conçu pour une production limitée, *Miss Blanche* et ses roses de papier rouge qui suggèrent, peut-être, la fragilité de l'amour, est un fauteuil d'aspect délicat. Kuramata combine en maître formes et matériaux inhabituels pour produire des dessins minimalistes qui vont à l'encontre des notions préconçues sur l'aspect et la fabrication d'un meuble.

Shiro Kuramata:
Armchair *Miss Blanche*, 1989
Sessel *Miss Blanche*, 1989
Fauteuil *Miss Blanche*, 1989

Morita's creations are luxury objects for the feelings, aiming to offer more than mere functionality. His preference for basic materials such as stone, steel and glass, together with his occasionally zoomorphic shapes, show a strong sense of Nature, for all his abstraction. He sees bright colours as artificial, and prefers dark shades.

Morita kreiert Luxusobjekte für die Gefühle. Sie wollen mehr bieten als bloße Funktionalität. Seine Vorliebe für elementare Materialien wie Stein, Stahl und Glas und seine zuweilen zoomorphen Formen haben bei aller Abstraktion einen starken Bezug zur Natur. Grelle Farben empfindet er als künstlich und benutzt am liebsten dunkle Töne.

Son style pourrait se nommer la "néo-confortabilité". Morita crée des objets de luxe qui veulent nous émouvoir, offrir davantage que la pure fonctionnalité. Sa préférence pour les matériaux élémentaires comme la pierre, l'acier et le verre et ses formes parfois zoomorphiques sont, toute abstraction retenue, très marquées par des références naturalistes. Il trouve les couleurs vives artificielles, et utilise plus volontiers des tons sombres.

Masaki Morita

*1950
Japan . Japon

Blue Sofa 1989
Blaues Sofa 1989
Canapé bleu 1989

Materials unknown
Materialien unbekannt
Matériaux non connus

Manufacturer unknown

Masaki Morita:
Red Sofa, 1989
Rotes Sofa, 1989
Canapé rouge, 1989

129

Alfredo Arribas

*1954

Spain . Spanien . Espagne

J. Greystoke chair 1990
Stuhl J. Greystoke 1990
Siège J. Greystoke 1990

Solid beech and anodised cast
aluminium frame with fabric-
covered, upholstered seat and
back

Rahmen Buche massiv und
galvanisiertes Gußaluminium;
Sitzfläche und Rückenlehne
gepolstert, mit Stoff bezogen

Hêtre massif et structure en fonte
d'aluminium anodisé, siège et
dossier rembourrés et recouverts
de tissu

**Carlos Jané Camacho, Spain,
from 1990**

Working primarily as an architect, Arribas launched his first industrial design,
the *J. Greystoke* chair, at the Vinçon
Gallery, Barcelona, in 1990. In this
elegant organic design, Arribas alludes
to wild animal forms and the earlier
work of Carlo Mollino, particularly
through his use of a bifurcated upholstered back.

Arribas, der vorwiegend als Architekt
arbeitet, stellte sein erstes Industriedesign, den Stuhl *J.-Greystoke*, 1990
in der Galerie Vinçon, Barcelona, vor.
Mit diesem eleganten, organischen
Entwurf spielt Arribas auf die Gestalten
wilder Tiere und auf die vorangegan-
genen Arbeiten von Carlo Mollino an,
vor allem durch die zweigeteilte gepolsterte Rückenlehne.

Architecte d'origine, Arribas exposa ce
siège, sa première intervention dans le
design, à la Galerie Vinçon de Barcelone, en 1990. A travers cet élégant
dessin organique, il fait allusion aux
formes de la vie sauvage et à certains
travaux antérieurs de Carlo Mollino, en
particulier dans son dossier «fourchu».

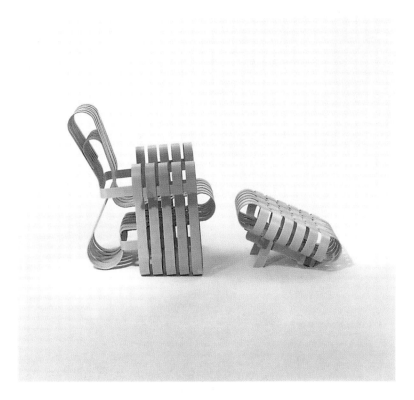

Frank O. Gehry

*1929
USA . Etats-Unis

Powerplay chair 1990 – 92
Stuhl Powerplay 1990 – 92
Siège Powerplay 1990 – 92

Bent and woven laminated wood

Geflecht aus gebogenen Schicht-
holzstreifen

Bois cintré, lamellé et entrelaçé

**Knoll Group, New York,
from 1992**

Michael Thonet, Alvar Aalto and Charles Eames all made revolutionary developments in the techniques employed for moulding and bending plywood. However, their designs either "had a heavy substructure and then webbing, or an intermediary structure for the seating." Gehry continues: "The difference in my chairs is that the (support) structure and the seat are formed of the same lightweight wood strips... (what) gives it extraordinary strength is the interwoven, basketlike character of the design."[34]

Michael Thonet, Alvar Aalto und Charles Eames entwickelten völlig neue Techniken zum Verformen und Biegen von schichtverleimtem Sperrholz, aber ihre Entwürfe hatten entweder »ein schweres Untergestell und dann noch ein Geflecht von Gurten oder eine Zwischenlösung für die Sitze«, sagt Gehry. »Meine Stühle unterscheiden sich dadurch, daß die (tragende) Konstruktion und die Sitzfläche aus den gleichen, leichten Holzstreifen geformt sind... (was) ihm (dem Stuhl) die ungewöhnliche Stärke verleiht, ist das korbartige Geflecht.«[34]

Pour Gehry, Michael Thonet, Alvar Aalto et Charles Eames apportèrent chacun des développements révolutionnaires aux techniques de moulage et de cintrage du contreplaqué. Cependant, leurs créations reposaient «soit sur une lourde sous-structure, puis sur une fixation, soit sur une structure intermédiaire pour le siège... La différence avec mon siège est que la structure (le support) et le siège sont constitués à partir des mêmes légères bandes de bois... ce qui lui donne son extraordinaire solidité est leur entrelaçage, cet aspect de «panier».»[34]

Frank O. Gehry at work, 1992
Frank O. Gehry bei der Arbeit, 1992
Frank O. Gehry au travail, 1992

Frank O. Gehry:
The Gehry Collection, 1992
Die Gehry Kollektion, 1992
La Collection Gehry, 1992

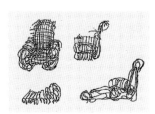

Frank O. Gehry:
Study for *Powerplay*, 1992
Studie für *Powerplay*, 1992
Etude pour *Powerplay*, 1992

Borek Sípek

*1949

Czech Republic .
Tschechische Republik .
République Tchèque

Sedlak chair 1992

Stuhl Sedlak 1992

Chaise Sedlak 1992

Cast-aluminium and stained
beech frame with integral
foam seat

Rahmen aus Gußaluminium und
massiver Buche, gebeizt; Sitzfläche aus Integralschaumstoff

Cadre en fonte d'aluminium et
hêtre massif teinté avec siège en
mousse

Vitra GmbH, Germany,
from 1992

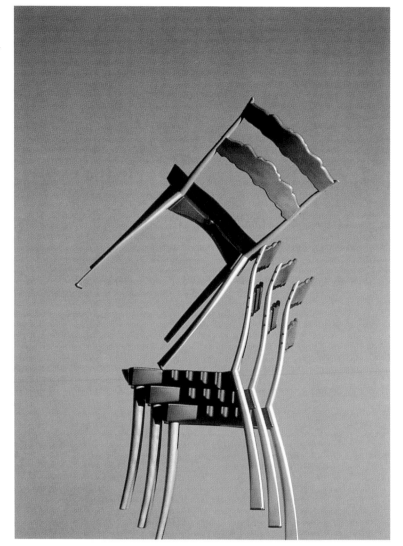

"*Sedlak* combines the decorative with the functional… The chair's parts can be dismantled and exchanged. The materials can be separated for recycling. Despite the fulfilment of functional requirements, *Sedlak* retains its special expression and is unmistakably identifiable as one of Sipek's designs."[35]

»Der Stuhl *Sedlak* kombiniert das De-korative mit dem Funktionalen… Man kann den Stuhl auseinandernehmen und die einzelnen Teile austauschen. Die Materialien können getrennt wie-derverwertet werden. Bei aller Funktio-nalität hat der Stuhl *Sedlak* einen ganz speziellen Charakter; er ist eindeutig als Sipek-Design identifizierbar.«[35]

«*Sedlak* marie le décoratif et le fonc-tionnel… Les éléments de la chaise peuvent être démontés et changés. Les matériaux peuvent se recycler. En dehors de ces qualités fonctionnelles achevées, elle conserve son expres-sion particulière et s'identifie sans risque d'erreur comme une création de Sípek.»[35]

Sedlak chairs in café
Sedlak-Stühle in einem Café
Chaises *Sedlak* au café

For recycling purposes the *Louis 20* chair has been constructed in two sections which are joined with screws rather than glue so that the materials remain unsullied by additives. This arrangement also facilitates the easy separation of the main elements. Designed to be used indoors or outdoors. the *Louis 20* can be stacked and is available with or without arms.

Um das Recycling zu ermöglichen, besteht die Konstruktion des Stuhls *Louis 20* aus zwei Teilen, die nicht geleimt, sondern durch Schrauben verbunden sind. Außerdem werden die Materialien dadurch nicht durch Zusatzstoffe verunreinigt und lassen sich leicht voneinander trennen. Der Stuhl läßt sich stapeln und eignet sich für drinnen und draußen; er ist mit und ohne Armlehnen erhältlich.

Pour être recyclable, cette chaise a été construite en deux sections assemblées par écrous et non collées afin que le matériau ne soit pas chimiquement pollué. Cet arrangement facilite également la séparation des principaux éléments. Conçues pour l'extérieur ou l'intérieur. les chaises peuvent s'empiler. *Louis 20* est disponible avec ou sans accoudoirs.

Philippe Starck

*1949
France . Frankreich

Louis 20 chair 1992
Stuhl Louis 20 1992
Chaise Louis 20 1992

Blasted polypropylene body with aluminium "bridge" rear leg section

Hochdruckgeformter Polypropylen-Körper; hinterer «Brücken»-Teil, einschließlich der Hinterbeine, aus Aluminium

Corps en polypropylène soufflé avec pieds arrière en «pont» en aluminium

Vitra GmbH, Germany, from 1992

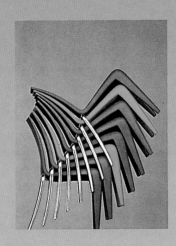

133

Alvar Aalto

Born in Kuortane, Finland, Alvar Aalto studied architecture at the Technical University of Helsinki from 1916 to 1921. Initially worked as an exhibition designer and later turned to architecture and furniture design in 1923 and 1925 respectively. He became a member of the Congrès Internationaux d'Architecture Moderne in 1928. In 1929 with Otto Korhonen he established an experimental plywood workshop in Turku. In 1935, he founded a furniture design company, Artek, with Harry and Marie Gullichsen and in the same year patented a cantilevered chair support made of wood. Aalto's work was shown to great acclaim in London at the exhibition of Finnish design held at Fortnum and Mason in 1933, at the Paris 1937 Exhibition and the New York 1939 World Fair. In 1957, he was awarded a gold medal by the Royal Institute of British Architects (RIBA).

Alvar Aalto wurde in Kuortane, Finnland, geboren und studierte von 1916 bis 1921 Architektur am Polytechnikum in Helsinki. Anfangs arbeitete er als Ausstellungsgestalter und wendete sich 1923 der Architektur und 1925 dem Möbelentwurf zu. 1928 wurde er Mitglied der Congrès Internationaux d'Architecture Moderne. 1929 eröffnete er zusammen mit Otto Korhonen eine Experimentierwerkstatt für Sperrholz in Turku. Zusammen mit Harry und Marie Gullichsen gründete er 1935 das Entwurfsstudio Artek für Möbel und ließ im gleichen Jahr einen freitragenden Stuhlrahmen aus Holz patentieren. Großen Erfolg hatte Aalto 1933 mit seinen Arbeiten auf einer Ausstellung für finnisches Design bei Fortnum and Mason in London sowie in den Jahren 1937 auf der Pariser Ausstellung und 1939 auf der New Yorker Weltausstellung. 1957 erhielt er vom Royal Institute of British Architects (RIBA) eine Goldmedaille.

Né à Kuortane, en Finlande, Alvar Aalto étudie l'architecture à l'Ecole Polytechnique d'Helsinki de 1916 à 1921. Initialement concepteur d'expositions (1923), il se tourne vers l'architecture et la création de mobilier (1925). Membre des Congrès Internationaux d'Architecture Moderne en 1928. En 1929, avec Otto Korhonen, il crée un atelier expérimental de contreplaqué à Turku. En 1935, il fonde, avec Harry et Marie Gullichsen, une société de création de mobilier, Artek, et dépose la même année le brevet d'une structure de chaise en porte-à-faux en contreplaqué. L'œuvre d'Aalto est présentée à Londres lors de l'exposition sur le design finlandais organisée par Fortnum and Mason en 1933, à l'Exposition de Paris de 1937 et à l'Exposition Universelle de New York en 1939, où elle reçoit un accueil remarqué. En 1957, lui est décernée la médaille d'or du Royal Institute of British Architects (RIBA).

Eero Aarnio

Born in Helsinki, Eero Aarnio studied at the Institute of Industrial Arts, Helsinki, graduating in 1957. He established his own design office in 1962 and has since worked primarily as an interior and industrial designer. In 1968, he was awarded an American Industrial Design award for the *Pastille* chair.

Eero Aarnio wurde in Helsinki geboren, er studierte am Institut für Angewandte Kunst in Helsinki bis 1957. Sein eigenes Designstudio gründete er 1962 und arbeitete als Innenarchitekt und Industriedesigner. 1968 erhielt er den American-Industrial-Design-Preis für den Stuhl *Pastille*.

Né à Helsinki, Eero Aarnio étudie à l'Institut d'Art Industriel d'Helsinki d'où il sort diplômé en 1957. Il ouvre son propre bureau de design en 1962 et, depuis, se consacre essentiellement au design industriel et domestique. En 1968, il reçoit un prix de l'American Industrial Design pour sa chaise *Pastille*.

Ron Arad

Born in Israel, Ron Arad studied at the Jerusalem Academy of Art from 1971 to 1973. Later, he studied at the Architectural Association, London, graduating in 1979. In 1981, he founded his own architectural design office-cum-showroom, One Off Ltd. in Covent Garden. The practice later moved to Chalk Farm, London. He is primarily known for his furniture designs; however, in recent years he has received several important architectural commissions, including the interior for the Tel Aviv Opera House in 1990.

Ron Arad wurde in Israel geboren und studierte von 1971 bis 1973 an der Kunstakademie von Jerusalem. Sein Studium bei der Architectural Association, London, schloß er 1979 mit Examen ab. 1981 gründete er ein eigenes Architekturstudio mit Ausstellungsraum, One Off Ltd., Covent Garden, London; die Werkstatt verlegte er später nach Chalk Farm, London. Er machte sich vor allem mit seinen Möbelentwürfen einen Namen, erhielt in der letzten Zeit aber auch wichtige Aufträge für Architekturprojekte, zu denen 1990 die Innenausstattung der Oper von Tel Aviv gehörte.

Né en Israël, Ron Arad fait ses études à l'Académie des Arts de Jérusalem de 1971 à 1973. Plus tard, il suit les cours de l'Architectural Association de Londres, dont il est diplômé en 1979. En 1981, il crée son propre bureau de design et showroom, One Off Ltd., à Covent Garden, qu'il transfère ensuite à Chalk Farm, toujours à Londres. Il se fait d'abord connaître pour ses créations de meubles, mais a cependant récemment reçu plusieurs importantes commandes architecturales, dont l'intérieur de l'Opéra de Tel Aviv en 1990.

This radical design group was founded in Florence by Andrea Branzi, Gilberto Corretti, Paolo Deganello and Massimo Morozzi in 1966 – the year the city was flooded. In 1968, Dario and Lucia Bartolini joined the group. Their early architectural "projections" such as No-Stop City attempted to reveal that by pushing rationalism to an extreme it becomes an utter absurdity. The intention of this, according to Branzi, was to "expose the underlying contradictions of the (Modern) movement, along with the fragile nature of its apparent unity of research". Their later proposals were more concerned with innovation and environments. The group exhibited at the Museum of Modern Art's "Italy: New Domestic Landscape" show of 1972.

Diese Designergruppe des sogenannten Radical Design wurde von Andrea Branzi, Gilberto Corretti, Paolo Deganello und Massimo Morozzi 1966 – im Jahr der großen Überschwemmung – in Florenz gegründet. 1968 schlossen sich Dario und Lucia Bartolini der Gruppe an. Mit ihren frühen architektonischen Projekten wie No-Stop City wollten sie demonstrieren, daß der Rationalismus, bis an seine äußersten Grenzen getrieben, ins Absurde umschlägt. Dabei verfolgten sie, wie Branzi erklärte, die Absicht, «die der Moderne innewohnenden Widersprüche und die Brüchigkeit ihrer anscheinend einheitlichen Forschungsansätze aufzudecken». Ihre späteren Entwürfe befaßten sich mehr mit Innovationen und Wohnlandschaften. Die Gruppe nahm 1972 an der Ausstellung «Italy: New Domestic Landscape» des Museum of Modern Art, New York, teil.

Ce groupe de design radical est créé par Andrea Branzi, Gilberto Corretti, Paolo Deganello et Massimo Morozzi à Florence en 1966, l'année de la grande inondation. En 1968, Dario et Lucia Bartolini le rejoignent. Leurs premières «projections» architecturales, comme le projet de la No-Stop City, essayent de montrer que le rationalisme poussé à l'extrême devient une absurdité complète. Selon Branzi, l'intention était «de mettre en lumière les contradictions sous-jacentes du mouvement (moderne), en même temps que la nature fragile de son apparente unité de recherche.» Leurs propositions ultérieures s'intéressent davantage à l'innovation et aux environnements. Le groupe expose au Museum of Modern Art, New York, à l'occasion de l'exposition «Italy: New Domestic Landscape», en 1972.

Hugo Henrik Alvar Aalto

1898 – 1976
Finland . Finnland . Finlande

Eero Aarnio

*1932
Finland . Finnland . Finlande

Ron Arad

*1951
Great Britain . Großbritannien .
Grande-Bretagne

Archizoom Associati

1966 – 74
Italy . Italien . Italie

Mario Bellini

Harry Bertoia

Born in Barcelona, Alfredo Arribas studied at the Superior Technical School of Architecture, Barcelona, graduating in 1977. He then began teaching there and at the Elisava School of Design. From 1977 to 1982 he collaborated with architects Basilio Tobias and Manuel Llano. In 1982, he became a member of INFAD and in 1987 and 1988 received FAD awards for Architecture and Interior Design. In 1990, he exhibited at the Frankfurt Autumn Fair and collaborated with Nigel Coates, Cesare Pergola and O. Vedrine on an architectural project in Florence.

Alfredo Arribas wurde in Barcelona geboren; er studierte an der Technischen Hochschule von Barcelona Architektur und machte 1977 sein Abschlußexamen. Anschließend unterrichtete er dort und an der Elisava-Schule für Design in Barcelona. Von 1977 bis 1982 arbeitete er mit Basilio Tobias und Manuel Llano zusammen. 1982 wurde er Mitglied von INFAD und erhielt 1987 und 1988 FAD-Auszeichnungen für Architektur und Innenausstattung. 1990 stellte er auf der Frankfurter Herbstmesse aus und arbeitete zusammen mit Nigel Coates, Cesare Pergola und O. Vedrine an einem Architekturprojekt in Florenz.

Né à Barcelone, Alfredo Arribas étudie à l'Ecole Technique Supérieure d'Architecture de Barcelone jusqu'à son diplôme en 1977. Il y enseigne ensuite, ainsi qu'à l'Ecole de Design Elisava. De 1977 à 1982, il collabore avec les architectes Basilio Tobias et Manuel Llano. En 1982, il devient membre de l'INFAD et reçoit, en 1987 et 1988, les prix d'architecture et de décoration de la FAD. En 1990, il expose à la Foire d'Automne de Francfort et collabore avec Nigel Coates, Cesare Pergola et O. Vedrine à un projet d'architecture à Florence.

Born in Milan, Mario Bellini studied architecture at the Polytechnic of Milan, graduating in 1959. From 1961 to 1963, he was design director at La Rinascente, the influential chain of department stores. In 1963, he founded an architectural office with Marco Romano and in 1973 established Studio Bellini, Milan. Since 1963 he has held the position of chief design consultant for Olivetti and from 1978 has been a research and design consultant for Renault. Between 1962 and 1965, he was the professor of design at the Istituto Superiore di Disegno Industriale, Venice, and since then has been a visiting lecturer to many design colleges, including the Royal College of Art, London. He has received numerous awards, including several Compassi d'Oro.

Mario Bellini wurde in Mailand geboren. Er studierte am Polytechnikum von Mailand, das er nach der Abschlußprüfung 1959 verließ. Von 1961 bis 1963 leitete er die Designabteilung der großen Warenhauskette La Rinascente. 1963 gründete er mit Marco Romano ein Architekturbüro, und 1973 eröffnete er das Studio Bellini in Mailand. Seit 1963 arbeitete er als Designberater bei Olivetti und seit 1978 als Forschungs- und Designberater bei Renault. Von 1962 bis 1965 lehrte er an der Hochschule für Industriedesign in Venedig und ist seither Gastprofessor an mehreren Design-Hochschulen, u.a. am Royal College of Art in London. Bellini hat zahlreiche Auszeichnungen erhalten, darunter mehrfach den Compasso d'Oro.

Milanais, Mario Bellini étudie l'architecture au Politecnico de Milan d'où il sort diplômé en 1959. De 1961 à 1963, il est directeur du design à La Rinascente, l'influente chaîne de grands magasins. En 1963, il fonde un cabinet d'architecture avec Marco Romano et plus tard, en 1973, le Studio Bellini, Milan. Depuis 1963, il est le principal consultant en design d'Olivetti et, à partir de 1978, consultant en recherches et design pour Renault. De 1962 à 1965, il est professeur de design à l'Instituto Superiore di Disegno Industriale de Venise et enseigne depuis dans de nombreuses écoles de design dont le Royal College of Art de Londres. Il a reçu de multiples distinctions dont plusieurs Compassi d'Oro.

Born in Wuppertal, Günter Belzig studied industrial design at the Werkkunstschule Wuppertal, graduating in 1966. From 1966 to 1970, he worked as a designer for Siemens. Since 1970 he has worked as a freelance designer. From 1971 to 1973, he was a visiting lecturer at the Fachhochschule München. From 1978 he has acted as a design consultant to the firm Richter Playground Equipment GmbH, Frasdorf.

Günter Belzig wurde in Wuppertal geboren, er studierte Industriedesign an der Werkkunstschule seiner Heimatstadt und schloß seine Ausbildung 1966 ab. Von 1966 bis 1970 arbeitete er als Designer für Siemens. Seit 1970 ist er freiberuflich tätig. Er war von 1971 bis 1973 Gastdozent an der Fachhochschule München und ist seit 1978 Designberater für die Firma Richter Playground Equipment GmbH, Frasdorf, einem Hersteller von Spielplatzgeräten.

Né à Wuppertal, Günter Belzig étudie le design industriel à la Werkkunstschule de Wuppertal dont il est diplômé en 1966. De 1966 à 1970, il travaille comme designer pour Siemens. Depuis 1970, il est designer free-lance. De 1971 à 1973 il a été conférencier invité à la Fachhochschule de Munich. A partir de 1978, il est designer consultant pour Richter Playground Equipment GmbH, de Frasdorf.

Born in Udine, Italy, Harry Bertoia emigrated with his family to America in 1930. In 1936, he graduated from the Cass Technical High School, Detroit, and from 1937 to 1939 trained on a scholarship at the Cranbrook Academy of Arts. He established the metalworking studio there and as head of that department taught from 1939 to 1943. Later, he worked with the Eameses at the Evans Products Company developing techniques for moulding plywood. After the war, he worked for a short period at the Eameses' Plyformed Products Company in Venice, California. His innovative wire chairs designed for Knoll International in 1951 were so commercially successful that the royalties from this group of designs allowed him to concentrate solely on his sculpting career.

Harry Bertoia wurde in Udine, Italien, geboren und wanderte 1930 mit seiner Familie in die Vereinigten Staaten aus. 1936 beendete er sein Studium an der Cass Technical High School in Detroit mit dem Abschlußexamen, und von 1937 bis 1939 erhielt er ein Stipendium der Cranbrook Academy of Arts. Anschließend richtete er dort das Cranbrook-Studio für Metallarbeiten ein, das er von 1939 bis 1943 leitete. Später arbeitete er mit Charles und Ray Eames zusammen bei der Evans Products Company, wo er Technologien für die Verformung von schichtverleimtem Sperrholz entwickelte. Nach dem Krieg arbeitete er kurze Zeit bei der Plyformed Products Company von Charles und Ray Eames in Venice, Kalifornien. Die innovativen Drahtstühle, die er 1951 für Knoll International entwarf, waren ein derart großer finanzieller Erfolg, daß ihm die Tantiemen zum Leben reichten und er sich ausschließlich der Bildhauerei widmen konnte.

Né à Udine, en Italie, il émigre en Amérique avec sa famille en 1930. En 1936, il est diplômé de la Cass Technical High School de Detroit et, de 1937 à 1939, bénéficie d'une bourse à la Cranbrook Academy of Arts. Il y fonde l'atelier de travail de métaux et y enseigne de 1939 à 1943, en tant que responsable de ce département. Il collabore plus tard avec les Eames à l'Evans Production Company, mettant au point des techniques de moulage du contreplaqué. Après la guerre, il travaille brièvement pour la Plyformed Products Company des Eames à Venice, en Californie. Ses chaises innovantes, en fil de métal, créées pour Knoll International en 1951, rencontrent un tel succès commercial que leurs royalties lui ont permis de se consacrer exclusivement à sa carrière de sculpteur.

Alfredo Arribas

*1954
Spain . Spanien . Espagne

Mario Bellini

*1935
Italy . Italien . Italie

Günter Belzig

*1941
Germany . Deutschland . Allemagne

Harry Bertoia

1915–78
USA . Etats-Unis

Marcel Breuer

Born in Hungary, Marcel Breuer spent a short time working in a Viennese architectural office before studying at the Bauhaus, Weimar, 1920–24. After graduating, he became master of the furniture workshop there and continued in that capacity when the Bauhaus moved to Dessau in 1925. He directed his own architectural firm in Berlin from 1928 to 1931 before leaving Germany where he spent a year in London, 1935–37, working first as an architect in partnership with F.R.S. Yorke and later as Controller of Design at Isokon. In 1937 he emigrated to the United States of America and was an associate professor at the School of Design at Harvard University from 1937 to 1946. Between 1937 and 1941 he shared an architectural practice in Cambridge, Massachusetts, with Walter Gropius. From 1946 he headed his own firm, Marcel Breuer & Associates, in New York until his retirement in 1976.

Marcel Breuer wurde in Ungarn geboren und arbeitete kurze Zeit in einem Wiener Architekturbüro, bevor er von 1920 bis 1924 am Bauhaus in Weimar studierte. Nach seiner Gesellenprüfung wurde er Leiter der Möbelwerkstatt; er behielt diese Position, als das Bauhaus 1925 nach Dessau umzog. 1928 ging er nach Berlin und eröffnete dort ein eigenes Architekturstudio. 1935 verließ er Deutschland und ließ sich zunächst in London nieder, wo er zusammen mit dem Architekten F.R.S. Yorke ein Architekturbüro gründete und etwas später als Chef der Designabteilung bei Isokon arbeitete. 1937 emigrierte er in die Vereinigten Staaten und erhielt eine Professur an der School of Design an der Harvard University, die er bis 1946 innehatte. Gemeinsam mit Walter Gropius eröffnete er 1937 ein Architekturbüro in Cambridge, Massachusetts, in dem beide bis 1941 tätig waren. 1946 gründete er in New York eine eigene Firma, Marcel Breuer & Associates, die er bis zu seinem Ruhestand 1976 selbst leitete.

Hongrois d'origine, Marcel Breuer travaille quelques temps dans un bureau d'architectes viennois avant de suivre les cours du Bauhaus, à Weimar, de 1920 à 1924. Diplômé, il devient responsable de l'atelier du mobilier et conserve ces fonctions lorsque le Bauhaus déménage pour Dessau en 1925. Il dirige son propre bureau d'architecture à Berlin de 1928 à 1931 avant de quitter l'Allemagne en 1935. Il passe deux ans à Londres (1935–37), d'abord comme architecte, en association avec F.R.S. Yorke, et plus tard comme contrôleur du dessin chez Isokon. En 1937, il émigre aux Etats-Unis et devient Professeur Associé à la School of Design de l'Université d'Harvard de 1937 à 1946. De 1937 à 1941, il partage un bureau d'architecte à Cambridge, Massachusetts, avec Walter Gropius. A partir de 1946, il dirige sa propre firme, Marcel Breuer & Associates à New York jusqu'à sa retraite en 1976.

Achille Castiglioni

Born in Milan, Achille Castiglioni trained at the Polytechnic of Milan. In 1944 he set up his own Como-based design office with his brothers, Livio, who left the partnership in 1952, and Pier Giacomo. In 1956 he became a founder of the Associazione Design Italiano. In 1957, the brothers held an exhibition entitled "Forme e Colori nella Casa d'Oggi" at the Olmo Villa, Como, which incorporated their highly influential "ready-made" designs. Since 1969, he has taught industrial design at the Polytechnic of Turin and has exhibited at every Milan Triennale since 1947. He has received the Compasso d'Oro award seven times, and was highly involved in the founding of the Italian A.D.I. awards.

Achille Castiglioni wurde in Mailand geboren und studierte am Polytechnikum von Mailand. 1944 gründete er zusammen mit seinen Brüdern Livio und Pier Giacomo ein Designstudio in Como. Livio verließ die Firma 1952. 1956 wurde Achille Gründungsmitglied der Associazione Design Italiano. 1957 veranstalteten die beiden Brüder in der Villa Olmo in Como eine Ausstellung mit dem Titel »Forme e Colori nella Casa d'Oggi«, in der sie auch einige ihrer berühmten »Ready-mades« zeigten. Seit 1969 lehrt Achille Castiglioni Industriedesign am Polytechnikum von Turin und hat seit 1947 auf jeder MailänderTriennale ausgestellt. Er wurde siebenmal mit dem Compasso d'Oro ausgezeichnet und machte sich verdient um die Stiftung des A.D.I.-Preises.

Né à Milan, Achille Castiglioni se forme au Politecnico de Milan et, en 1944, ouvre un bureau de design à Côme avec ses frères, Livio – qui quittera l'association en 1952 – et Pier Giacomo. En 1956, il fait partie des fondateurs de l'Associazione Design Italiano. En 1957, les deux frères tiennent une exposition intitulée »Forme e Colori nella Casa d'Oggi« à la Villa Olmo, à Côme, incluant leurs projets de »ready-made« qui exercent déjà une grande influence. Depuis 1947, il a exposé à la Triennale de Milan et enseigné le design industriel à l'Ecole Polytechnique de Turin à partir de 1969. Il a reçu plusieurs Compassi d'Oro et s'est beaucoup impliqué dans la création des prix A.D.I. italiens.

Osvaldo Borsani

Son of the craftsman Gaetano Borsani, who won a silver medal at the first Monza Triennale in 1927, Osvaldo and his brother, Fulgenzio, founded Tecno in 1952; the company had formerly been known as the Arredamento Borsani in Varedo and prior to this, Atelier Varedo. From 1952 to the present day, Osvaldo has been the main designer for Tecno, a firm committed to the research and development of high quality furniture for the office environment.

Osvaldo Borsanis Vater, Gaetano Borsani, war Handwerker und wurde bei der ersten Triennale von Monza, 1927, mit einer Silbermedaille ausgezeichnet. Zusammen mit seinem Bruder Fulgenzio gründete Osvaldo 1952 die Firma Tecno, die aus der Werkstatt seines Vaters, dem Atelier Varedo und dessen späterem Unternehmen Arredamento Borsani in Varedo, hervorging. Seit 1952 ist Osvaldo erster Designer der Firma Tecno, die sich auf die Entwicklung qualitativ hochwertiger Büroeinrichtungen spezialisiert hat.

Fils de l'artisan Gaetano Borsani qui avait remporté la médaille d'argent de la première Triennale de Monza en 1927, Osvaldo et son frère Fulgenzio fondèrent Tecno en 1952, société initialement connue sous le nom d'Atelier Varedo puis d'Arredamento Borsani de Varedo. De 1952 à ce jour, Osvaldo est le principal designer de Tecno dont les activités se concentrent sur la recherche et le développement de mobilier de bureau de haute qualité.

Mario Botta

Born in Mendrisio, Switzerland, Mario Botta trained at the Academy of Fine Arts, Milan before studying architecture at the Istituto Universitario di Architettura in Venice. Prior to founding his own architectural practice in Lugano, he worked in the offices of Le Corbusier. Since 1982, he has designed furniture for the Italian manufacturer, Alias. His *Seconda* chair is in the permanent collections of The Museum of Modern Art, New York, and the Victoria & Albert Museum, London.

Mario Botta wurde in Mendrisio, Schweiz, geboren und erhielt seine Ausbildung an der Akademie der bildenden Künste in Mailand. Er studierte am Istituto Universitario d'Architettura in Venedig Architektur. Bevor er in Lugano sein eigenes Architekturbüro eröffnete, arbeitete er im Architekturbüro Le Corbusiers. Seit 1982 entwirft er Möbel für den italienischen Hersteller Alias. Sein Stuhl *Seconda* wurde vom Museum of Modern Art, New York, und vom Victoria & Albert Museum, London, angekauft.

Né à Mendrisio, en Suisse, Mario Botta se forme à l'Académie des Beaux-Arts de Milan avant d'étudier l'architecture à l'Istituto Universitario di Architettura de Venise. Avant de créer son propre cabinet à Lugano, il travaille dans les bureaux de Le Corbusier. A partir de 1982, il crée des meubles pour le fabricant italien Alias. Sa chaise *Seconda* figure dans la collection permanente du Museum of Modern Art, New York, et du Victoria & Albert Museum de Londres.

Osvaldo Borsani

*1911
Italy . Italien . Italie

Mario Botta

*1943
Switzerland . Schweiz . Suisse

Marcel Breuer

1902–81
Germany . Deutschland . Allemagne

Achille Castiglioni

*1918
Italy . Italien . Italie

Pier Giacomo Castiglioni was born in Milan and studied at the polytechnic there, where he took his doctorate. In 1945, he set up a design office with his younger brother Achille, specialising in lighting, but also designing furniture and technical equipment. Their famous "Phonola" radio with its plastic casing was designed in 1938. Pier Giacomo and Achille Castiglioni won international acclaim for their major contributions to furniture and industrial design.

Pier Giacomo Castiglioni wurde in Mailand geboren und studierte am dortigen Polytechnikum, wo er mit Promotion abschloß. Seit 1945 führte er ein gemeinsames Designbüro mit seinem jüngeren Bruder Achille, wobei er sich auf Beleuchtung spezialisierte, aber auch Möbel und technisches Gerät entwarf. Berühmt wurde ihr Radio »Phonola« mit Kunststoffgehäuse aus dem Jahre 1938. Mit bedeutenden Möbel- und Industriedesign erlangten Pier Giacomo und Achille Castiglioni weltweite Anerkennung.

Pier Giacomo Castiglioni est né à Milan. Il y fait ses études à l'Ecole Polytechnique d'où il sort diplômé. Depuis 1945, il dirige, avec son frère cadet Achille, un studio de design spécialisé dans les luminaires mais également en mobilier et appareils divers. Leur poste de radio «Phonola» en plastique (1938) leur apporte la célébrité. A travers des meubles et des travaux d'esthétique industrielle importants, Pier Giacomo et Achille Castiglioni se feront connaître dans le monde entier.

Wendell Castle studied sculpture at the University of Kansas and graduated in 1961. The leading exponent of the Craft Revival in the United States of America, Castle founded his own school for craftsmanship in wood in 1980. After brief experimentation with fibreglass in the late 1960s, he went on to create extraordinary illusionistic sculptural furniture through the use of virtuoso "trompe-l'œil" carving techniques. In recent years he has concentrated on historically based designs produced in exquisitely worked exotic materials.

Wendell Castle studierte Bildhauerei an der Universität von Kansas, die er 1961 nach dem Abschlußexamen verließ. Als führender Vertreter der Craft Revival in den USA gründete er 1980 eine eigene Schule für handwerkliche Holzbearbeitung. Gegen Ende der 60er Jahre hat er kurze Zeit mit Fiberglas experimentiert, sich dann aber wieder der Herstellung seiner skulpturalen Möbel mit den virtuos gearbeiteten, unglaublich wirklichkeitsgetreuen Schnitzereien gewidmet. In letzter Zeit hat er sich hauptsächlich auf Entwürfe mit historischem Gehalt in hervorragend verarbeiteten exotischen Hölzern konzentriert.

Wendell Castle étudie la sculpture à l'Université du Kansas d'où il sort diplômé en 1961. Représentant notable du Craft Revival aux Etats-Unis, Castle crée sa propre école de travail du bois en 1980. Après de brèves expériences avec la fibre de verre à la fin des années 60, il crée d'extraordinaires meubles-sculptures faisant appel à des techniques de travail sur bois en trompe-l'œil qui révèlent un talent de virtuose. Ces dernières années, il s'est principalement consacré à des créations faisant référence à l'histoire et produites dans des matériaux exotiques travaillés avec beaucoup de délicatesse.

Joe Colombo

Born in Milan, Joe Colombo initially trained as a painter at the Accademia di Belle Arti (Brera Academy) before studying architecture at the Polytechnic of Milan. From 1951 to 1955, he worked independently as a painter and sculptor, establishing the Nuclear Painting Movement and later becoming a founding member of the Art Concret Group. In 1962, he opened his own design office, working among others for Kartell, O-Luce, Comfort and Bayer. In 1970, he, Pierre Paulin and Sori Yanagi were co-authors of "New Form Furniture: Japan".

Joe Colombo, gebürtiger Mailänder, studierte an der Accademia di Belle Arti (Brera-Akademie) Malerei, bevor er am Polytechnikum von Mailand ein Architekturstudium aufnahm. Von 1951 bis 1955 arbeitete er als freier Maler und Bildhauer. Er gründete das Nuclear Painting Movement und gehörte später zu den Gründungsmitgliedern der Art Concret Group. 1962 eröffnete er ein eigenes Designstudio und arbeitete unter anderem für Kartell, O-Luce, Comfort und Bayer. 1970 schrieb er zusammen mit Pierre Paulin und Sori Yanagi das Buch »New Form Furniture: Japan«.

Né à Milan, Joe Colombo étudie d'abord la peinture à l'Accademia di Belle Arti de Brera avant de se mettre à l'architecture au Politecnico de Milan. De 1951 à 1955, il travaille sur le mode libéral, comme peintre et sculpteur, lançant le mouvement de la Peinture Nucléaire et devenant plus tard membre fondateur de l'Art Concret Group. En 1962, il crée son bureau de design et travaille, entre autres, pour Kartell, O-Luce, Comfort et Bayer. En 1970, il écrit avec Pierre Paulin et Sori Yanagi «New Form Furniture: Japan».

Born in Zurich, Hans Coray studied at the University there before embarking on a varied career as a figurative artist. He designed the Landi stacking chair for the outside terraces of the Swiss National Exhibition held in 1938. He designed several other pieces of furniture during the 1950s before devoting his time completely to the fine arts.

Hans Coray wurde in Zürich geboren. Er studierte an der Universität seiner Heimatstadt, bevor er seine vielseitige künstlerische Laufbahn begann. Er entwarf den Stapelstuhl Landi für die Außenterrassen der Schweizerischen Nationalausstellung von 1938. In den 50er Jahren konzipierte er diverse andere Möbelstücke, widmete sich dann aber ausschließlich den bildenden Künsten.

Né à Zurich, Hans Coray y étudie à l'université avant de se lancer dans une carrière diversifiée d'artiste figuratif. Il dessine la chaise empilable Landi pour les terrasses extérieures de l'Exposition Nationale Suisse de 1938. Il crée plusieurs autres éléments de mobilier pendant les années 50 avant de se consacrer entièrement aux beaux-arts.

Pier Giacomo Castiglioni

1913–68
Italy . Italien . Italie

Wendell Castle

*1932
USA . Etats-Unis

Joe Colombo

1930–71
Italy . Italien . Italie

Hans Coray

*1906
Switzerland . Schweiz . Suisse

Robin Day

Born in High Wycombe, Robin Day worked for a local furniture manufacturer before training at the Royal College of Art, London, graduating in 1938. He and his wife, Lucienne (the renowned textile designer) opened their own design office in 1948. In the same year, he won first prize with Clive Latimer for the design of a storage unit at The Museum of Modern Art's "International Competition for Low-Cost Furniture Design". In 1949, he was appointed design director at Hille International and has subsequently worked as a design consultant for the company.

Robin Day wurde in High Wycombe geboren und war in der heimischen Möbelbranche tätig, bevor er sein Studium am Royal College of Art in London aufnahm und 1938 mit der Abschlußprüfung beendete. Er und seine Frau Lucienne (die bekannte Textildesignerin) eröffneten 1948 ihr erstes Designstudio. Im selben Jahr gewann er zusammen mit Clive Latimer für eine gemeinsam entworfene Regaleinheit den ersten Preis beim »International Competition for Low-Cost Furniture Design« des Museum of Modern Art, New York. 1949 ernannte ihn die Firma Hille International, für die er später als Designberater tätig war, zum Designdirektor.

Né à High Wycombe, Robin Day travaille pour un fabricant local de meubles avant d'étudier au Royal College of Art, à Londres (diplômé en 1938). Avec sa femme Lucienne (créatrice textile renommée), il ouvre propre bureau de design en 1948. La même année, il remporte, avec Clive Latimer, le premier prix du «International Competition for Low-Cost Furniture Design» du Museum of Modern Art pour un élément de rangement. En 1949, il est nommé directeur du design chez Hille International et travaille depuis régulièrement pour cette société.

Born in Ferrara, Michele De Lucchi studied in Padua and later at the University of Florence, graduating in 1975. He subsequently taught there. He designed for Studio Alchimia and in the 1980s for Memphis, being responsible for the introduction of geometric motifs on the plastic laminates used by Memphis. In 1979, he was appointed as a consultant by Olivetti, Ivrea, Italy. Currently, he is concentrating on product design.

Michele De Lucchi wurde in Ferrara geboren. Er studierte zunächst in Padua, anschließend nahm er ein Architekturstudium an der Universität von Florenz auf und schloß es 1975 ab. Seitdem lehrte er an der gleichen Universität. Er entwarf zunächst für Alchimia und in den 80er Jahren für Memphis. Die geometrischen Motive auf den Kunststofflaminaten, die Memphis herausbrachte, stammen von ihm. 1979 ernannte ihn Olivetti, Ivrea, Italien, zum Designberater. Zur Zeit ist er hauptsächlich als Produktdesigner tätig.

Né à Ferrare, Michele De Lucchi fait ses études à Padoue, puis à l'Université de Florence (diplômé en 1975) où il enseignera plus tard. Il travaille pour Studio Alchimia et, dans les années 80, pour Memphis. Il est à l'origine de l'introduction des motifs géométriques sur les plastiques lamifiés du groupe. En 1979, il est nommé consultant auprès d'Olivetti. Actuellement, il intervient essentiellement dans la conception de produits.

A design practice that was founded in Milan in 1966 by Jonathan De Pas, Donato D'Urbino, Paolo Lomazzi and Carla Scolari. All these designers were born in the 1930s and trained at the Politecnico di Milano. They received considerable recognition in the 1960s and 1970s for their *Blow* chair and later *Joe* chair. In the 1970s they concentrated their efforts on furniture designs that were flexible, interchangeable and adaptable. They have designed furniture for among others, Driade, BBB Bonacina, Palina. Zanotta and Poltronova as well as lighting for Stilnovo.

Das Designstudio wurde 1966 von Jonathan De Pas, Donato D'Urbino, Paolo Lomazzi und Carla Scolari in Mailand gegründet. Alle vier Designer wurden in den 30er Jahren geboren und studierten am Polytechnikum in Mailand. Ihre Sessel *Blow* und *Joe* verschafften ihnen in den 60er und 70er Jahren große Anerkennung. In den 70er Jahren konzentrierten sich ihre Entwürfe auf vielseitig einsetzbare, austauschbare und anpassungsfähige Möbel. Sie haben unter anderem Möbel für Driade, BBB Bonacina, Palina, Zanotta und Poltronova sowie Lampen für Stilnovo entworfen.

Studio de design fondé à Milan en 1966 par Jonathan de Pas, Donato D'Urbino, Paolo Lomazzi et Carla Scolari, tous nés au cours des années 30 et formés au Politecnico de Milan. Ils connaissent un succès considérable dans les années 60 et 70 avec leur chaise *Blow* et plus tard la chaise *Joe*. Dans les années 70, ils se consacrent à la conception de mobiliers à usages multiples, interchangeables et adaptables. Ils ont créé des meubles pour, entre autres, Driade, BBB Bonacina, Palina, Zanotta, Poltronova et des luminaires pour Stilnovo.

Tom Dixon

Born in 1959, he runs his own metal workshop in London, where he creates one-off and limited edition furniture designs. Dixon has an extremely expressive style and likes to use "objets trouvés". He has exhibited his work worldwide, particularly in Japan.

Tom Dixon wurde 1959 geboren. Er führt eine eigene Metallwerkstatt in London, wo er Möbel als Unikate oder in geringer Stückzahl entwirft. Dixons Design ist sehr ausdrucksstark, er verwendet dabei gerne »objets trouvés«. Dixon hat seine Arbeiten weltweit ausgestellt, mit Schwerpunkt in Japan.

Tom Dixon est né en 1959. Il dirige son propre atelier de travail du métal à Londres où il réalise des meubles en un seul exemplaire ou en séries très limitées. Le design de Dixon est très expressif, faisant volontiers appel à des objets «trouvés». Dixon a exposé ses travaux dans le monde entier et particulièrement au Japon.

Robin Day

*1915
Great Britain . Großbritannien .
Grande-Bretagne

Michele De Lucchi

*1951
Italy . Italien . Italie

De Pas, D'Urbino, Lomazzi & Scolari

founded . gegründet . fondé 1966
Italy . Italien . Italie

Tom Dixon

*1959
Great Britain . Großbritannien .
Grande-Bretagne

Charles Eames

Ray Eames

Born in St. Louis, Charles Eames studied architecture at the Washington University. In 1936, he received a fellowship at the Cranbrook Academy of Arts, Michigan. His colleagues there included Harry Bertoia, Eero Saarinen and Ray Kaiser, whom he married in 1941. During the Second World War he and his wife produced plywood splints and litters, developing a new method of bending plywood over three geometric planes into complex curves. In 1940, Eames and Eero Saarinen designed the winning entry for The Museum of Modern Art "Organic Design in Home Furnishings" competition. In 1946, Eames was given MoMA's first one-man show (New Furniture by Charles Eames). Charles and Ray Eames worked closely with the manufacturer Herman Miller, creating highly innovative, rational furniture designs. Later, the Eameses concentrated on film-making, photography and exhibition design; their patrons for such projects included the US Government and IBM.

Charles Eames wurde in St. Louis, Missouri, geboren und studierte an der dortigen Washington University Architektur. 1936 erhielt er ein Stipendium der Cranbrook Academy of Arts, Michigan, an der er später lehrte. Zu seinen Kollegen dort zählten Harry Bertoia, Eero Saarinen und Ray Kaiser, die er 1941 heiratete. Während des 2. Weltkriegs stellten er und seine Frau für die US Navy Arm- und Beinschienen sowie Krankentragen aus Sperrholz her. Für dieses Projekt entwickelten sie eine neue Methode, schichtverleimtes Sperrholz dreidimensional zu verformen. 1940 gewannen Charles Eames und Eero Saarinen den vom Museum of Modern Art veranstalteten Wettbewerb »Organic Design in Home Furnishings«. 1946 widmete ihm das Museum of Modern Art die erste Einzelausstellung (New Furniture by Charles Eames). Charles und Ray Eames arbeiteten eng mit dem Hersteller Herman Miller zusammen, mit dem sie ein sehr fortschrittliches, rationales Möbeldesign entwickelten. Später wandten sie sich dem Film, der Photographie und der Ausstellungsgestaltung zu. Zu ihren Kunden zählten die US-Regierung und der IBM-Konzern.

Né à Saint-Louis, Charles Eames étudie l'architecture à la Washington University de St. Louis. En 1936, il reçoit une bourse pour la Cranbrook Academy of Arts, Michigan, où il enseignera plus tard. Parmi ses collègues figurent Harry Bertoia, Eero Saarinen et Ray Kaiser qu'il épouse en 1941. Pendant la Seconde Guerre mondiale, les Eames mettent au point une nouvelle méthode de courbures complexes du contreplaqué selon trois plans. De 1939 à 1940, il travaille dans le cabinet d'architecture d'Eliel Saarinen. En 1940, Eames et Eero Saarinen remportent le concours du Museum of Modern Art, New York »Organic Design in Home Furnishings«. En 1946, Eames est l'objet de la première rétrospective personnelle consacrée à un designer par le MoMA. En collaboration avec sa femme, Ray, Eames crée des meubles hautement innovateurs et rationnels. Plus tard ils concevront des films, des jouets, des photographies et des expositions pour des clients comme le gouvernement américain ou IBM.

Born Bernice Alexandra Kaiser (in 1954 legally changed to Ray Bernice Alexandra Kaiser) in Sacramento, California. In 1933, she graduated from the May Friend Bennett School in Millbrook, New York, and began to study painting at Hans Hofmann's recently opened school. 1937 her work was exhibted in the first American Abstract Artists group show staged at the Riverside Museum, New York. In 1940, she commenced weaving classes at Cranbrook Academy of Arts, Michigan, under the instruction of Marianne Strengel. At this time Charles Eames was head of the Industrial Design Department at Cranbrook. A year later, after Charles Eames divorced his first wife, the couple were married in Chicago. Later the same year, they moved to California and began experimenting to find better methods of moulding plywood – and so began one of the greatest husband-and-wife design collaborations of the century.

Bernice Alexandra Kaiser (1954 änderte sie ihren Namen in Ray Bernice Alexandra Kaiser) wurde in Sacramento, Kalifornien, geboren. Nach ihrem Abschluß (1933) an der May Friend Bennett School in Millbrook, New York, studierte sie Malerei bei Hans Hofmann an der School of Art. 1937 nahm sie an der ersten Gruppenausstellung der American Abstract Artists im Riverside Museum, New York, teil. 1940 schrieb sie sich für die Webkurse der Cranbrook Academy of Arts, Michigan, ein, die von Marianne Strengel geleitet wurden (zu diesem Zeitpunkt war Charles Eames Direktor der Abteilung für Industriedesign). Ein Jahr später, nachdem sich Charles Eames von seiner Frau hatte scheiden lassen, heiratete er Ray in Chicago. Im gleichen Jahr zogen die beiden nach Kalifornien und begannen mit wissenschaftlichen Experimenten, um bessere Methoden der Schichtholzverformung zu entwickeln. So begann die Zusammenarbeit des Ehepaares, die zu einer der größten Doppelkarrieren auf dem Gebiet des Designs im 20. Jahrhundert führte.

Née Bernice Alexandra Kaiser (modifié officiellement en 1954 en Ray Bernice Alexandra Kaiser) à Sacramento, Californie. En 1933, elle reçoit le diplôme de la May Friend Bennett School de Millbrook, New York, et commence à étudier la peinture auprès de Hans Hofmann. En 1937, son travail est présenté lors de la première exposition de groupe des American Abstract Artists, organisée au Riverside Museum à New York. En 1940, elle commence un cours de tissage à la Cranbrook Academy of Arts, Michigan sous la direction de Marianne Strengel (à cette époque, Charles Eames dirigeait le département de design industriel de Cranbrook). Un an plus tard, après que Charles Eames ait divorcé de sa première femme, le couple se marie à Chicago. Au cours de la même année, ils s'installent en Californie et commencent leurs recherches sur les procédés de moulage du contreplaqué et c'est ainsi que débuta l'une des plus célèbres coopérations entre mari et femme de l'histoire du design de ce siècle.

All trained as architects, Jorge Ferrari-Hardoy, Antonio Bonet & Juan Kurchan designed a sling chair for their own offices based on an earlier design by the British civil engineer, Joseph Beverley Fenby, for a wooden folding chair with a canvas seat. The Museum of Modern Art's curator of industrial design, Edgar Kaufmann Jr., ordered the first two *BFK* chairs, or as they are more commonly known, *Hardoy* chairs, to arrive in the United States. Initially the chair was manufactured by Artek-Pascoe until the Second World War stopped production. Some time after 1945, Knoll International, under a royalty agreement with Hardoy, started producing the chair again, only to be plagued with unlicensed copies entering the market. A lawsuit ensued which Knoll lost, opening the market to legal but unlicensed versions of this chair.

Alle drei sind ausgebildete Architekten. Sie haben für ihre Büros einen freitragenden Stuhl entworfen, der auf einem Entwurf des britischen Bauingenieurs Joseph Beverley Fenby für einen Klappstuhl aus Holz mit einer Sitzfläche aus Segeltuch zurückgeht. Die ersten beiden *BFK*-Stühle, besser bekannt unter dem Namen *Hardoy*-Stühle, die in die Vereinigten Staaten geliefert wurden, bestellte Edgar Kaufmann Jr., Kurator für Industriedesign des Museum of Modern Art. Anfangs stellte Artek-Pascoe den Stuhl her, bis die Produktion wegen des Zweiten Weltkriegs eingestellt werden mußte. Nach 1945 einigte sich Knoll International mit Hardoy und begann, den Stuhl in Lizenz herzustellen. Doch zu ihrem großen Ärger kamen auch Plagiate auf den Markt. Die Firma strengte einen Prozeß an, den sie verlor, und die ihrem Stuhl nachempfundenen Versionen wurden nun legal verkauft.

Tous architectes, ils créèrent une chaise suspendue pour leurs propres bureaux, d'après le dessin antérieur d'un ingénieur britannique, Joseph Beverley Fenby, pour une chaise de bois à siège de toile. Le curateur du design au Museum of Modern Art, Edgar Kaufmann Jr., commanda les deux premières chaises *BFK* (plus connues sous le nom de *Hardoy* chair) livrées aux USA. Au départ, le siège fut fabriqué par Artek-Pascoe jusqu'à ce que la Seconde Guerre mondiale en fasse cesser la production. Peu après 1945, Knoll International remit la chaise en production sous licence jusqu'à ce que des copies non autorisées commencent à envahir le marché. Un procès s'ensuivit, que perdit Knoll, ouvrant le marché à des copies légales, mais non licenciées, de ce siège.

Born in Lyons, André Dubreuil studied at the Inchbald School of Design, London in 1969. From 1973 to 1976, he worked as a freelance interior designer, before operating his own antiques business (1977–82). In 1983, he started experimenting with trompe-l'œil effects and in 1985 commenced furniture design. Since then, he has exhibited his classicist furniture designs in London, Paris, New York, Tokyo and Brussels.

André Dubreuil wurde in Lyon geboren und nahm 1969 sein Studium an der Inchbald School of Design in London auf. Von 1973 bis 1976 arbeitete er als freiberuflicher Innenarchitekt, anschließend war er als Antiquitätenhändler tätig (1977–82). 1983 begann er, mit Trompe-l'œil-Effekten zu experimentieren, und 1985 wandte er sich dem Entwurf von Möbeln zu. Seit dieser Zeit hat er seine von klassischem Stil beeinflußten Modelle in London, Paris, New York, Tokio und Brüssel ausgestellt.

Né à Lyon, André Dubreuil fait ses études à la Inchbald School of Design de Londres en 1969. De 1973 à 1976, il travaille comme décorateur indépendant avant d'ouvrir un magasin d'antiquités (1977–82). En 1983, il s'essaye aux effets de trompe-l'œil et, en 1985, commence à dessiner des meubles. Depuis lors, il a exposé ses meubles d'esprit classique à Londres, Paris, New York, Tokyo et Bruxelles.

André Dubreuil

*1951
France . Frankreich

Charles Eames

1907–78
USA . Etats-Unis

Ray Eames

1913–88
USA . Etats-Unis

Jorge Ferrari-Hardoy,

Antonio Bonet & Juan Kurchan

founded . gegründet . fondé 1935
Argentine . Argentinien

141

The Italian designer trio Piero Gatti (*1940), Cesare Paolini (1937–83) and Franco Teodoro (*1939) have been working in the field of architecture, town planning, product development, photography and graphics since 1965. In 1969, Gatti, Paolini and Teodoro designed the multiple award winning *Sacco* – a bag-like leather seat filled with polyester granules which adapted perfectly to the body. The design trio took part in numerous trade fairs, competitions and exhibitions at home and abroad.

Das italienische Designertrio Piero Gatti (*1940), Cesare Paolini (1937–83) und Franco Teodoro (*1939) arbeitet seit 1965 auf dem Gebiet der Architektur, des Städtebaus, der Produktentwicklung, Fotografie und Grafik. Im Jahre 1969 entwarfen Gatti, Paolini und Teodoro den vielfach prämierten *Sacco*, einen mit Polyesterkugeln gefüllten Sitzsack aus Leder, der sich dem Sitzenden perfekt anpaßt. Das Designertrio nahm mit seinen Entwürfen an zahlreichen Messen, Wettbewerben und Ausstellungen im In- und Ausland teil.

Le trio de designers italiens Piero Gatti (né en 1940), Cesare Paolini (1937–83) et Franco Teodoro (né en 1939) intervient depuis 1965 dans les domaines de l'architecture, de l'urbanisme, de la mise au point de produits, de la photographie et de l'art graphique. En 1969, ils présentent le *Sacco*, un fauteuil de cuir en forme de sac rempli de billes de polyester qui s'adapte parfaitement aux positions de son occupant, et maintes fois primé depuis. Ils participent à de nombreuses foires, prix et expositions en Italie comme à l'étranger.

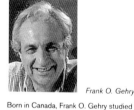

Frank O. Gehry

Born in Canada, Frank O. Gehry studied architecture at the University of Southern California, Los Angeles, graduating in 1954. From 1956 to 1957, he pursued postgraduate studies at Harvard University, Cambridge, Massachusetts. In 1962, he established his own architectural office in Los Angeles. He has received many prestigious architectural commissions, including the Vitra Design Museum, Weil am Rhein, Germany.

Frank O. Gehry wurde in Canada geboren. Er studierte an der University of Southern California, Los Angeles, die er 1954 nach dem Abschlußexamen verließ. Von 1956 bis 1957 setzte er sein Studium an der Harvard University, Cambridge, Massachusetts, fort. 1962 eröffnete er ein eigenes Architekturbüro in Los Angeles. Er erhielt einige sehr repräsentative Architekturaufträge, zu denen auch der Entwurf des Vitra Design Museums in Weil am Rhein zählt.

Né au Canada, Frank O. Gehry étudie l'architecture à l'University of Southern California, Los Angeles, dont il obtient le diplôme en 1954. De 1956 à 1957, il poursuit ses études à Harvard et en 1962 ouvre son propre cabinet d'architecte à Los Angeles. Il a reçu de nombreuses commandes prestigieuses dont le Vitra Design Museum de Weil am Rhein, en Allemagne.

During the Second World War, Paul Goldman designed and manufactured products for the US military including tubular moulded plywood masts. His Massachusetts-based company, Plycraft, continued to manufacture furniture to his designs during the post-war years. He has recently retired to Miami, and one of his nephews has taken over the administration of Plycraft USA.

Während des Zweiten Weltkriegs arbeitete Paul Goldman für das US-Militär. Er entwarf und produzierte unter anderem Schiffsmasten aus Sperrholz. In der Nachkriegszeit stellte seine in Massachusetts ansässige Firma Plycraft weiterhin Möbel nach seinen Entwürfen her. Kürzlich hat er sich in Miami zur Ruhe gesetzt; einer seiner Neffen übernahm die Leitung von Plycraft USA.

Paul Goldman dessine et fabrique des produits pour l'armée américaine, dont des mâts tubulaires en contreplaqué moulé, pendant la Seconde Guerre mondiale. Sa société du Massachusetts, Plycraft, continua à produire des meubles réalisés selon ses plans pendant les années d'après-guerre. Il s'est récemment retiré à Miami et l'un de ses neveux a repris la direction de Plycraft USA.

Born in Ireland and from an affluent and artistic family background, Eileen Gray studied at the Slade School of Fine Arts (1898). In 1902, she moved to France and studied drawing at the Académies Colarossi and Julian, Paris. Later, she trained in the art of lacquer with the Japanese craftsman, Sougawara. She spent much of the World War I in London and only returned to Paris in 1918. Prior to 1919, she had worked solely as a furniture designer; however, in that year she began to work on interior design. In 1922, she opened the Galerie Jean Désert as a showcase for her own work. The same year she also came into contact with the De Stijl movement. In 1923, J.J.P. Oud and Walter Gropius wrote a very favourable review of her interior – a bedroom-boudoir for Monte Carlo – at the Salon des Artistes Décorateurs. From 1926 onwards, she worked as an architect and exhibited several architectural projects in Le Corbusier's Pavillon des Temps Nouveaux at the 1937 Paris Exhibition.

Eileen Gray wurde in Irland geboren. Sie entstammte einer wohlhabenden Künstlerfamilie und begann ihr Studium 1898 an der Slade School of Fine Arts. 1902 ging sie nach Frankreich und studierte Malerei an der Académie Colarossi und der Académie Julian in Paris. Später ließ sie sich von dem Japaner Sougawara in japanischer Lackkunst unterrichten. Während des Ersten Weltkriegs hielt sie sich fast ununterbrochen in London auf und kehrte erst 1918 nach Paris zurück. Bis 1919 arbeitete sie als freie Möbelentwerferin, danach als Innenarchitektin. 1922 eröffnete sie die Galerie Jean Désert als Schaufenster für ihre eigenen Entwürfe. Im selben Jahr kam sie in Kontakt mit der De-Stijl-Bewegung. J.J.P. Oud und Walter Gropius veröffentlichten eine begeisterte Rezension ihres »Monte-Carlo«-Zimmers, ein Schlafzimmer/Boudoir, das sie im Salon des Artistes Décorateurs von 1923 ausstellte. Ab 1926 arbeitete sie ausschließlich als Innenarchitektin und stellte einige ihrer Projekte in Le Corbusiers Pavillon des Temps Nouveaux der Pariser Weltausstellung von 1937 vor.

Née en Irlande, dans une famille aisée et de goûts artistiques, Eileen Gray étudie à la Slade School of Fine Arts (1898). En 1902, elle s'installe à Paris et suit des cours de dessin aux Académies Colarossi et Julian. Plus tard, elle se forme à l'art de la laque avec le spécialiste japonais Sougawara. Elle passe la plus grande partie de la Première Guerre mondiale à Londres et ne revient à Paris qu'en 1918. Avant 1919, elle n'avait travaillé que sur des projets de meubles et commence à s'intéresser à la décoration. En 1922, elle ouvre la Galerie Jean Désert pour présenter son travail. La même année, elle entre en contact avec le groupe De Stijl. En 1923, J.J.P. Oud et Walter Gropius commentent favorablement sa participation au Salon des Artistes-Décorateurs, une chambre-boudoir à Monte-Carlo. A partir de 1926, elle travaille comme architecte et présente plusieurs projets architecturaux dans le Pavillon des Temps Nouveaux de Le Corbusier lors de l'Exposition de Paris de 1937.

Gatti, Paolini & Teodoro

since . seit . depuis 1965
Italy . Italien . Italie

Frank O. Gehry

*1929
USA . Etats-Unis

Paul Goldman

*1912
USA . Etats-Unis

Eileen Gray

1878–1976
France . Frankreich

Born in Moravia, Josef Hoffmann studied architecture in Munich before training under Otto Wagner at the Akademie der bildenden Künste in Vienna. From 1896–99, he worked in Otto Wagner's practice. In 1885, Hoffmann founded the Siebener Club, which included Joseph Maria Olbrich and Koloman Moser as members. In 1897, he joined the Vienna Secession, designing the "Ver Sacrum" room for the 1898 exhibition. From 1899–1941, he was professor of architecture at the Kunstgewerbeschule Vienna. His work was influenced by Charles Rennie Mackintosh's designs. He visited England in 1902 with Koloman Moser and founded the Wiener Werkstätte with him in 1903. Commissions include the Palais Stoclet, Brussels (1905–11) and the Purkersdorf Sanatorium (1903–06). In 1905 he left the Vienna Secession and with Gustav Klimt formed the Kunstschau. His many international exhibitions included the 1914 Deutsche Werkbund Exhibition in Cologne, the 1925 Exposition des Arts Décoratifs in Paris and the 1930 Exhibition in Stockholm.

Josef Hoffmann wurde in Mähren geboren. Er studierte Architektur in München, bevor er seine Ausbildung an der Akademie der bildenden Künste in Wien bei Otto Wagner begann, dessen Mitarbeiter er von 1896 bis 1899 war. 1885 gründete Hoffmann den Siebener Club, zu dessen Mitgliedern auch Joseph Maria Olbrich und Koloman Moser zählten. 1897 schloß er sich der Wiener Sezession an und entwarf zur ersten Ausstellung 1898 den »Ver Sacrum«-Raum. Von 1899 bis 1941 hatte er eine Professur an der Wiener Kunstgewerbeschule inne. Seine Arbeiten waren stark von den geometrischen, gelängten Formen der Entwürfe Mackintoshs beeinflußt. 1902 bereiste er zusammen mit Koloman Moser England. 1903 gründeten sie die Wiener Werkstätte. Zu den wichtigsten Aufträgen Hoffmanns zählen u.a. das Palais Stoclet (1905–11) und das Sanatorium »Westend« in Purkersdorf bei Wien (1903–06). 1905 gründete er zusammen mit Gustav Klimt die Kunstschau. Er nahm an zahlreichen internationalen Ausstellungen teil, wie der Kölner Werkbundausstellung von 1914, der Pariser Exposition des Arts Décoratifs von 1925 und der Stockholmer Ausstellung von 1930.

Né en Moravie, Josef Hoffmann étudie l'architecture à Munich avant de travailler pour Otto Wagner à Vienne. En 1895, il entre au cabinet de Wagner où il travaillera jusqu'en 1899. Il fonde le Siebener Club en 1885, rejoint la Sècession Viennoise en 1897 et prend part en 1898 à la première exposition du mouvement, concevant la salle «Ver Sacrum». En 1899, il est nommé professeur d'architecture à la Wiener Kunstgewerbeschule. Son oeuvre a été fortement influencée par la géométrie et l'élongation de Charles Rennie Mackintosh. Il visite l'Angleterre vers 1902 en compagnie de Koloman Moser avec lequel il crée les Wiener Werkstätte. Il conçoit entre autres le palais Stoclet (Bruxelles, 1905–11) et le Purkersdorf Sanatorium (1903–06). En 1905, il fonde avec Gustav Klimt le Kunstschau. Nombreuses expositions internationales dont la Kölner Werkbundausstellung de 1914, l'Exposition des Arts Décoratifs de Paris en 1925 et l'exposition de Stockholm de 1930.

Arne Jacobsen

Born in Copenhagen, Arne Jacobsen initially trained as a mason before studying architecture at the Royal Danish Academy of Arts, Copenhagen, graduating in 1927. From 1927 until 1930, he worked in the architectural office of Paul Holsoe. In 1930, he established his own design office, which he headed until his death in 1971, and worked independently as an architect, interior, furniture, textile and ceramics designer. He was professor of Architecture at the Royal Academy of Arts, Copenhagen, from 1956 onwards. His best known projects are St. Catherine's College, Oxford, and the SAS Hotel, Copenhagen.

Arne Jacobsen wurde in Kopenhagen geboren. Vor seiner Ausbildung zum Architekten an der Königlichen Kunstakademie in Kopenhagen, die er 1927 nach dem Abschlußexamen verließ, machte er eine Maurerlehre. Von 1927 bis 1930 arbeitete er in dem Architekturbüro von Paul Holsoe. 1930 gründete er ein eigenes Designstudio, das er bis zu seinem Tod 1971 leitete. Er war als Architekt, Innenarchitekt, Möbel-, Textil- und Keramikdesigner tätig. 1956 erhielt er eine Professur an der Königlichen Kunstakademie in Kopenhagen. Seine bekanntesten Werke sind das St. Catherines College, Oxford, und das SAS-Hotel in Kopenhagen.

Né à Copenhague, Arne Jacobsen reçoit une formation de maçon avant d'étudier l'architecture à l'Académie Royale des Arts de Copenhague d'où il sort diplômé en 1927. De 1927 à 1930, il travaille pour l'architecte Paul Holsoe. En 1930, il ouvre son propre cabinet qu'il dirigera jusqu'à sa mort en 1971 et travaille comme architecte, décorateur, créateur de mobilier, de textiles et de céramique. Il fut professeur d'architecture à l'Académie Royale des Arts de Copenhague à partir de 1956. Ses projets les plus connus sont le College St. Catherine à Oxford et l'hôtel SAS à Copenhague.

Pierre Jeanneret was born in Geneva, where he studied architecture at the Ecole des Beaux-Arts from 1913 to 1915 and from 1918 to 1921. He worked with the Perret brothers until 1923 and, from 1923–40 collaborated with his cousin Le Corbusier, whose designs he produced. Later, Jeanneret went on to work with Jean Prouvé, Charlotte Perriand, G. Blanchon and A. Masson. From 1951–65, Jeanneret was involved primarily in architectural projects. He was director of the School of Architecture at Chandigarh in India.

Pierre Jeanneret wurde in Genf geboren. Von 1913–15 und von 1918–21 studierte er Architektur an der Ecole des Beaux-Arts in Genf. Anschließend arbeitete er bis 1923 im Büro der Brüder Perret, von 1923–40 in Kooperation mit seinem Cousin Le Corbusier, dessen Entwürfe er ausführte. Jeanneret arbeitete später auch mit Jean Prouvé, Charlotte Perriand, G. Blanchon und A. Masson zusammen. Von 1951–65 war Jeanneret vor allem mit architektonischen Projekten befaßt. Er leitete als Direktor die Architekturschule von Chandigarh in Indien.

Pierre Jeanneret est né à Genève où il étudie l'architecture à l'Ecole des Beaux-Arts de 1913 à 1915 et de 1918 à 1921. Il débute dans le cabinet des frères Perret jusqu'en 1923, puis, de 1923 à 1940, collabore avec son cousin Le Corbusier dont il exécute les projets. Il travaille plus tard avec Jean Prouvé, Charlotte Perriand, G. Blanchon et A. Masson. De 1951 à 1965 Jeanneret se consacre à des projets architecturaux. Il a été directeur de l'école d'architecture de Chandigarh, en Inde.

The American designers all studied at the Pratt Institute, New York. In 1949 they began a 6-year partnership with Erwine and Estelle Lavernes' company, Laverne International Ltd. As a team they designed their *New Furniture Group*, which comprised of chairs, sofas and tables including the *3LC* chair which won an American Industrial Design award in 1952. Ross Littell now lives in Denmark, where he designs for Unikavaev and De Padova, while Douglas Kelley currently resides in London.

Die amerikanischen Designer haben alle am New Yorker Pratt Institut studiert. 1949 begann eine sechsjährige Zusammenarbeit mit Erwine und Estelle Laverne für deren Firma Laverne International Ltd. Gemeinsam entwarfen sie eine *New Furniture Group*, die aus Sofas, Stühlen und Tischen bestand. Hierzu gehörte auch der *3LC*-Stuhl, mit dem sie 1952 den American-Industrial-Designpreis gewannen. Ross Littell lebt heute in Dänemark, wo er für Unikavaev und De Padova tätig ist, während Douglas Kelley zur Zeit in London lebt.

Les designers américains ont tous étudié au Pratt Institut de New York. A partir de 1949 ils ont collaboré pendant six ans avec la société Laverne international Ltd créée par Erwine et Estelle Laverne. Ils ont conçu ensemble le *New Furniture Group* composé de chaises, de canapés et de tables. La chaise *3LC*, qui reçut le prix du design industriel américain en 1952, faisait partie de ce groupe. Ross Littell vit aujourd'hui au Danemark où il intervient pour Unikavaev et De Padova, tandis que Douglas Kelley vit à Londres.

Josef Hoffmann

1870–1956
Austria . Österreich . Autriche

Arne Jacobsen

1902–71
Denmark . Dänemark . Danemark

Pierre Jeanneret

1896–1967
Switzerland . Schweiz . Suisse

Katavolos, Littell & Kelley

*1924, *1924, *1928
USA . Etats-Unis

Rodney Kinsman

Born in London, Rodney Kinsman studied furniture design at the Central School of Art, London. In 1966, he established OMK Design, initially with Jurek Olejnik and Bryan Morrison. Since then, he has headed this furniture design company and is also now the chief design consultant at Kinsman Associates. In 1983, he was awarded a fellowship by the Society of Industrial Artists and Designers.

Rodney Kinsman wurde in London geboren. Er studierte Möbeldesign an der Central School of Art, London. 1966 gründete er die Firma OMK Design, zu der anfangs auch Jurek Olejnik und Bryan Morrison gehörten. Seither leitet er die Firma, die sich auf Möbeldesign spezialisiert hat, und arbeitet außerdem als erster Designberater bei Kinsman Associates. 1983 wurde er von der Society of Industrial Artists and Designers als Mitglied aufgenommen.

Né à Londres, Rodney Kinsman étudie le design de mobilier à la Central School of Art de Londres. En 1966, il fonde OMK Design, avec, au départ, Jurek Olejnik et Bryan Morrison. Depuis, il dirige cette entreprise de création de meubles tout en étant le principal designer consultant de Kinsman Associates. En 1983, il est admis comme membre de la Society of Industrial Artists and Designers.

Rodney Kinsman

*1943
Great Britain . Großbritannien .
Grande-Bretagne

Born in Oster Vra, Poul Kjaerholm studied at the School of Arts and Crafts in Copenhagen, where he taught from 1952 to 1956. From 1955 to 1976, he also taught at the Royal Danish Academy of Arts, Copenhagen. He has worked independently, designing for, among others, Fritz Hansen and E. Kold Christensen. He was awarded a Grand Prix at both the 1957 and 1960 Milan Triennales and a Lunning Prize in 1958.

Poul Kjaerholm wurde in Oster Vra geboren. Er studierte an der Kunstgewerbeschule in Kopenhagen, an der er von 1952 bis 1956 lehrte. Von 1955 bis 1976 lehrte er an der Königlichen Kunstakademie in Kopenhagen. Er arbeitete als freischaffender Designer unter anderem für Fritz Hansen und E. Kold Christensen. Auf der Triennale von Mailand wurde er 1957 und 1960 mit dem Grand Prix ausgezeichnet und erhielt 1958 den Lunning-Preis.

Né à Oster Vra, Poul Kjaerholm fait ses études à l'Ecole des Arts Décoratifs de Copenhague où il enseigne de 1952 à 1956. De 1955 à 1976, il professe également à l'Académie Royale des Arts de Copenhague. Il a travaillé comme consultant pour, parmi d'autres, Fritz Hansen et E. Kold Christensen, et a reçu le Grand Prix des Triennales de Milan de 1957 et 1960, ainsi que le Prix Lunning en 1958.

Poul Kjaerholm

*1929
Denmark . Dänemark . Danemark

Shiro Kuramata

Born in Tokyo, Shiro Kuramata studied architecture and later cabinet-making at the Tokyo Technical High School of Art and the Kuwasawa Institute of Design. He subsequently founded his own design practice in 1965. In the early 1980s he produced designs for Memphis and in the latter half of the decade for, among others, Vitra, Toyo Sash Co. and Kokuyo Co. His reputation was established mainly through interior design work, such as his shop projects for Seibu, Esprit and Issey Miyake. In 1981, he was awarded the Japanese Cultural Design Prize.

Shiro Kuramata wurde in Tokio geboren. Er studierte zunächst Architektur an der Technischen Kunsthochschule und danach Kunsttischlerei am Kuwasawa-Institut für Design in Tokio. Nach dem Studium gründete er 1965 ein eigenes Designstudio. Zu Beginn der 80er Jahre fertigte er Entwürfe für Memphis, und in der zweiten Hälfte der 80er Jahre arbeitete er unter anderem für Vitra, die Toyo Sash Co. und die Kokuyo Co. Seinen Ruf als Designer verdankt er vor allem seinen Arbeiten für die Innenausstattung diverser Firmen wie Seibu, Esprit und Issey Miyake. 1981 wurde er mit dem japanischen Preis für Kultur-Design ausgezeichnet.

Né à Tokyo, Shiro Kuramata étudie l'architecture puis l'ébénisterie à l'Ecole technique Supérieure de Tokyo et à l'Institut de Design Kuwasawa. Il crée ensuite son propre bureau en 1965. Au début des années 80, il crée pour Memphis et, dans la seconde moitié de la décennie, pour Vitra, Toyo Sash Co. et Kokuyo Co., entre autres. Sa célébrité vient principalement de son travail d'architecture intérieure et en particulier de ses magasins pour Seibu, Esprit et Issey Miyake. En 1981 lui est décerné le Prix japonais du Design Culturel.

Shiro Kuramata

1934–91
Japan . Japon

Danny Lane

Born in America, Danny Lane emigrated with his parents to Britain in 1975. He apprenticed with the stained glass craftsman, Patrick Reyntiens, before studying painting at the Central School of Art, London, graduating in 1980. In 1981, he set up a studio in the East End of London and in 1983 established his own company, Glassworks. During the 1980s he exhibited work at Ron Arad's One Off showroom in Covent Garden, London.

Danny Lane wurde in den Vereinigten Staaten geboren und emigrierte 1975 mit seinen Eltern nach Großbritannien. Er absolvierte eine Lehre bei dem Glasmaler Patrick Reyntiens und studierte anschließend Malerei an der Central School of Art in London, die er 1980 nach dem Abschlußexamen verließ. 1981 eröffnete er ein eigenes Studio im Londoner East End, und 1983 gründete er seine Firma Glassworks. In den 80er Jahren stellte er seine Arbeiten im Ausstellungsraum von Ron Arads One Off in Covent Garden, London, aus.

Né aux Etats-Unis, Danny Lane émigre avec ses parents en Grande-Bretagne en 1975. Il fait son apprentissage auprès du maître-verrier Patrick Reyntiens avant d'étudier la peinture à la Central School of Art, à Londres, dont il obtient le diplôme en 1980. En 1981, il monte un studio dans l'East End à Londres et, en 1983, crée sa propre société, Glassworks. Pendant les années 80 il expose son travail dans le showroom de Ron Arad, One Off, à Covent Garden.

Danny Lane

*1955
Great Britain . Großbritannien .
Grande-Bretagne

144

Le Corbusier

Charles Edouard Jeanneret-Gris, known as Le Corbusier, was born in La Chaux-de-Fonds, Switzerland, where he studied architecture. In 1908 he went to Paris to work in the architectural practice of Auguste Perret. In 1910, while studying the teaching of design, he met Wolf Dohrn, Peter Behrens and Hermann Muthesius. From 1912 to 1914, he taught at L'Eplattenier's Nouvelle Section at the La Chaux-de-Fonds art school. In 1917, he moved to Paris, where he and the painter Amédée Ozenfant coined the postcubist Purism movement. Le Corbusiers book "Vers une nouvelle Architecture" was published in 1923. He designed the L'Esprit Nouveau pavilion at the 1925 Paris Exhibition and exhibited furniture designs at the 1929 Salon d'Automne which Thonet subsequently produced. He was a member of the Congrès Internationaux d'Architecture Moderne and acknowledged as a leading architect of his day.

Charles Edouard Jeanneret-Gris wurde in La Chaux-de-Fonds, Schweiz, geboren, wo er Möbeldesign studierte. 1908 arbeitete er in Paris in Auguste Perrets Architekturbüro. 1910 und 1911 hielt er sich in Deutschland auf und kam dort mit den Ideen führender Designer in Berührung: Er lernte Wolf Dohrn, den Direktor der Dresdner Werkstätte, Hermann Muthesius und Peter Behrens kennen, in dessen Büro er für kurze Zeit tätig war. Von 1912–14 lehrte er an der Kunsthochschule von La Chaux-de-fonds Architektur. Zurück in Paris, entwikkelte er mit dem Maler Amédée Ozenfant die postkubistische Kunstrichtung des Purismus. 1923 erschien Le Corbusiers Buch »Vers une nouvelle Architecture«, in dem er seine Ideen über modernes Bauen darlegte. Für die Pariser Exposition Internationale des Arts Décoratifs von 1925 entwarf Le Corbusier den Pavillon L'Esprit Nouveau, und auf dem Pariser Herbstsalon von 1929 stellte er seine Möbelentwürfe aus. Daraufhin übernahm die Firma Thonet die Produktion. Le Corbusier war Mitglied der Congrès Internationaux d'Architecture Moderne und galt als einer der führenden Architekten seiner Zeit.

Charles-Edouard Jeanneret-Gris, dit Le Corbusier, est né à La Chaux-de-Fonds en Suisse. Il se rend en 1908 à Paris et travaille chez Auguste Perret. En 1910, il étudie l'enseignement du dessin en Allemagne. Rencontre Wolf Dohrn, directeur des Dresdner Werkstätte, ainsi que Hermann Muthesisus et Peter Behrens. De 1912 à 1924, il enseigne à l'école de La Chaux-de-Fonds. En 1917, il s'installe à Paris et lance avec le peintre Amédée Ozenfant le Purisme. Le Corbusier écrit en 1923 son livre »Vers une nouvelle architecture«. Il conçoit le pavillon de l'Esprit Nouveau pour l'Exposition de 1925 à Paris et montre ses dessins de mobilier au Salon d'Automne de 1929. Ces meubles furent par la suite produits par Thonet. Il fut un membre actif des Congrès Internationaux d'Architecture Moderne. Le Corbusier passe pour être l'un des grands architectes de son temps.

Charles Rennie Mackintosh

Born in Brno, Adolf Loos studied at Liberec and later at the Dresden Institute of Technology. He lived in America from 1893 to 1896. On his return to Vienna, he worked for a year with the architect, Carl Mayreder. From 1897, he wrote extensively on design and architectural matters. In 1908, his famous article "Ornament and Crime" ("Ornament und Verbrechen") was published, in which he linked the use of excessive decoration to a debasement of society. In 1912 he founded an architectural school, and from 1920 to 1922, Loos was chief housing architect of Vienna.

Adolf Loos wurde in Brünn geboren. Er studierte in Liberec und später an der Technischen Hochschule von Dresden. Von 1893 bis 1896 lebte er in den Vereinigten Staaten. Nach seiner Rückkehr nach Wien arbeitete er ein Jahr lang bei dem Architekten Carl Mayreder. 1897 begann er eine rege publizistische Tätigkeit über Design- und Architekturfragen. 1908 erschien sein berühmter Artikel »Ornament und Verbrechen«, in dem er die exzessive Verwendung von Ornamenten mit dem Niedergang der Gesellschaft verknüpfte. 1912 gründete er eine »Bauschule«, und von 1920 bis 1922 war er Chefarchitekt des Siedlungsamtes der Stadt Wien.

Né à Brno, Adolf Loos étudie à Liberec, et plus tard, à l'Ecole Technique Supérieure de Dresde. Il vit en Amérique de 1893 à 1896 et,à son retour à Vienne, travaille pendant un an chez l'architecte Carl Mayreder. A partir de 1897, il écrit abondamment sur le design et l'architecture. En 1908, dans un article célèbre »Ornement et Crime«, il fait le lien entre la surabondance de la décoration et la décadence de la société. En 1912, il fonde une école d'architecture et, de 1920 à 1922,est architecte en chef de la ville de Vienne pour les programmes de logement.

Born in Glasgow, in 1884 Charles Rennie Mackintosh entered the practice of local architect, John Hutchinson, and in 1889 he joined the architectural office of Honeyman & Keppie. By 1896, he was designing furniture for Messrs. Guthrie & Wells and exhibiting with H.J. MacNair and Frances & Margret Macdonald as "The Four". In 1897, he won the competition for the new Glasgow School of Art building. The same year he was commissioned to decorate Miss Cranstons's Buchanan Street Tea Rooms. In 1900, the year he married Margaret Macdonald, he exhibited at the Vienna Secession Exhibition. In 1903, he received the commission for Hill House, Helensburgh from the publisher, W.W. Blackie. In 1904, he designed the Willow Street Tea Rooms for Miss Cranston. His last major work, the School of Art Library (1909), received little attention. In 1916, he moved to London and then, in 1923, to France, where he painted until his death in 1928.

Charles Rennie Mackintosh wurde in Glasgow geboren. 1884 trat er als Praktikant in das Büro des Glasgower Architekten John Hutchinson ein und wurde 1889 Mitarbeiter in dem Architekturbüro Honeyman & Keppie. 1896 begann er für die Firma Guthrie & Wells Möbel zu entwerfen und zusammen mit H.J. MacNair und Frances und Margaret Macdonald als »The Four« Arbeiten auszustellen. 1897 gewann er den Wettbewerb für den Entwurf einer neuen Kunstschule in Glasgow. Im gleichen Jahr wurde er mit der Innenausstattung von Miss Cranston's Tea Rooms in der Buchanan Street und mit dem Möbelentwurf für ihre Tea Rooms in der Glasgower Argyle Street beauftragt. 1900 heiratete er Margaret Macdonald und nahm an der Ausstellung der Wiener Sezession teil. 1903 beauftragte ihn der Verleger W.W. Blackie mit dem Bau seiner Villa Hill House in Helensburgh. 1904 entwarf er für Miss Cranston die Tea Rooms in der Willow Street. Sein letztes Hauptwerk, die Bibliothek der Kunstschule von Glasgow (1909), fand wenig Beachtung. 1916 ließ er sich in London nieder, bevor er 1923 nach Frankreich übersiedelte, wo er sich bis zu seinem Tod 1928 der Malerei widmete.

Né à Glasgow, en 1884 Charles Rennie Mackintosh commence à travailler pour un architecte local, John Hutchinson, puis pour Honeyman & Keppie en 1889. En 1986, il dessine des meubles pour Guthrie & Wells et expose avec H.J. MacNair, Frances et Margaret Macdonald sous le nom de «The Four». En 1897, il remporte le concours pour la construction de la nouvelle école d'Art de Glasgow et la même année est retenu pour décorer Miss Cranston's Tea Rooms de Buchanan Street et créer le mobilier de Miss Cranston's Tea Rooms d'Argyle Street. En 1900, participe à l'exposition de la Sécession Viennoise. La même année il épouse Margaret Macdonald. En 1903, l'éditeur W.W. Blackie le choisit pour construire sa maison, Hill House, à Helensburgh. En 1904 il décore Miss Cranston's Tea Rooms de Willow Street. Sa dernière œuvre importante, la Bibliothèque de l'Ecole d'Art, fut à peine remarquée lors de son ouverture en 1909. En 1916, il s'installe à Londres et, en 1923, il part pour la France, où il peindra jusqu'à sa mort.

Erwine and Estelle Laverne studied painting under the direction of Hans Hofmann at the Students' Art League, New York (as did Ray Eames). Together they founded their own manufacturing and retailing company in 1938, Laverne Originals. Owing to its spatial qualities, their moulded perspex furniture was extremely popular with interior designers in the late 1950s, and can be seen to predict the direction furniture design would take in the 1960s.

Erwine und Estelle Laverne studierten, wie auch Ray Eames, bei Hans Hofmann an der Student's Art League in New York. 1938 gründeten beide die Produktions- und Vertriebsfirma Laverne Originals. Ihre Plexiglasmöbel waren gegen Ende der 50er Jahre wegen ihrer Raumqualitäten außerordentlich beliebt; sie nahmen das Möbeldesign der 60er Jahre vorweg.

Erwine et Estelle Laverne étudient la peinture sous la direction de Hans Hofmann à la Students' Art League de New York (comme Ray Eames). Ensemble, ils fondent leur propre société de production et de distribution en 1938, Laverne Originals. Leurs meubles de perspex moulé furent extrêmement appréciés par les décorateurs à la fin des années 50 pour leurs qualités spatiales qui présageaient la direction qu'allait prendre le design de mobilier dans les années 60.

Erwine & Estelle Laverne

*1909 & *1915
USA . Etats-Unis

Le Corbusier

1887–1965
France . Frankreich

Adolf Loos

1870–1933
Austria . Österreich . Autriche

Charles Rennie Mackintosh

1868–1928
Great Britain . Großbritannien .
Grande-Bretagne

Vico Magistretti

Born in Milan, Vico Magistretti studied architecture at the Polytechnic of Milan, graduating in 1945. From 1946, he has worked independently for among others, Cassina, O-Luce, Artemide, Knoll International and Olivetti. He was a commission member for the 1960 and 1964 Milan Triennales and also for the 1959 and 1960 Compasso d'Oro awards. Since 1980, he has been a visiting lecturer at the Royal College of Art, London. He has received numerous awards throughout his career, including two Grands Prix and a Gold Medal at the 1948 and 1954 Milan Triennales and the Compasso d'Oro in 1967 and 1969.

Vico Magistretti wurde in Mailand geboren. Er studierte am Polytechnikum von Mailand Architektur und verließ die Akademie 1945 nach dem Abschlußexamen. Seit 1946 arbeitet er als freier Designer unter anderem für Cassina, O-Luce, Artemide, Knoll International und Olivetti. 1960 und 1964 gehörte er zur Jury der Mailänder Triennale und 1959 und 1960 zur Jury des Compasso d'Oro. Seit 1980 lehrt er als Gastprofessor am Royal College of Art, London. Er erhielt während seiner Laufbahn diverse Preise, darunter zweimal den Grand Prix und einmal eine Goldmedaille auf der Mailänder Triennale (1948 und 1954), außerdem zweimal den Compasso d'Oro (1967 und 1969).

Né à Milan, Vico Magistretti étudie l'architecture à l'Ecole Polytechnique de Milan et en est diplômé en 1945. A partir de 1946, il travaille comme consultant pour, entre autres, Cassina, O-Luce, Artemide, Knoll International et Olivetti. Il fait partie d'une commission pour les Triennales de Milan de 1960 et 1964 et pour les prix du Compasso d'Oro de 1959 et 1960. Depuis 1980, il est conférencier invité au Royal College of Art, à Londres. Il a reçu de nombreuses distinctions tout au long de sa carrière, dont deux Grands Prix et une médaille d'or aux Triennales de Milan de 1948 et 1954, et le Compasso d'Oro en 1967 et 1969.

Born in Värnamo, Bruno Mathsson was trained in his father Karl's cabinet-making workshop. From 1933, he designed furniture primarily for his father's business. In 1936, he was given a one-man show at the Röhsska Konstlöjdmuseet in Gothenburg, Sweden. A year later, he took part in the Paris 1937 Exhibition "Arts et Techniques Appliqués à la Vie Moderne". He was awarded the Gregor Paulsson Medal in Stockhólm, in 1955. From 1945 to 1958, he mainly practised architecture, designing several simple structures from glass, wood and concrete for use as summer-houses and school rooms. From 1958, he designed furniture in collaboration with Piet Hein. He exhibited his furniture designs in Stockholm, Oslo, Dresden and New York in 1963, 1976, 1976 and 1982 respectively.

Bruno Mathsson wurde in Värnamo geboren. Sein Vater Karl bildete ihn in seiner eigenen Werkstatt als Kunsttischler aus. 1933 begann er, für das Geschäft seines Vaters Möbel zu entwerfen. 1936 veranstaltete das Röhsska Konstslöjdmuseet in Göteborg eine Einzelausstellung für ihn. 1937 stellte er auf der Ausstellung »Arts et Techniques Appliqués à la Vie Moderne« in Paris aus. 1955 wurde ihm in Stockholm die Gregor-Paulsson-Medaille verliehen. Von 1945-58 widmete er sich hauptsächlich der Architektur und entwarf eine Anzahl einfacher Bauten aus Glas, Holz und Beton, die als Sommerhäuser oder Schulräume benutzt wurden. 1958 begann er zusammen mit Piet Hein Möbel zu entwerfen. Seine Arbeiten wurden ausgestellt: 1963 in Stockholm, 1976 in Oslo und Dresden sowie1982 in New York.

Né à Värnamo, Bruno Mathsson se forme tout d'abord dans l'atelier de son père, Karl, ébéniste. A partir de 1933, il crée des meubles, essentiellement pour ce dernier. En 1936, il est l'objet d'une exposition personnelle au Röhsska Konstlöjdmuseet de Göteborg et prend part à l'exposition de Paris «Arts et Techniques Appliqués à la Vie Moderne» de 1937. Il a reçu la Médaille Gregor Paulsson à Stockholm en 1955. De 1945 à 1958, il pratique surtout l'architecture, créant plusieurs structures simples à partir de verre, de bois et de béton pour des maisons d'été et des salles de classe. A partir de 1958, il dessine des meubles en collaboration avec Piet Hein. Il a exposé ses dessins de mobilier à Stockholm (1963), Oslo (1976), Dresde (1976) et New York (1982).

Born in Santiago, Roberto Sebastian Matta Echaurren studied architecture at Chile's Catholic University before working in Le Corbusier's office in Paris. In 1937, he met René Magritte, Joan Miró and Pablo Picasso and later, other members of the Surrealist movement. In 1938, he exhibited his first drawings as an artist. He was interested in automatism and he often suffused his work with references to alchemy and cosmology. In 1939, he was persuaded by Marcel Duchamp to leave Paris for New York. In 1940, he had a one-man show at the Julien Levy Gallery, New York. In 1948, he returned to Paris, via Rome, and in the late 1950s turned his attention to sculpture. In the the 1960s and 1970s he became more politically active and campaigned against the Chilean junta that had overthrown Salvador Allende. During this period he designed several pieces of furniture for Gavina, Italy, and tapestries that were manufactured by the Atelier Yvette Cauquil-Prince, France.

Roberto Sebastian Matta Echaurren wurde in Santiago geboren. Er studierte an der Katholischen Universität seiner Heimatstadt Architektur und arbeitete anschließend für Le Corbusier in Paris. 1937 lernte er René Magritte, Joan Miró und Pablo Picasso kennen und etwas später weitere Mitglieder der surrealistischen Bewegung. 1938 stellte er seine ersten Zeichnungen als bildender Künstler aus. Der Automatismus faszinierte ihn, und seine Arbeiten durchzogen häufig alchimistische und kosmologische Anspielungen. 1939 überredete ihn Marcel Duchamp, Paris zu verlassen und nach New York zu gehen. 1940 hatte er in der Galerie von Julien Levy in New York eine Einzelausstellung. 1948 kehrte er über Rom nach Paris zurück, und gegen Ende der 50er Jahre wandte er sich der Bildhauerei zu. In den 60er und 70er Jahren wurde er politisch aktiv und beteiligte sich an Kampagnen gegen die chilenische Junta, die Salvador Allende gestürzt hatte. Während dieser Zeit entwarf er diverse Möbel für Gavina, Italien, und Tapisserien, die vom Atelier Yvette Cauquil-Prince in Frankreich realisiert wurden.

Né à Santiago, Roberto Sebastian Matta Echaurren étudie l'architecture à l'Université Catholique de Santiago avant de travailler pour Le Corbusier à Paris. En 1937, il rencontre René Magritte, Joan Miró et Pablo Picasso, puis des membres du mouvement surréaliste. En 1938, il expose ses premiers dessins d'artiste. Il s'intéresse à l'automatisme et introduit souvent dans son œuvre des références à l'alchimie et à la cosmologie. En 1939, Marcel Duchamp le persuade de quitter Paris pour New York où il tient une exposition personnelle à la Julien Levy Gallery, en 1940. En 1948, il retourne à Paris, via Rome, et à la fin des années 50 s'intéresse à la sculpture. Dans les années 60 et 70, il devient politiquement plus actif et participe à la campagne contre la junte chilienne qui a renversé Salvador Allende. Pendant cette période, il crée plusieurs meubles pour Gavina (Italie) et des tapisseries tissées par l'Atelier Yvette Cauquil-Prince, en France.

Alessandro Mendini

Born in Milan, Alessandro Mendini worked for Nizzoli Associati until 1970. From 1970 to 1976, he was the editor of "Casabella" and founded the journal "Modo". In 1973, he became a founding member of Global Tools, a school of counter architecture and design. In the late 1970s he was the primary designer at Studio Alchimia. In 1979, he became editor of "Domus" and the same year, received a Compasso d'Oro award. Since 1983, he has been a design lecturer at the Hochschule für Angewandte Kunst, Vienna.

Alessandro Mendini wurde in Mailand geboren. Er arbeitete bis 1970 für Nizzoli Associati. Von 1970 bis 1976 war er Chefredakteur der Zeitschrift »Casabella« und gründete die Zeitschrift »Modo«. 1973 war er Mitbegründer von Global Tools, einer Schule für Gegendesign und -architektur. In den späten siebziger Jahren war er der führende Designer von Studio Alchimia. 1979 wurde er Herausgeber der Zeitschrift »Domus« und erhielt im selben Jahr den Compasso d'Oro. Seit 1983 lehrt er Design an der Hochschule für Angewandte Kunst in Wien.

Né à Milan, Alessandro Mendini travaille pour Nizzoli Associati jusqu'en 1970, date à laquelle il devient rédacteur-en-chef du magazine «Casabella» (jusqu'en 1976), avant de créer le journal «Modo». En 1973, il est membre-fondateur de Global Tools, école d'anti-architecture et d'anti-design. A la fin des années 70, il est le principal créateur du Studio Alchimia et, en 1979, devient rédacteur-en-chef de «Domus». La même année, il reçoit un Compasso d'Oro. Depuis 1983, il enseigne le design à la Hochschule für Angewandte Kunst de Vienne.

Vico Magistretti

*1920
Italy . Italien . Italie

Bruno Mathsson

*1907
Sweden . Schweden . Suède

Roberto Sebastian Matta Echaurren

*1911
Chile . Chili

Alessandro Mendini

*1931
Italy . Italien . Italie

Born in Aachen, Ludwig Mies van der Rohe
initially trained as a builder and later worked
as a draftsman of stucco ornaments for a
local architectural office. In 1905, he moved
to Berlin and studied under Bruno Paul,
designing his first building in 1907. In
1908, Mies joined Peter Behrens' architectural practice, staying there until 1911. In
1919, he joined the revolutionary Novembergruppe, promoting Modernism through
his architectural proposals. In 1926, he was
made vice-president of the Deutscher
Werkbund and a year later, organised the
Stuttgart Exhibition. He designed the German pavilion for the 1929 Barcelona Exhibition and the Tugendhat house, Brno,
Czechoslovakia, between 1929 and 1930.
In 1931, he exhibited at the Berlin Building
Exhibition and granted Thonet-Mundus exclusive marketing rights for chair designs. In
1930, he became the last director of the
Bauhaus. In 1938, he emigrated to America
and took up a teaching post at the Armour
Institute (now Illinois Institute of Technology) in Chicago.

*Ludwig
Mies van der Rohe*

Ludwig Mies van der Rohe wurde in
Aachen geboren. Nach seiner Ausbildung
als Baumeister arbeitete er als Zeichner von
Stuckornamenten bei einem Aachener Architekten. 1905 ging er nach Berlin und
arbeitete dort bei Bruno Paul. 1907 entwarf
er sein erstes Gebäude. Von 1908 bis
1911 war er Mitarbeiter von Peter Behrens.
1919 schloß er sich der revolutionären Novembergruppe an und leitete deren Archi-
tektursektion. 1926 wurde er Vizepräsident
des Deutschen Werkbundes und war verantwortlich für die Weißenhofsiedlung in
Stuttgart 1927. 1929 entwarf er den
deutschen Pavillon für die Internationale
Ausstellung von Barcelona und 1929/30
das Tugendhat-Haus in Brünn. 1931 nahm
er teil an der Berliner Bauausstellung und
unterzeichnete einen Vertrag mit Thonet-
Mundus, der er die Exklusivrechte für die
Vermarktung von 15 Stuhlentwürfen über-
trug. 1930 wurde er (letzter) Direktor des
Bauhauses. 1938 emigrierte er in die Vereinigten Staaten und erhielt eine Professur
am Armour Institute (heute Illinois Institute
of Technology) in Chicago.

Né à Aix-la-Chapelle, il reçoit une formation
de constructeur. En 1905, il part pour Berlin et étudie sous la direction de Bruno
Paul. En 1908, il entre chez Peter Behrens
où il restera jusqu'en 1911. En 1919, il
s'implique de plus en plus dans le groupe
révolutionnaire Novembergruppe, promou-
vant le Modernisme à travers des propositions architecturales. En 1926, il devient
vice-président du Deutscher Werkbund et,
un an plus tard, organise l'exposition de
Stuttgart. Il dessine le pavillon allemand de
l'Exposition de Barcelone de 1929 et la
maison Tugendhat à Brno, en Tchécoslo-
vaquie (1929–1930). En 1931, il participe
à l'exposition de Berlin sur le bâtiment et
signe un contrat avec Thonet-Mundus, leur
donnant les droits exclusifs sur quinze de
ses dessins de sièges. En 1930, il est le
dernier directeur du Bauhaus et responsable du déménagement de l'école de
Dessau à Berlin. En 1938, il émigre en
Amérique et prend un poste d'enseignant à
l'Armour Institute, aujourd'hui Illinois Institute of Technology, à Chicago.

Carlo Mollino

Carlo Mollino was born in Turin, the son of
the city's most prominent architect-engi-
neer, Eugenio Mollino. He studied engineering before enrolling at Ceradini's Regia
School of Architecture. From 1952 until
1968, he taught a course in the history of
architecture at the Faculty of Architecture in
Turin. During his career, he worked as an
independent architect, furniture designer,
interior designer, photographer, fashion
designer, writer and designer of racing
cars, including the "Osca 1100" – the win-
ner of its class at the Le Mans 24-hour race
of 1954.

Carlo Mollino wurde in Turin als Sohn des
bekanntesten Ingenieurs und Architekten
der Stadt, Eugenio Mollino, geboren. Er
begann ein Ingenieurstudium, studierte
dann aber Architektur an Ceradinis Architekturschule. Von 1952 bis 1968 las er Ar-
chitekturgeschichte an der Universität von
Turin. Während seiner vielseitigen beruf-
lichen Laufbahn arbeitete er als freier Architekt, Möbeldesigner, Innenarchitekt, Photograph, Modedesigner, Schriftsteller und
Entwerfer von Rennwagen. Er entwarf unter
anderem den »Osca 1100« – den Klassen-
gewinner des 24-Stunden-Rennens von Le
Mans, 1954.

Né à Turin et fils du plus célèbre architecte
de la ville, Eugenio Mollino. Il étudie d'abord
l'ingénierie avant d'entrer à l'Ecole d'Architecture Ceradini. De 1952 à 1968, il enseigne un cours sur l'histoire de l'architecture à la Faculté d'Architecture de Turin. Il
sera à la fois architecte indépendant, dessinateur de mobilier, décorateur, photo-
graphe, créateur de mode, écrivain et dessinateur de voitures de course (son »Osca
1100« remporta les 24 heures du Mans
dans sa catégorie en 1954).

Masaki Morita was born in Kumamoto in
1950. He met his wife Marjatta in Finland in
1974. In 1975, he graduated from the Kurasawa Design School in Tokyo and founded
the Design M studio the following year. In
1980, he was awarded the Japan Commercial Design Association prize. Although for
a long time an adherent of the minimalism
of Shiro Kuramata, Kuramata's omnipres-
ence proved restrictive and Morita sought
to redefine his own style. Morita's designs
are conceptual without being minimalist
and, in contrast to the monofunctionalism of
European utility objects have an inherently
multivalent symbolism.

Masaki Morita wurde 1950 in der Präfektur
Kumamoto geboren. Während eines Finn-
landaufenthaltes lernte er 1974 seine Frau
Marjatta kennen. 1975 schloß er sein De-
signstudium an der Kusawa-Schule in Tokio
ab. Im Folgejahr gründete er das Studio
»Design M«. Für seine Entwürfe erhielt er
1980 den Preis der »Japan Commercial
Design Association«. Lange Zeit orientierte
sich Moritas Schaffen am Vorbild des Alt-
meisters Shiro Kuramata. Die Omnipräsenz
Kuramatas ließ jüngeren Entwerfern allerdings kaum Spielraum, was schließlich zu
einer Abkehr Moritas vom Minimalismus
Kuramatas und zu einer Neudefintion seines
Stils führte. Seine Entwürfe sind konzep-
tionell, ohne minimalstisch zu sein und
zeichnen sich im Gegensatz zum Monofunk-
tionalismus europäischer Gebrauchsgegen-
stände durch die ihnen innewohnende
Mehrdeutigkeit aus.

Masaki Morita est né en 1950 dans la Pré-
fecture de Kumamoto. C'est au cours d'un
séjour en Finlande, en 1974, qu'il rencontre
sa femme, Marjatta. En 1975, il termine ses
études de design à l'Ecole Kurasawa de
Tokyo et ouvre l'année suivante son propre
studio »Design M«. En 1980 il reçoit pour
ses travaux le prix de l'Association japonaise d'Esthétique Industrielle. Longtemps,
les créations de Morita ont été inspirées par
le grand maître Shiro Kuramata. Mais
l'omniprésence de celui-ci sur la scène
japonaise ne laissant que peu d'espace à
des créateurs plus jeunes, pousse Morita à
s'éloigner de l'influence de minimalisme
pour aboutir à un style qui lui est propre.
Ses projets sont conceptuels, sans être
minimalistes, et s'opposent dans leur poly-
sémie intrinsèque au monofonctionnalisme
des objets usuels européens.

Jasper Morrison studied at Kingston Polytechnic and later at the Royal College of
Art, London, graduating in 1985. In 1986,
he founded his own design practice and
has since designed furniture for Zeus, Idée,
SCP and Cappellini. The prototypes for his
furniture are in the collection of the Vitra
Design Museum.

Jasper Morrison studierte am Kingston
Polytechnikum und am Royal College of Art,
London, das er 1985 nach der Abschlußprüfung verließ. 1986 gründete er ein eigenes Designstudio und ist seither als Entwerfer für Zeus, Idée, SCP und Cappellini
tätig. Die Prototypen seiner Möbel sind im
Vitra Design Museum zu sehen.

Jasper Morrison étudie à la Kingston Polytechnic et plus tard au Royal College of Art,
à Londres, dont il est diplômé (1985). En
1986, il ouvre son propre bureau et crée
depuis des meubles pour Zeus, Idée, SCP
et Cappellini. Des prototypes de ses
meubles se trouvent dans la collection du
Vitra Design Museum.

Ludwig Mies van der Rohe

1886–1969
Germany . Deutschland . Allemagne

Carlo Mollino

1905–73
Italy . Italien . Italie

Masaki Morita

*1950
Japan . Japon

Jasper Morrison

*1959
Great Britain . Großbritannien .
Grande-Bretagne

George Nelson

Born in Connecticut, George Nelson studied architecture at Yale University, graduating in 1931. In 1932, while on a fellowship at the American Academy in Rome, he was awarded the Prix de Rome for architecture. As a design theorist and architectural critic, he was extremely influential during the postwar years – he is credited with the invention of the integrated office system and the concept of the shopping mall. From 1935 to 1944, he was editor of "Architectural Forum". Between 1936 and 1944, he and William Hanby ran an architectural practice in New York. In 1946, he became design director of Herman Miller and encouraged Charles and Ray Eames to design furniture for the company. A year later, with Gordon Chadwick, he formed George Nelson Associates, specializing in industrial design. His major furniture designs for Herman Miller include the *Basic Storage Components* (1946), the *Comprehensive Storage System* (1958) and, with Bob Propst, the *Action Office I* system (1965).

George Nelson wurde in Connecticut geboren. Er studierte Architektur an der Yale Universität und machte 1931 sein Abschlußexamen. Als Stipendiat der American Academy in Rom (1932) gewann er den Prix de Rome für Architektur. In der Nachkriegszeit war er als Designtheoretiker und Architekturkritiker sehr einflußreich – ihm werden die Erfindung des Großraumbüros und des Einkaufzentrums zugeschrieben. Von 1935 bis 1944 war er Herausgeber der Zeitschrift »Architectural Forum«. Zusammen mit William Hanby betrieb er von 1936 bis 1944 ein Architekturbüro in New York. 1946 wurde er Designdirektor bei Herman Miller, und in dieser Eigenschaft ermutigte er Charles und Ray Eames, Möbel für die Firma zu entwerfen. Ein Jahr später gründete er gemeinsam mit Gordon Chadwick das Architekturstudio George Nelson Associates, das auf Industriedesign spezialisiert war. Er entwarf mehrere bedeutende Möbelstücke für Herman Miller, darunter die *Basic Storage Components* von 1946, das *Comprehensive Storage System* von 1958 und mit Bob Propst das System *Action Office I* von 1965.

Né dans le Connecticut, George Nelson étudie l'architecture à l'Université de Yale (diplôme en 1931). En 1932, il reçoit le Prix de Rome d'architecture. Théoricien du design et critique d'architecture, il fut extrêmement influent pendant les années d'après-guerre. On lui attribue l'invention du système de bureaux intégrés et le concept de centre commercial. De 1935 à 1944, il est rédacteur en chef d' «Architectural Forum». Entre 1936 et 1944, avec William Hanby, il ouvre et dirige un cabinet d'architecture à New York. En 1946, il est directeur du design d'Herman Miller et, à ce titre, incite Charles et Ray Eames à créer des meubles pour cette société. Un an plus tard, avec Gordon Chadwick, il crée le cabinet d'architecture George Nelson Associates spécialisé dans le design industriel. Il conçoit plusieurs meubles importants pour Herman Miller, dont les *Basic Storage Components* de 1946, le *Comprehensive Storage System* de 1958 et, avec Bob Propst, le système *Action Office I* de 1965.

Born in Vienna, Koloman Moser studied painting at the Akademie der bildenden Künste in 1888 and later attended the Wiener Kunstgewerbeschule. In 1897, he became a founding member of the Vienna Secession and two years later began teaching at the Wiener Kunstgewerbeschule. His furniture designs were shown at the 1900 Secession Exhibition and the 1900 Paris Exhibition. In 1903, with Josef Hoffmann and Fritz Wärndorfer, Moser founded the Wiener Werkstätte. In 1907 he fell out with Wärndorfer and subsequently left the cooperative. From 1908 until his death, he was mainly active as a painter.

Koloman Moser wurde in Wien geboren. Er begann 1888 sein Studium der Malerei an der Akademie der bildenden Künste in Wien und studierte anschließend an der Wiener Kunstgewerbeschule. Er war Gründungsmitglied der Wiener Sezession (1897) und begann 1899 eine Lehrtätigkeit an der Kunstgewerbeschule. Seine Möbelentwürfe wurden auf der Ausstellung der Wiener Secession von 1900 und auf der Pariser Weltausstellung von 1900 gezeigt. 1903 gründete er zusammen mit Josef Hoffmann und Fritz Wärndorfer die Wiener Werkstätte, die er aber 1907 wieder verließ, nachdem er sich mit Wärndorfer entzweit hatte. Von 1908 bis zu seinem Tod war er hauptsächlich als Maler tätig.

Né à Vienne, Koloman Moser étudie la peinture à la Akademie der bildenden Künste de Vienne en 1888 avant de suivre les cours de la Wiener Kunstgewerbeschule. En 1897, il est membre-fondateur de la Sécession Viennoise et, deux ans plus tard, commence à enseigner à la Wiener Kunstgewerbeschule. Ses dessins de meubles sont présentés à l'exposition de la Sécession de 1900 et à l'Exposition de Paris de 1900. En 1903, avec Josef Hoffmann et Fritz Wärndorfer, Moser fonde la Wiener Werkstätte. En 1907, il se brouille avec Wärndorfer et quitte la coopérative. De 1908 à sa mort, il se consacre essentiellement à la peinture.

Born in Paris, Olivier Mourgue studied interior design at the Ecole Boulle and furniture-making at the Ecole Nationale des Beaux-Arts, Paris, graduating in 1960. Additionally, he trained from 1958 to 1961 in Sweden and Finland and worked for Maurice Holland, Nordiska Kompaniet, Stockholm, in 1960. In 1963, he worked as an interior designer for the Agence d'Architecture Intérieure Gautier-Delaye, Paris. In 1966, he established his own studio in Paris. Closing the studio in 1976, he moved to Brittany and became a professor at the School of Fine Arts in Brest.

Olivier Mourgue wurde in Paris geboren. Er studierte Innenarchitektur an der Ecole Boulle (1954–58) und anschließend Möbeldesign an der Ecole Nationale des Beaux-Arts in Paris, die er 1960 nach dem Abschlußexamen verließ. Gleichzeitig studierte er von 1958 bis 1961 in Schweden und Finnland und arbeitete 1960 bei Maurice Holland, Nordiska Kompaniet, Stockholm. 1963 war er als Innenarchitekt für die Agence d'Architecture Intérieure Gautier-Delaye in Paris tätig. 1966 eröffnete er in Paris ein eigenes Studio. 1976 löste er es wieder auf, zog in die Bretagne und nahm eine Professur an der Ecole de Beaux-Arts in Brest an.

Né à Paris, Olivier Mourgue étudie la décoration intérieure à l'Ecole Boulle et l'ébénisterie à l'Ecole Nationale des Beaux-Arts dont il est diplômé en 1960. De 1958 à 1961, il poursuit sa formation en Suède et en Finlande et travaille auprès de Maurice Holland, de la Nordiska Kompaniet, Stockholm, en 1960. En 1963 il est décorateur pour l'Agence d'Architecture Intérieure Gautier-Delaye à Paris et fonde, en 1966, son propre studio qu'il ferme en 1976 pour partir en Bretagne et devenir professeur à l'Ecole des Beaux-Arts de Brest.

Peter Murdoch

Peter Murdoch trained at the Royal College of Art, graduating in 1963. In 1968, he established his own design office in London. He is primarily known for his work in graphics, signage and corporate identity. In 1968, he designed, in collaboration with Lance Wyman, the graphics for the Olympics in Mexico City. He has acted as design consultant to Hille International.

Peter Murdoch studierte am Royal College of Art in London und beendete das Studium 1963 mit dem Abschlußexamen. 1968 gründete er ein eigenes Designstudio in London. Er wurde vor allem bekannt durch seine graphischen Arbeiten, seine Piktogramme und seine Arbeiten auf dem Gebiet der Corporate Identity. 1968 entwarf er in Zusammenarbeit mit Lance Wyman die graphische Gestaltung der Olympischen Spiele von Mexico City. Er ist Design-Berater bei Hille International.

Peter Murdoch est formé au Royal College of Art à Londres dont il reçoit le diplôme en 1963. En 1968, il ouvre son bureau de design à Londres et se fait tout d'abord connaître pour ses travaux dans les domaines du graphisme, de la signalétique et de l'identité institutionnelle. En 1968, il signe, en collaboration avec Lance Wyman, l'image graphique des J.O. de Mexico. Il est intervenu comme consultant pour Hille International.

Koloman Moser

1868–1918
Austria . Österreich . Autriche

Olivier Mourgue

*1939
France . Frankreich

Peter Murdoch

*1940
Great Britain . Großbritannien .
Grande-Bretagne

George Nelson

1907–86
USA . Etats-Unis

Pierre Paulin

Pierre Paulin studied stone-carving and clay-modelling at the Ecole Camondo. He began designing furniture for Thonet in 1954 and Artifort from 1958. From 1967 to 1968, he designed a series of chairs using foam upholstery and polyester seats which were developed by Mobilier National. In 1968, he was commissioned to refurbish the Louvre and the following year was awarded an American Industrial Design award for the *Ribbon* chair, *Model No. 582*. In 1970, he designed seating for Expo '70 in Osaka and in 1971, he redesigned the private apartments of the Elysée Palace. In 1975, he founded ADSA + Partners and the practice was joined by Roger Tallon and Michel Schreiber in 1984. He was commissioned in 1983 to design furniture for the presidential office at the Elysée Palace.

Pierre Paulin erhielt seine Ausbildung als Steinmetz und Bildhauer an der Ecole Camondo. 1954 begann er, Möbel für Thonet zu entwerfen und 1958 für Artifort. Zwischen 1967 und 1968 entwarf er eine Stuhlserie mit Schaumstoffpolsterung und Polyestersitzen, die von Mobilier National hergestellt wurde. 1968 erhielt er den Auftrag, den Louvre neu auszustatten, und im darauffolgenden Jahr wurde ihm der American-Industrial-Design-Preis für seinen *Ribbon*-Stuhl, *Modell Nr. 582*, verliehen. 1970 entwarf er die Sitzmöbel für die Expo '70 in Osaka, und 1971 erhielt er den Auftrag, die Privaträume des Präsidenten im Elysée-Palast neu zu gestalten. 1975 gründete er ADSA + Partners, ein Unternehmen, dem sich 1984 Roger Tallon und Michel Schreiber anschlossen. 1983 wurde er beauftragt, Möbel für das Arbeitszimmer des Präsidenten im Elysée-Palast zu entwerfen.

Pierre Paulin étudie la sculpture sur pierre et le modelage de glaise à l'Ecole Camondo. Il commence à dessiner des meubles pour Thonet en 1954 et Artifort, à partir de 1958. De 1967 à 1968, il crée une série de chaises à rembourrage de mousse et de sièges en polyester qui seront mis au point par le Mobilier national. En 1968, il reçoit une commande de meubles pour le Louvre et l'année suivante se voit décerner un prix de l'American Industrial Design pour le siège *Ribbon*, modèle n° 582. En 1970, il crée des sièges pour l'Expo '70 d'Osaka et en 1971, redécore les appartements privés du palais de l'Elysée. En 1975, il fonde ADSA + Partners avant d'être rejoint par Roger Tallon et Michel Schreiber en 1984. Le palais de l'Elysée lui commande de nouveaux meubles pour le bureau présidentiel.

Verner Panton

Verner Panton trained at the Royal Danish Academy of Fine Arts, Copenhagen, and initially worked in Arne Jacobsen's architectural practice. He established his own design office in 1955 and is credited with the design of the very first single-form injection-moulded plastic chair – the *Stacking* chair designed in 1960. He now lives in Switzerland.

Verner Panton studierte an der Königlich-Dänischen Kunstakademie in Kopenhagen. Zunächst arbeitete er im Architekturbüro von Arne Jacobsen, bis er 1955 ein eigenes Designstudio einrichtete. Ihm wird das 1960 entworfene Modell des *Stapelstuhls* zugeschrieben, des ersten Plastikstuhls, der aus einem Stück nach dem Spritzgußverfahren gefertigt wurde. Panton lebt heute in der Schweiz.

Formé à l'Académie Royale des Beaux-Arts de Copenhague, Verner Panton commence à travailler pour le cabinet d'architecture d'Arne Jacobsen. Il ouvre son propre studio de design en 1955 et est crédité de la conception du tout premier siège en plastique moulé – la *Stacking* chair ou la chaise empilable – qu'il dessina en 1960. Il réside actuellement en Suisse.

Charlotte Perriand was born in Paris, where she studied at the Ecole des Beaux-Arts. Around 1927, she began working with Pierre Jeanneret and Le Corbusier, but also designed furniture independently. She took part in the 1927 Salon d'Automne in Paris, showing chromed steel furniture. In 1929, she presented an interior with sofas and cupboards. Together with Le Corbusier and Pierre Jeanneret, she created furniture for the 1935 International Exhibition in Brussels. From 1939 to 1941 she lived in Japan, where she strove to achieve a synthesis of modern furniture production with Japanese craftsmanship.

Charlotte Perriand wurde in Paris geboren und studierte an der dortigen Ecole des Beaux-Arts. Seit etwa 1927 arbeitete sie mit Pierre Jeanneret und Le Corbusier zusammen, sie entwarf aber auch selbständig Möbel. Am Salon d'Automne 1927 in Paris nahm sie mit Möbeln aus verchromtem Stahl teil, 1929 präsentierte sie ein Interieur mit Kanapees und Schränken. In Kooperation mit Le Corbusier und Pierre Jeanneret kreierte sie Möbel für die Internationale Ausstellung 1935 in Brüssel. Von 1939 bis 1941 lebte sie in Japan, wo sie sich um eine Synthese moderner Möbelherstellung mit japanischem Kunsthandwerk bemühte.

Charlotte Perriand est née à Paris où elle fait ses études à l'Ecole des Beaux-Arts. A partir de 1927 environ, elle travaille avec Pierre Jeanneret et Le Corbusier mais dessine également ses propres meubles. Elle participe au Salon d'Automne de Paris, en 1927, avec des meubles en acier chromé et, en 1929, présente un intérieur avec des canapés et des rangements. En coopération avec Le Corbusier et Pierre Jeanneret, elle crée des meubles pour l'Exposition Internationale de l'Ameublement de Bruxelles, en 1935. De 1939 à 1941, elle vit au Japon où elle s'efforce de trouver une synthèse entre les techniques modernes de production de meubles et l'artisanat japonais.

Jorge Pensi was born in Buenos Aires. In 1977, he became a founding member of Grupo Berenguer, Design, Form & Communication, together with Alberto Liévore, Oriol Pibernat and Norberto Chaves. Since 1979, he has worked with Perobell and the SIDI group and contributed to the journal "On Diseño". His furniture is manufactured by Amat S.A., Spain, and Thonet, Germany, while his designs for lighting are produced by B-Lux, Spain.

Jorge Pensi wurde in Buenos Aires geboren. 1977 wurde er Gründungsmitglied der Grupo Berenguer, Design, Form & Communication, zu der auch Alberto Liévore, Oriol Pibernat und Norberto Chaves gehörten. Seit 1979 arbeitet er mit Perobell und der SIDI-Gruppe zusammen und schreibt Beiträge für die Zeitschrift «On Diseño». Seine Möbel werden von Amat S.A., Spanien, und Thonet, Deutschland, hergestellt, seine Beleuchtungskörper von B-Lux, Spanien.

Jorge Pensi est né à Buenos Aires. En 1977, il fonde, avec Alberto Liévore, Oriol Pibernat et Norberto Chaves le Grupo Berenguer, Design, Form & Communication. Depuis 1979, il a travaillé avec Perobell et le groupe SIDI et écrit pour le magazine «On Diseño». Ses meubles sont réalisés par Amat S.A., en Espagne, et Thonet, en Allemagne, ses luminaires par B-Lux, en Espagne.

Verner Panton

*1926
Denmark . Dänemark . Danemark

Pierre Paulin

*1927
France . Frankreich

Charlotte Perriand

*1903
France . Frankreich

Jorge Pensi

*1946
Spain . Spanien . Espagne

149

Gaetano Pesce

Gaetano Pesce studied architecture at the University of Venice from 1959 to 1965 while also training at the Institute of Industrial Design, Venice from 1961 to 1965. Since then he has worked as a freelance designer, artist and film-maker. His furniture designs are always revolutionary in either the materials or methods of production they adopt.

Gaetano Pesce studierte von 1959 bis 1965 Architektur an der Universität Venedig und absolvierte von 1961 bis 1965 auch eine Ausbildung am dortigen Institut für Industriedesign. Seitdem arbeitet er als freiberuflicher Designer, Künstler und Filmemacher. Seine Möbelentwürfe sind immer revolutionär, entweder im Hinblick auf die verwendeten Materialien oder die Herstellungsverfahren.

Gaetano Pesce étudie l'architecture à l'Université de Venise de 1959 à 1965 tout en suivant les cours de l'Institut de Design Industriel de Venise de 1961 à 1965. Il travaille depuis comme designer indépendant, artiste et réalisateur de films. Ses dessins de meubles sont toujours révolutionnaires que ce soit pour les matériaux ou les méthodes de production qu'ils adoptent.

Giancarlo Piretti studied at the Institute of Art, Bologna, before working for Castelli, Italy. He subsequently became the company's director of research and design. In the 1980s he designed, with Emilio Ambasz, the *Dorsal* and the *Vertebra*, ergonomically conceived seating systems.

Giancarlo Piretti hat an der Kunstakademie von Bologna studiert. Er begann seine berufliche Laufbahn bei der Firma Castelli und wurde nach einiger Zeit zum Direktor für Forschung und Design ernannt. In den 80er Jahren entwarf er zuammen mit Emilio Ambasz die nach ergonomischen Gesichtspunkten konzipierten Sitzmöbel *Dorsal* und *Vertebra*.

Giancarlo Piretti étudie à l'Institut d'Art de Bologne avant de travailler pour Castelli dont il deviendra directeur pour la recherche et le design. Dans les années 80, avec Emilio Ambaz, il crée *Dorsal* et *Vertebra*, deux lignes de sièges ergonomiques.

Warren Platner

Born in Baltimore, Warren Platner studied architecture at Cornell University, Ithaca, New York, graduating in 1941. From 1945 to 1950, he worked in the design office of Raymond Loewy and the architectural practices of I.M. Pei and Kevin Roche & John Dinkeloo. From 1960 to 1965, he worked for Eero Saarinen & Associates, Birmingham, Michigan. In 1965, he established his own firm, Platner Associates, New Haven, Connecticut and since then has worked primarily as an architect.

Warren Platner wurde in Baltimore geboren. Er studierte an der Cornell University, Ithaka, New York, und machte dort 1941 sein Examen. Von 1945 bis 1950 arbeitete er im Design-Studio von Raymond Loewy und in den Architektur-büros von I.M. Pei und Kevin Roche & John Dinkeloo. Von 1960 bis 1965 war er bei Saarinen & Associates in Birmingham, Michigan, tätig. 1965 gründete er die Firma Platner Associates, New Haven, Connecticut, und seitdem ist er vorwiegend als Architekt tätig.

Né à Baltimore, Warren Platner est diplômé d'architecture de la Cornell University, Ithaca, New York, en 1941. De 1945 à 1950, il travaille dans la firme de design de Raymond Loewy, puis pour I.M. Pei, Kevin Roche & John Dinkeloo. De 1960 à 1965, il collabore avec Eero Saarinen & Associates, Birmingham, Michigan, avant de créer sa propre firme, Platner Associates, New Haven, Connecticut, en 1965. Il se consacre depuis essentiellement à l'architecture.

Gio Ponti

Gio Ponti studied architecture at the Politecnico di Milano, graduating in 1921. He initially became a ceramics designer for Richard Ginori and also practiced architecture. In 1928, he founded the prestigious design journal "Domus" and from 1925 to 1979 was the director of the Monza Biennale. From 1936 to 1961, he taught at the Politecnico di Milano. During the 1950s he collaborated on several furniture designs and interior schemes with Piero Fornasetti. Until his death in 1979, he was a regular contributor to "Domus" and "Casabella".

Gio Ponti studierte Architektur am Polytechnikum in Mailand und schloß sein Studium 1921 ab. Anfangs entwarf er für Richard Ginori Keramik und war als Architekt tätig. 1928 gründete er die renommierte Design-Zeitschrift »Domus« und von 1925 bis 1979 leitete er die Biennale in Monza. Von 1936 bis 1961 lehrte er am Polytechnikum in Mailand. In den 50er Jahren entwarf er zusammen mit Piero Fornasetti einige Möbel und Inneneinrichtungen. Bis zu seinem Tod im Jahre 1979 schrieb er regelmäßig für »Domus« und »Casabella«.

Gio Ponti étudie l'architecture au Politecnico de Milan dont il est diplômé en 1921. Il commence par créer des céramiques pour Richard Ginori tout en pratiquant l'architecture. En 1928, il fonde le prestigieux journal de design »Domus« et, de 1925 à 1979, est le directeur de la Biennale de Monza. De 1936 à 1961, il enseigne au Politecnico de Milan et, pendant les années 50, collabore avec Piero Fornasetti sur plusieurs projets de meubles et d'aménagements intérieurs. Jusqu'à sa mort, en 1979, il écrit régulièrement dans »Domus« et »Casabella«.

Gaetano Pesce

*1939
Italy . Italien . Italie

Giancarlo Piretti

*1940
Italy . Italien . Italie

Warren Platner

*1919
USA . Etats-Unis

Gio Ponti

1891–1979
Italy . Italien . Italie

Jean Prouvé came from a highly artistic background. His grandfather had worked as a ceramicist with Emile Gallé's father and his own father, Victor, collaborated with Emile Gallé and Louis Majorelle on the design of ceramics and marquetry respectively. From 1917 to 1920, Jean Prouvé trained as a blacksmith and afterwards attended the Ecole Supérieure de Nancy. In 1923, he opened his own workshop and a year later was designing and producing modern steel chairs. In the late 1920s he worked for Le Corbusier and became a founding member of the Union des Artistes Modernes. In 1931 he established a manufacturing company, Les Ateliers Jean Prouvé. After 1950, he abandoned furniture design in favour of architecture.

Jean Prouvé stammte aus einer alten Künstlerfamilie: sein Großvater hat als Keramikkünstler mit Emile Gallés Vater zusammengearbeitet, und sein Vater Victor assistierte Emile Gallé bei Keramikentwürfen und Louis Majorelle bei Marketerieentwürfen. Von 1917 bis 1920 absolvierte Jean Prouvé eine Lehre als Schmied und danach die Ecole Supérieure de Nancy. 1923 gründete er seine erste Werkstatt, und ein Jahr später entwarf und produzierte er moderne Stahlstühle. Gegen Ende der 20er Jahre arbeitete er für Le Corbusier und wurde Gründungsmitglied der Union des Artistes Modernes. 1931 gründete er eine Produktionsfirma, Les Ateliers Jean Prouvé. Nach 1950 gab er das Möbeldesign zugunsten der Architektur auf.

Jean Prouvé est né d'une famille d'artistes. Son grand-père avait travaillé comme céramiste avec le père d'Emile Gallé et son père, Victor, avec Emile Gallé et Louis Majorelle, à la création de céramique et de marquetteries. De 1917 à 1920, Jean Prouvé reçoit une formation de forgeron puis suit les cours de l'Ecole Supérieure de Nancy. En 1923, il ouvre son propre atelier et, un an plus tard, dessine et produit des sièges modernistes en acier. A la fin des années 20, il travaille pour Le Corbusier et devient membre-fondateur de l'Union des Artistes Modernes. En 1931, il crée une usine de production, les Ateliers Jean Prouvé. Après 1950, il abandonne le mobilier pour l'architecture.

Born in Hanau, he trained in silversmithing and metalwork at the Staatliche Zeichenakademie, Hanau, and later studied metal and glass design at the Werkschule, Cologne. Additionally, he trained in these latter disciplines under Elisabeth Treskow in Paris. Since 1953, he has been an independent designer in Ulm, Hamburg and Saarbrücken. He has designed various pieces of kitchen equipment and cutlery for Hessische Metallwerke, Ziegenhain. He is a founder and co-editor of "Szene" magazine and a founding member of the Vereinigung Deutscher Industrie-Designer.

Peter Raacke wurde in Hanau geboren. Seine Ausbildung als Goldschmied erhielt er an der Staatlichen Zeichenakademie in Hanau und studierte anschließend an der Werkschule in Köln Metall- und Glasdesign. Zusätzlich vertiefte er seine Kenntnisse in diesen Fächern bei Elizabeth Treskow in Paris. Seit 1953 ist er als freier Designer in Ulm, Hamburg und Saarbrücken tätig. Für die Hessischen Metallwerke in Ziegenhain hat er diverse Küchenutensilien und Bestecke entworfen. Er ist Gründer und Mitherausgeber der Zeitschrift «Szene» und Gründungsmitglied der Vereinigung Deutscher Industrie-Designer.

Né à Hanau, il apprend l'orfèvrerie et le travail du métal à la Staatliche Zeichenakademie de cette ville, puis étudie le dessin du métal et du verre à la Werkschule de Cologne. Il poursuit sa formation à Paris, auprès d'Elizabeth Teskow. Depuis 1953, il est intervenu comme designer indépendant à Ulm, Hambourg et Sarrebruck et a créé divers équipements pour la cuisine et de la coutellerie pour Hessische Metallwerke de Ziegenhain. Il est fondateur et co-éditeur du magazine «Szene» et membre-fondateur de la Vereinigung Deutscher Industrie-Designer.

Ernest Race

Born in Newcastle-upon-Tyne, Ernest Race studied interior design at the Bartlett School of Architecture, London, from 1932 to 1935. Afterwards, he worked as a draftsman for the progressive lighting company, Troughton & Young. In 1937, he went to Madras, India, to visit his missionary aunt who ran a weaving centre there. On his return, he opened a shop in London to sell his aunt's textiles which had been woven to his designs. In 1945, with the engineer J.W. Noel Jordan, he founded Ernest Race Ltd., with the intention of mass producing low-cost, high-quality contemporary furniture. In 1953, Race was made a Royal Designer for Industry. From 1954 onwards, he worked as a freelance designer.

Ernest Race wurde in Newcastle-upon-Tyne geboren. Er studierte von 1932 bis 1935 an der Bartlett School of Achitecture in London Innenarchitektur. Anschließend arbeitete er als Zeichner für die Firma Troughton & Young, Hersteller moderner Beleuchtungskörper. 1937 ging er nach Madras, Indien, um seine Tante zu besuchen, die dort als Missionarin ein Webzentrum betrieb. Nach seiner Rückkehr eröffnete er ein Ladengeschäft in London, um die Textilien seiner Tante zu verkaufen, die nach seinen Entwürfen gewebt worden waren. 1945 gründete er zusammen mit dem Ingenieur J.W. Noel Jordan die Firma Ernest Race Ltd., um hochwertige moderne Möbel als kostengünstige Massenware produzieren zu können. 1953 wurde Race der Titel Royal Designer for Industry verliehen. 1954 begann er als freier Designer zu arbeiten.

Né à Newcastle-upon-Tyne, Ernest Race étudie l'architecture intérieure à la Bartlett School of Architecture, à Londres, de 1932 à 1935. Il est ensuite engagé comme dessinateur par la société de luminaires d'avant-garde Troughton & Young. En 1937, il part pour Madras, rendre visite à une tante missionnaire qui y dirige un centre de tissage. De retour à Londres, il ouvre une boutique pour vendre les textiles que sa tante réalise selon ses dessins. En 1945, il fonde, avec l'ingénieur J.W. Noel Jordan, Ernest Race Ltd. avec l'intention de produire en série des meubles contemporains de haute qualité et de prix peu élevé. En 1953, Race est fait «Royal designer for Industry». A partir de 1954, il devient designer indépendant.

Born in Munich, Richard Riemerschmid studied fine art at the Munich Academy from 1888 to 1890. He exhibited at the 1897 Munich Glaspalast Exhibition and designed furniture for the Munich Vereinigte Werkstätten für Kunst im Handwerk, alongside Bruno Paul and Bernhard Pankok. In 1899, he designed furniture for Hermann Obrist and worked with him at the 1900 Paris Exhibition. He taught at the Nuremberg School of Art from 1902 to 1905 and in 1904, at the St. Louis Exhibition, exhibited an interior he had designed for the school's rector. His first machine-made furniture was produced in a Dresden workshop and was shown at the 1905 Deutsche Werkstätten Exhibition in Dresden. He became a founding member of the Deutscher Werkbund in 1907 and began teaching at the Berlin Kunstgewerbemuseum. Between 1912 and 1924, he was the director of the Vereinigte Werkstätten für Kunst im Handwerk in Munich and from 1926 to 1931 the principal of the Werkschule in Cologne.

Richard Riemerschmid wurde in München geboren. Er studierte von 1888 bis 1890 an der Kunstakademie seiner Heimatstadt bildende Kunst. 1897 beteiligte er sich an der Ausstellung im Münchner Glaspalast, und ein Jahr später entwarf er, neben Bruno Paul und Bernhard Pankok, Möbel für die Vereinigten Werkstätten für Kunst im Handwerk, München. 1899 arbeitete er mit Hermann Obrist zusammen und für die Pariser Weltausstellung von 1900. Von 1902 bis 1905 lehrte er an der Nürnberger Kunstschule und stellte 1904 auf der Weltausstellung von St. Louis ein Interieur aus, das er für den Direktor der Schule entworfen hatte. Die ersten Möbel, die er für die Massenproduktion entworfen hatte, wurden in den Dresdner Werkstätten für Handwerkskunst seines Schwagers Karl Schmidt hergestellt und 1905 auf der Ausstellung der Deutschen Werkstätten in Dresden gezeigt. 1907 wurde er Mitbegründer des Deutschen Werkbundes und begann eine Lehrtätigkeit am Berliner Kunstgewerbemuseum. Von 1912 bis 1924 leitete er die Vereinigten Werkstätten München, und von 1926 bis 1931 war er Direktor der Werkschule in Köln.

Né à Munich, Richard Riemerschmid étudie les beaux-arts à l'Académie de sa ville de 1888 à 1890. Il expose au Palais de Verre de Munich en 1897 et, un an plus tard, avec Bruno Paul et Bernhard Pankok, dessine des meubles pour les Vereinigte Werkstätten für Kunst im Handwerke de Munich . En 1899, il crée des meubles pour Hermann Obrist et collabore avec lui pour l'Exposition de Paris de 1900. Il enseigne à l'Ecole d'Art de Nuremberg de 1902 à 1905 et en 1904, pour l'Exposition de Saint Louis, il présente l'aménagement de l'appartement du recteur de l'école. Son premier meuble conçu pour être fabriqué par une machine est produit à Dresde dans l'atelier de son beau-frère, Karl Schmidt, et sera présenté à l'Exposition des Deutsche Werkstätten de Dresde en 1905. Il est membre-fondateur du Deutscher Werkbund en 1907 et commence à enseigner au Kunstgewerbemuseum de Berlin. De 1912 à 1924, il dirige les Vereinigte Werkstätten de Munich et de 1926 à 1931 dirige la Werkschule de Cologne.

Jean Prouvé

1901–84
France . Frankreich

Peter Raacke

*1928
Germany . Deutschland . Allemagne

Ernest Race

1913–64
Great Britain . Großbritannien .
Grande-Bretagne

Richard Riemerschmid

1868–1957
Germany . Deutschland . Allemagne

Gerrit Rietveld

Born in Utrecht, the son of a cabinetmaker, Gerrit Rietveld worked in his father's workshop from the age of eleven. In 1911, he became an independent cabinetmaker and began architectural drawing classes given by P.J.C. Klaarhamer. He designed the *Red-and-blue-chair* 1917/18 and in 1919 became one of the first members of the De Stijl movement. His celebrated chair design was first published in "De Stijl" magazine and in 1923 it was included in an exhibition at the Bauhaus. During the 1920s his most important architectural commission was the Schröder House (1924). In 1927, he designed experimental fibreboard and plywood furniture, subsequently manufactured by Metz & Co, Amsterdam. During the depression, Rietveld designed low-cost furniture constructed from packing-crate components. In 1942 he designed a stamped aluminium chair and in 1957 produced a series of bent-metal chairs. For his final design, however, the *Steltman* chair of 1963, he returned to the use of solid wood elements and geometric formalism.

Gerrit Rietveld wurde in Utrecht als Sohn eines Möbelschreiners geboren. Mit elf Jahren begann er, in der Werkstatt seines Vaters zu arbeiten. 1911 machte er sich als Schreiner selbständig und besuchte Kurse in Bauzeichnen bei P.J.C. Klaarhamer. Von 1917 bis 1918 entwarf er den *Rot-Blau-Stuhl* und wurde 1919 eines der ersten Mitglieder der De-Stijl-Bewegung. Sein berühmter Stuhlentwurf wurde zum erstenmal in der Zeitschrift »De Stijl« veröffentlicht und in die Bauhaus-Ausstellung von 1923 aufgenommen. Zu Rietvelds wichtigsten Architekturaufträgen gehörte das Schröder-Haus (1924). 1927 machte er experimentelle Möbelentwürfe aus Spanplatten und Sperrholz, die von Metz & Co, Amsterdam, realisiert wurden. Während der Depression entwarf er Möbel aus Lattenkistenelementen, um den Bedarf an Niedrigpreisprodukten zu decken. 1942 entwarf er einen Stuhl aus gepreßtem Aluminiumblech, und 1957 schuf er eine Serie von Stühlen aus gebogenem Metallrohr. Mit seinem letzten Entwurf, dem *Steltman*-Stuhl von 1963, kehrte er zu Massivholzelementen und zum geometrischen Formalismus zurück.

Né à Utrecht, fils d'un ébéniste, Gerrit Rietveld travaille dans l'atelier de son père dès l'âge de onze ans. En 1911, il se met à son compte et commence à étudier le dessin d'architecture aux cours de P.J.C. Klaarhamer. Il dessine le *fauteuil rouge-et-bleu*, en 1917/18, et en 1919 devient l'un des premier membres du Mouvement De Stijl. Son célèbre dessin de siège fut d'abord publié dans le magazine »De Stijl« et fut inclu en 1923 dans une exposition au Bauhaus. Pendant les années 20, sa commande d'architecture la plus importante fut la Maison Schröder (1924). En 1927, il dessine un mobilier expérimental en aggloméré et contreplaqué qui sera plus tard produit par Metz & Co, à Amsterdam. Pendant la crise économique, en réponse à la demande de produits bon marché, il crée une série de meubles à partir de caisses d'emballage. En 1942, il dessine un siège d'aluminium embouti et, en 1957, des modèles en métal cintré. Pour ses derniers dessins, cependant – le siège *Steltman* de 1963 – il revient au bois massif et au formalisme géométrique.

Eero Saarinen was the son of the celebrated Finnish architect and first President of the Cranbrook Academy of Art, Eliel Saarinen. Born in Helsinki, he emigrated with his family to the United States in 1923. Initially studied sculpture at the Académie de la Grande Chaumière in Paris (1929/30) and later architecture at Yale University in New Haven, Connecticut, graduating in 1934. He received a scholarship there which enabled him to travel to Europe (1934/35). On his return, he taught at the Cranbrook Academy of Art. In 1937, he began a collaboration with Charles Eames which culminated in a series of highly progressive and prize-winning furniture designs for The Museum of Modern Art's 1940 "Organic Design in Home Furnishings" competition. He later produced several highly successful furniture designs for Knoll International. He worked in his father's architectural office until Eliel's death in 1950. His greatest architectural project was the remarkable TWA terminal at John F. Kennedy Airport, New York.

Eero Saarinen ist der Sohn des berühmten finnischen Architekten und ersten Präsidenten der Cranbrook Academy of Art, Eliel Saarinen. Er wurde in Helsinki geboren und emigrierte 1923 mit seiner Familie in die Vereinigten Staaten. Er absolvierte ein Bildhauerstudium an der Pariser Académie de la Grande Chaumière (1929/30) und studierte Architektur an der Yale University in New Haven, Connecticut, die er 1934 nach dem Abschlußexamen verließ. In Yale erhielt er ein Stipendium, das ihm eine Reise nach Europa ermöglichte (1934/35). Nach seiner Rückkehr lehrte er an der Cranbrook Academy of Arts. 1937 begann seine Zusammenarbeit mit Charles Eames, die in einer Vielzahl sehr innovativer Möbelentwürfe kulminierte, die 1940 bei dem Wettbewerb »Organic Design in Home Furnishings« des Museum of Modern Art, New York, preisgekrönt wurden. In den darauffolgenden Jahren schuf Saarinen für Knoll International diverse, sehr erfolgreiche Möbelentwürfe. Bis zu seines Vaters Tod 1950 arbeitete er in dessen Architekturbüro. Sein größtes Architekturprojekt war der großartige TWA-Terminal im John F. Kennedy Airport, New York.

Fils du célèbre architecte finlandais et premier président de la Cranbrook Academy of Arts, Eliel Saarinen. Né à Helsinki, il émigre avec sa famille aux Etats-Unis en 1923. Après avoir étudié la sculpture à l'Académie de la Grande Chaumière, Paris (1929/30) il apprend l'architecture à Yale, dont il sera diplômé en 1934. Il reçoit une bourse qui lui permet de voyager en Europe (1934/35). A son retour, il commence à enseigner à la Cranbrook Academy of Arts. En 1937, débute sa collaboration avec Charles Eames qui les conduira à une série de meubles très avant-gardistes qui remporteront de nombreux prix lors du concours »Organic design in home furnishings« du Museum of Modern Art de New York, en 1940. Il réalisera plus tard plusieurs des meubles pour Knoll qui connaîtront un grand succès. Il travaille dans le cabinet de son père jusqu'à la mort de celui-ci en 1950. Son plus grand projet architectural reste le remarquable terminal TWA de l'aéroport Kennedy, à New York.

Eero Saarinen

Borek Sípek

Born in Prague, Borek Sipek studied furniture design at the School of Arts and Crafts, Prague, graduating in 1968. Later he studied architecture at the Kunsthochschule, Hamburg and philosophy at the University of Stuttgart. From 1977 to 1979, he taught at the University of Hanover and was a lecturer in design theory from 1979 to 1983 at the University of Essen. In 1984, together with David Palterer, he founded the Amsterdam-based design company, Alterego, and has since designed for, among others, Driade, Sawaya & Moroni, Vitra and Cleto Munari. In 1990, he was appointed Professor of Architecture at the Academy of Arts, Prague.

Borek Sípek wurde in Prag geboren. Er studierte an der Kunstgewerbeschule in Prag und machte 1968 sein Abschlußexamen. Anschließend besuchte er die Kunstakademie in Hamburg und studierte Philosophie an der Stuttgarter Universität. Von 1977 bis 1979 lehrte er an der Universität Hannover und war von 1979 bis 1983 Dozent für Designtheorie an der Universität Essen. 1984 gründete er zusammen mit David Palterer das Designstudio Alterego mit Sitz in Amsterdam und arbeitete unter anderem für Driade, Sawaya & Moroni, Vitra und Cleto Munari. 1990 erhielt er eine Professur für Architektur an der Prager Kunstakademie.

Né à Prague, Borek Sípek étudie le dessin de mobilier à l'Ecole des Arts Appliqués de Prague (diplôme en 1968). Il suit plus tard des cours d'architecture à l'Université de Hambourg et de philosophie à celle de Stuttgart. De 1977 à 1979, il enseigne à l'Université de Hanovre et est chargé de cours en théorie du design de 1979 à 1983 à l'Université de Essen. En 1984, il fonde avec David Palterer une société de design, Alterego, à Amsterdam et est intervenu depuis pour Driade, Sawaya & Moroni, Vitra et Cleto Munari, entre autres. En 1990, il est nommé Professeur d'Architecture à l'Académie des Arts de Prague.

Franca Stagi studied architecture at the Milan Polytechnic, graduating in 1962. Her collaboration with the designer Cesare Leonardi in Modena began the same year. In 1968 and 1969, they presented their furniture at the Milan Furniture Fair and in 1970 at the London "Design for Living, Italian Style" exhibition.

Franca Stagi studierte am Polytechnikum in Mailand Architektur und schloß ihre Ausbildung 1962 ab. Im gleichen Jahr begann ihre Zusammenarbeit mit dem Designer Cesare Leonardi in Modena. Sie stellten ihre Möbel 1968 und 1969 auf der Möbelmesse in Mailand und 1970 bei der Londoner Ausstellung »Design for Living, Italian Style« aus.

Franca Stagi étudie à l'Ecole Polytechnique de Milan d'où elle sort en 1962 pour commencer, la même année, à collaborer avec le designer Cesare Leonardi, à Modène. Ils exposent leurs meubles à la Foire du Meuble de Milan en 1968 et 1969 et, en 1970, lors de l'exposition londonienne »Design for Living, Italian Style«.

Gerrit Thomas Rietveld

1888–1964
Netherlands . Niederlande . Pays-Bas

Eero Saarinen

1910–61
USA . Etats-Unis

Borek Sípek

*1949
Czech Republic . Tschechische Republik . République Tchèque

Franca Stagi

*1937
Italy . Italien . Italie

Philippe Starck

Born in Purmerend, Mart Stam studied drawing at the Rijksnormaalschool vor Tekenonderwijs in Amsterdam from 1917 to 1919. He worked as a draftsman for a Rotterdam architectural practice until 1922, when he moved to Berlin. In 1923, he took part in an exhibition at the Bauhaus. In 1925, he returned to Amsterdam via Paris and a year later made his first cantilevered chair. His chair designs were shown at the 1928 "Der Stuhl" exhibition in Stuttgart. He became a founding member, with Gerrit Rietveld and Hendrik Petrus Berlage, of the Congrès Internationaux d'Architecture Moderne in 1927. From 1931 to 1932 he worked in Russia as a town planner and from 1948 to 1952 he taught architecture and design in Dresden and Berlin. He retired in 1966 and moved to Switzerland.

Mart Stam wurde in Purmerend geboren. Nach seiner künstlerischen Ausbildung an der Zeichenschule Rijksnormaalschool voor Tekenonderwijs in Amsterdam (1917–19) arbeitete er bis 1922 als Zeichner in einem Architekturbüro in Rotterdam und ging anschließend nach Berlin. 1923 nahm er an der Bauhaus-Ausstellung teil. 1925 kehrte er über Paris nach Amsterdam zurück und entwarf ein Jahr später seinen ersten freitragenden Stuhl. Seine Stuhlentwürfe wurden 1928 auf der Stuttgarter Ausstellung "Der Stuhl" gezeigt. 1927 wurde er, neben Gerrit Rietveld und Hendrik Petrus Berlage, Gründungsmitglied der Congrès Internationaux d'Architecture Moderne. Von 1931 bis 1932 arbeitete er in der Sowjetunion als Stadtplaner. Von 1948 bis 1952 lehrte er Architektur und Design in Dresden und Berlin. 1966 zog er sich vom Berufsleben zurück und ließ sich in der Schweiz nieder.

Né à Purmerend, Mart Stam étudie le dessin à Amsterdam de 1917 à 1919 à la Rijksnormaalschool vor Tekenonderwijs. Il travaille ensuite comme dessinateur pour un cabinet d'architecture de Rotterdam jusqu'en 1922, date de son départ pour Berlin. En 1923, il participe à une exposition du Bauhaus. Il retourne à Amsterdam en 1925, via Paris, et, un an plus tard, réalise sa première chaise en porte-à-faux. Ses dessins de sièges sont présentés à l'exposition de Stuttgart de 1928 "Der Stuhl". Il est membre-fondateur, avec Gerrit Rietveld et Hendrik Petrus Berlage, des Congrès Internationaux d'Architecture Moderne en 1927. De 1931 à 1932, il travaille en Russie comme urbaniste et, de 1948 à 1952, enseigne l'architecture et le design à Dresde et Berlin. Il se retire en Suisse en 1966.

Born in Paris, Philippe Starck studied at the Ecole Nissin de Camondo. In 1965, he won the La Villette furniture competition and in 1968 was commissioned by L. Venturi and later Quasar to design inflatable furniture. He subsequently founded one of the first companies to produce such furniture. In 1969, he was appointed art director of the Pierre Cardin studio, where he produced sixty-five furniture designs. In 1979, he founded his own manufacturing company, Starck Products. He has worked as a product, furniture and interior designer and in 1982 was selected to design the refurbishment of the President's private apartments at the Elysée Palace. He has designed furniture for Vitra, Disform, Driade, Baleri and Idée. In 1986 he became a visiting lecturer to the Domus Academy, Milan.

Philippe Starck wurde in Paris geboren und studierte an der Ecole Nissin de Camondo. 1965 gewann er den Möbelwettbewerb La Villette und erhielt 1968 von L. Venturi und später von Quasar den Auftrag, aufblasbare Möbel zu entwerfen. Daraufhin gründete Starck eine der ersten Firmen, die derartige Möbel produzierten. 1969 wurde er Art Direktor im Studio Pierre Cardin, für das er fünfundsechzig Möbelentwürfe schuf. 1979 gründete er eine eigene Produktionsfirma, Starck Products. Sein Arbeitsgebiet umfaßt Produkt- und Möbeldesign und Innenausstattung. 1982 wurde er beauftragt, die Privaträume des Präsidenten im Elysée-Palast neu zu gestalten. Er hat Möbel für Vitra, Disform, Driade, Baleri und Idée entworfen. 1986 erhielt er eine Gastprofessur an der Domus-Akademie in Mailand.

Né à Paris, Philippe Starck suit les cours de l'Ecole Nissin de Camondo. Dès 1965, il remporte un concours de mobilier pour La Villette et, en 1968, se voit commander des projets pour des meubles gonflables par L. Venturi, puis Quasar. Il crée sur cette lancée l'une des premières sociétés spécialisées dans ce type de mobilier. En 1969, il est nommé directeur artistique du Studio Pierre Cardin pour lequel il réalisera soixante-cinq projets de meubles. En 1979 il fonde sa propre société de fabrication, Starck Products. Il intervient comme designer de produits, de meubles et décorateur et, en 1982, participe aux nouveaux aménagements des appartements privés du palais de l'Elysée. Il a créé des meubles pour Vitra, Disform, Driade, Baleri et Idée. En 1986, il devient chargé de cours associé à l'Académie Domus, Milan.

Stiletto Studios has devoted himself to experimental graphics and art since 1981, and describes himself as a practising designer. Since 1986 his works have appeared at numerous international exhibitions in Vienna, Paris, Ljubljana, St. Petersburg, Los Angeles, New York, Stuttgart and Frankfurt. Thanks to a P.S. One artist's grant he was able to spend 1988/89 in New York. In 1991 he opened a practice for design faults and amongst other things is responsible for organising and running the prodomo in Vienna. In 1992 he co-operated with the Verband der Systemberater für Produktgestaltung Design-Labor Bremerhaven e.V. on the design case study "Das Sichtbarmachen des Vorhandenen" using the Zschopau motorcycle works as an example.

Stiletto Studios bezeichnet sich selbst als Designpraktiker und beschäftigt sich seit 1981 mit experimenteller Graphik und Kunst. Seit 1986 ist er mit seinen Arbeiten auf zahlreichen internationalen Ausstellungen in Wien, Paris, Ljubljana, St. Petersburg, Los Angeles, New York, Stuttgart und Frankfurt vertreten. Dank eines P.S. One-Künstlerstipendiums verbringt er die Jahre 1988/89 in New York. 1991 eröffnet er ein Studio für Gestaltungsschäden und ist u.a. verantwortlich für die Organisation und Durchführung der Prodomo in Wien. In Zusammenarbeit mit dem Verband der Systemberater für Produktgestaltung Design-Labor Bremerhaven e.V. erstellt er 1992 die Design-Fallstudie "Das Sichtbarmachen des Vorhandenen" am Beispiel der Motorradwerke Zschopau.

Stiletto Studios se consacre depuis 1981 au graphisme et aux activités artistiques expérimentales, se décrivant lui-même comme un praticien du design. Depuis 1986, ses travaux ont été présentés dans de nombreuses expositions internationales à Vienne, Paris, Ljubljana, Saint Petersbourg, Los Angeles, New York, Stuttgart et Frankfort. Grâce à une bourse, il passe l'année 1988/89 à New York. En 1991, il ouvre un bureau de fautes en matière de design et devient, entre autres, responsable de l'organisation et la réalisation de Prodomo à Vienne. En collaboration avec l'Union des conseils en systèmes pour l'esthétique industrielle Design-Labor Bremerhaven e.V., il réalise en 1992 l'étude de cas de design «Rendre visible le présent» en prenant pour exemple l'usine de moto de Zschopau.

Kazuhide Takahama

Born in Japan, Kazuhide Takahama has lived in Bologna since 1963. He met Dino Gavina at the Tenth Milan Triennale in 1954. Gavina subsequently asked him to design a series of modular sofa. The first of his designs to be produced was the *Naeko* sofa, however the later *Marcel*, *Raymond* and *Suzanne* sofas were to be even more successful.

Kazuhide Takahama wurde in Japan geboren und lebt seit 1963 in Bologna. 1954 lernte er Dino Gavina bei der Zehnten Triennale in Mailand kennen. Später bat ihn Gavina, eine Reihe von Modular-Sofas zu entwerfen. Das erste Möbelstück, das nach seinen Entwürfen hergestellt wurde, war das *Naeko*-Sofa. Die späteren Sofa-Modelle *Marcel*, *Raymond* und *Suzanne* sollten allerdings noch erfolgreicher werden.

Né au Japon, Kazuhide Takahama vit à Bologne depuis 1963. Il rencontre à la Xème Triennale de Milan, en 1954, Dino Gavina qui lui demande de créer pour lui un sofa modulaire. Le premier de ces projets à être réalisé est le sofa *Naeko*. Les modèles ultérieurs, *Marcel*, *Raymond* et *Suzanne* connurent encore plus de succès.

Mart Stam

1899–1986
Netherlands . Niederlande . Pays-Bas

Philippe Starck

*1949
France . Frankreich . France

Stiletto Studios

*1959
Germany . Deutschland . Allemagne

Kazuhide Takahama

*1930
Japan . Japon

153

Born in Milan, Giuseppe Terragni studied architecture at the Polytechnic of Milan, graduating in 1926. He was one of the founders of Gruppo Sette and in 1927 began working in Como. In 1928, he took part in the first exhibition of Rational Architecture in Rome. From 1932 to 1936, he designed the Casa del Fascio, Como, and in 1936 the Asilo Sant'Elia. At the outbreak of World War II he was enlisted in the army and in 1943 he returned to Italy from the Russian front, having suffered a nervous breakdown. Tragically, he died a few days later.

Giuseppe Terragni wurde in Mailand geboren. Sein Studium am Polytechnikum seiner Heimatstadt schloß er 1926 ab. Er war einer der Mitbegründer der Gruppo Sette (1927) und begann seine berufliche Laufbahn in Como. 1928 beteiligte er sich an der ersten Ausstellung Rationale Architektur in Rom. Von 1932 bis 1936 arbeitete er an den Entwürfen für die Casa del Fascio in Como, und 1936 gestaltete er das Asilo Sant'Elia. Bei Ausbruch des Zweiten Weltkriegs wurde er in die italienische Armee eingezogen. 1943 kehrte er von der russischen Front wegen eines Nervenzusammenbruchs nach Italien zurück, wo er wenige Tage später starb.

Né à Milan, Giuseppe Terragni obtient le diplôme du Politecnico de Milan en 1926. Co-fondateur du Gruppo Sette, il commence à travailler à Côme en 1927 et , en 1928, prend part à la première exposition d'Architecture Rationnelle à Rome. De 1932 à 1936, il dessine la Casa del Fascio, à Côme, et en 1936 l'Asilo Sant'Elia. A la déclaration de guerre, il s'engage dans l'armée et en 1943, victime d'une profonde dépression, il meurt quelques jours après son retour.

Michael Thonet was born in Boppard am Rhein, where he established a workshop in 1819. In 1842, he was granted a patent for his new process for bending wood laminates and in 1849 set up his own furniture-manufacturing factory. He exhibited his furniture and won a bronze medal at the 1851 Great Exhibition in London. In the early 1900s several progressive Viennese architects, including Josef Hoffmann, designed furniture for Thonet. Le Corbusier was the first to use *Thonet* chairs in a "modern" architectural setting.

Michael Thonet wurde in Boppard am Rhein geboren, wo er 1819 eine Werkstatt eröffnete. 1842 erhielt er ein Patent für seine Methode, schichtverleimtes Sperrholz zu verformen, und 1849 gründete er eine eigene Firma, die seine Möbel produzierte. Auf der Londoner Weltausstellung von 1851 erhielt er für seine Möbel eine Bronzemedaille. Zu Beginn des 20. Jahrhunderts entwarfen einige der fortschrittlichen Wiener Architekten wie Josef Hoffmann Möbel für Thonet. Le Corbusier war der erste, der *Thonet*-Stühle in einer »modernen« architektonischen Umgebung verwendete.

Michael Thonet est né à Boppard am Rhein, où il crée son premier atelier en 1819, il dépose un brevet de cintrage de lamellé de bois en 1842 et crée sa propre manufacture de meubles en 1849. Il expose ses meubles et remporte une médaille de bronze à l'exposition de Londres de 1851. Au début des années 1900, plusieurs architectes d'avant-garde viennois, dont Josef Hoffmann, dessineront des meubles pour Thonet. Le Corbusier fut le premier à placer des sièges de *Thonet* dans un intérieur moderne.

Michael Thonet

Born in Antwerp, Henry van de Velde studied painting at the Académie des Beaux-Arts in Antwerp (1881–84) and later in Paris (1884/85). In 1886 he joined "Als ik Kan" and helped to found "L'Art Indépendant", both Antwerp-based art societies. In 1892, he gave up painting for design and two years later published "Déblaiement de l'Art", which pleaded for a unification of the arts. In 1907, he became a founder member of the Deutscher Werkbund. However, he left the group in 1914 after a disagreement with Hermann Muthesius over the latter's rigorous adherence to industrial standardization. In 1917, he emigrated to Switzerland and in 1920 moved to Holland. From 1926 to 1936, he was the Professor of Architecture at the University of Ghent. In 1947, he moved back to Switzerland and lived there until his death.

Henry van de Velde wurde in Antwerpen geboren. Er studierte Malerei an der Académie des Beaux-Arts in Antwerpen (1881–84) und in Paris (1884/85). 1886 wurde er Mitglied der Antwerpener Kunstvereinigungen »Als ik Kan« und »L'Art Indépendant«. 1892 gab er die Malerei zugunsten des Designs auf und veröffentlichte zwei Jahre später seine Schrift »Déblaiement de l'Art«, in der er für die Vereinigung der bildenden und der angewandten Künste plädierte. 1907 wurde er Gründungsmitglied des Deutschen Werkbundes, den er aber 1914 wieder verließ, nachdem er sich mit Hermann Muthesius wegen dessen kompromißlosen Eintretens für die Typisierung von Industrieprodukten überworfen hatte. 1917 emigrierte er in die Schweiz, und 1920 ging er nach Holland. Von 1926 bis 1936 war er Professor für Architektur an der Universität von Gent. 1947 kehrte er in die Schweiz zurück und lebte dort bis zu seinem Tod.

Henry van de Velde est né à Anvers, où il étudie la peinture à l'Académie des Beaux-Arts (1881–84) et plus tard à Paris (1884/85). En 1886, il rejoint l'«Als ik Kan» et aide à la création de «L'Art Indépendant», deux sociétés artistiques basées à Anvers. En 1892, il abandonne la peinture pour le design et deux ans plus tard publie «Déblaiement de l'Art», qui plaide pour une unification des arts. Il est membre fondateur du Deutscher Werkbund en 1907, mais quitte le groupe en 1914 en désaccord avec Hermann Muthesius sur la rigueur de l'adhésion de celui-ci à la standardisation industrielle. Il émigre en Suisse en 1917, puis en Hollande en 1920. De 1926 à 1936, il est professeur d'architecture à l'Université de Gand. Il retourne en Suisse en 1947 où il demeurera jusqu'à sa mort.

Hans Wegner trained as a cabinet-maker before attending the Copenhagen School of Arts and Crafts, where he later lectured from 1946 to 1953. From 1938 to 1942, he worked as a furniture designer in Arne Jacobsen and Erik Moller's architectural practice. In 1943, he set up his own office in Gentofte and collaborated with Borge Mogensen in the design of an apartment shown at the 1946 Cabinetmakers' Exhibition in Copenhagen. Throughout his long career, he has designed furniture extensively for Johannes Hansen and Fritz Hansen. The Royal Society of Arts, London, made him an Honorary Royal Designer for Industry in 1959.

Nach seiner Ausbildung als Kunsttischler besuchte Hans Wegner die Kunstgewerbeschule in Kopenhagen, an der er später, von 1946 bis 1953, lehrte. Von 1938 bis 1942 arbeitete er als Möbeldesigner im Architekturbüro von Arne Jacobsen und Erik Moller. 1943 gründete er ein eigenes Studio in Gentofte und entwarf zusammen mit Borge Mogensen eine Innenausstattung, die 1946 auf der Ausstellung der Kunsttischler in Kopenhagen gezeigt wurde. Während seiner langen Laufbahn gestaltete er Möbelentwürfe für Johannes Hansen und Fritz Hansen. Die Royal Society of Arts, London, verlieh ihm 1959 den Titel Honorary Royal Designer for Industry.

Hans Wegner est formé à l'ébénisterie avant de suivre les cours de l'Ecole des Arts Appliqués de Copenhague où il en seignera de 1946 à 1953. De 1938 à 1942, il travaille comme dessinateur de meubles dans les cabinets d'architecture d'Arne Jacobsen et d'Erik Moller. En 1943, il monte son propre cabinet à Gentofte et collabore avec Borge Mogensen à la conception d'un appartement présenté à l'Exposition d'ébénisterie de Copenhague en 1946. Au cours de sa longue carrière, il a créé de nombreux meubles pour Johannes Hansen et Fritz Hansen. The Royal Society of Arts, de Londres, l'a fait »Honorary Royal Designer for Industry« en 1959.

Giuseppe Terragni

1904–43
Italy . Italien . Italie

Michael Thonet

1796–1871
Austria . Österreich . Autriche

Henry van de Velde

1863–1957
Belgium . Belgien . Belgique

Hans Wegner

*1914
Denmark . Dänemark . Danemark

*Frank
Lloyd Wright*

Frank Lloyd Wright trained at the Engineering School of Wisconsin before working in the architectural office of J.L. Silsbee. From 1888 to 1893, he worked as a draftsman with Louis Sullivan. In 1889, he began his own practice as an architect and by 1900 had designed over fifty houses and their interiors. In 1897, he helped to found the Chicago Arts and Crafts Society. Like Charles Voysey, he believed that the machine could be used for the betterment of society when employed sympathetically. Influenced by Japanese forms, his designs were more sophisticated than those of fellow Arts & Crafts designer, Gustav Stickley. In 1909, he travelled to Europe, and on his return his house, *Taliesin*, became an architectural school. In 1955, he designed the *Taliesin* line of furniture which was intended for the mass-market and manufactured by the Heritage Henredon Company.

Frank Lloyd Wright studierte Ingenieurwesen an der Engineering School of Wisconsin. Danach trat er in das Architekturbüro von J.L. Silsbee ein und arbeitete von 1888 bis 1893 bei dem Architekten Louis Sullivan als Zeichner. 1889 eröffnete er ein eigenes Architekturstudio, und 1900 hatte er bereits über fünfzig Häuser nebst Innenausstattung entworfen. 1897 wurde er Mitbegründer der Chicago Arts and Crafts Society. Wie Charles Voysey glaubte auch er, daß die Maschine zur Verbesserung der Gesellschaft beitragen könne, wenn man sie nur entsprechend ihrer speziellen Eigenschaften einsetzte. Er stand der japanischen Formenwelt nahe, das gab seinen Entwürfen eine gewisse Eleganz, verglichen mit denen des Arts-and-Crafts-Designers Gustav Stickley. 1909 reiste er nach Europa, und nach seiner Rückkehr richtete er in seinem Haus *Taliesin* eine Architekturschule ein. 1955 entwarf er eine Möbelkollektion für die Massenproduktion, die er nach seinem Haus *Taliesin* benannte und die von der Heritage Henredon Company produziert wurde.

Frank Lloyd Wright est formé à l'Engineering School of Wisconsin, avant de travailler dans le cabinet d'architecte de J.L. Silsbee, puis de collaborer, comme dessinateur, avec Louis Sullivan, de 1888 à 1893. En 1889, il se met à son compte en tant qu'architecte et, vers 1900, aura dessiné plus de cinquante maisons et leur intérieur. En 1897, il aide à la fondation de la Chicago Arts and Crafts Society. Comme Charles Voysey, il croit que la machine peut servir à améliorer la société si elle est employée avec intelligence. Influencé par les formes japonaises, ses dessins sont plus sophistiqués que ceux de son confrère en Arts and Crafts, Gustav Stickley. En 1909, il voyage en Europe et à son retour, sa maison, *Taliesin*, devient une école d'architecture. En 1955, il dessine une ligne de mobilier *Taliesin*, destinée à la grande consommation et fabriquée par la Heritage Henredon Company.

Sori Yanagi trained at the Tokyo National University of Fine Arts and Music, graduating in 1940. He became an assistant to Charlotte Perriand from 1940 to 1942 while she was working in Japan. In 1951, he won the "Japanese Competition for Industrial Design" and a year later founded the Yanagi Industrial Design Institute. In 1977, he became the director of the Japan Folk Crafts Museum, Tokyo.

Sori Yanagi studierte an der Staatlichen Universität für Kunst und Musik in Tokio und schloß sein Studium 1940 ab. Von 1940 bis 1942 war er Assistent von Charlotte Perriand, die zu der Zeit in Japan arbeitete. 1951 gewann er den Wettbewerb »Japanese Competition for Industrial Design«, und ein Jahr später gründete er das Yanagi-Institut für Industriedesign. 1977 wurde er Direktor des Japanischen Museums für Volkskunst in Tokio.

Sori Yanagi est formé à l'Université Nationale des Beaux-Arts et de Musique de Tokyo dont il est diplômé en 1940. De 1940 à 1942, assistant de Charlotte Perriand pendant le séjour de celle-ci au Japon. En 1951, il remporte le «Concours japonais de design industriel» et, un an plus tard, fonde le Yanagi Industrial Design Institute. En 1977, il devient directeur du Musée des Arts Populaires Japonais, à Tokyo.

Marco Zanuso

Born in Milan, Marco Zanuso studied architecture at the Polytechnic, graduating in 1939. In 1945, he established his own design practice and was a director of "Domus" magazine. From 1947 to 1949 he was chief editor of the journal "Casabella". In 1948, he was commissioned by the Pirelli company to design seating with foam rubber upholstery – one example, the *Lady* chair, was awarded a gold medal at the 1951 Milan Triennale. In 1957, he formed a design collaboration with Richard Sapper. From this fruitful partnership was born the innovative *Child's chair* of 1961, which was the first sizeable object produced in non-reinforced plastic.

Marco Zanuso wurde in Mailand geboren. Sein Architekturstudium am Polytechnikum seiner Heimatstadt schloß er 1939 mit der Abschlußprüfung ab. 1945 gründete er ein eigenes Designstudio und trat in die Geschäftsleitung der Zeitschrift »Domus« ein. Von 1947 bis 1949 war er Chefredakteur der Zeitschrift »Casabella«. 1948 erhielt er von Pirelli den Auftrag, Sitzmöbel mit Schaumstoffpolsterung zu entwerfen. Einer seiner Entwürfe, der *Lady*-Stuhl, erhielt auf der Triennale von Mailand 1951 eine Goldmedaille. 1957 tat er sich mit Richard Sapper zu einer Arbeitsgemeinschaft zusammen. Ein Produkt dieser fruchtbaren Zusammenarbeit ist der innovative *Kinderstuhl* von 1961 – das erste Objekt von Bedeutung, das aus nichtverstärktem Kunststoff hergestellt wurde.

Né à Milan, Marco Zanuso sort du Politecnico avec un diplôme d'architecture en 1939. En 1945, il ouvre son cabinet de design et dirige le magazine «Domus». De 1947 à 1949, il est rédacteur en chef du journal «Casabella». En 1948 il reçoit commande de Pirelli pour un siège rembourré de mousse de caoutchouc. La chaise *Lady* recevra une médaille d'or à la Triennale de Milan de 1951. En 1957, il commence à former équipe avec Richard Sapper. De ce partenariat naîtra la *Chaise d'enfant* de 1961, premier objet d'une certaine dimension produit en matière plastique non-renforcée.

Frank Lloyd Wright

1869–1959
USA . Etats-Unis

Sori Yanagi

*1915
Japan . Japon

Marco Zanuso

*1916
Italy . Italien . Italie

Notes . Anmerkungen

Introduction

1. **Frank Russell, Philippe Garner, John Read**, A Century of Chair Design, Academy Editions, London 1980, p. 9

2. **Institute of Contemporary Arts**, The Modern Chair: Twentieth Century British Chair Design, ICA, London 1988, p. 4

3. **(Herwin Schaefer) – Helena Hayward**, World Furniture, Hamlyn, London 1965, p. 295

4. **George Nelson**, Chairs, Whitney Publications Inc., New York 1953, pp. 28–29

5. Ibid., pp. 30–33

6. Ibid., p. 33

7. Frank Gehry: New Bentwood Furniture Designs, The Montreal Museum of Decorative Arts, p. 90

8. The Art Journal – Vol. XI, George Virtue, London 1849, p. 95

9. **Institute of Contemporary Arts**, The Modern Chair: Twentieth Century British Chair Design, ICA, London 1988, p. 12

10. Ibid., p. 18

11. **The Whitechapel Art Gallery**, Modern Chairs 1918–1970, Lund Humphries, London 1970, p. 9

12. **Reyer Kras**, Gerrit Rietveld: A Centenary Exhibition, Barry Friedman, New York 1988, p. 28

13. **(Niels Diffrient) – Kathryn Hiesinger, George Marcus**, Design Since 1945, Thames & Hudson, London 1983, p. 14

14. **The Whitechapel Art Gallery**, Modern Chairs, 1918–1970, Lund Humphries, London 1970, tav. 7

Catalogue descriptions

1. **Derek E. Ostergard**, Bent Wood and Metal Furniture: 1850–1946, The American Federation of Arts, New York 1987, p. 214

2. **Fiona MacCarthy**, British Design Since 1880: A Visual History, Lund Humphries, London 1982, p. 54

3. **Institute of Contemporary Arts**, The Modern Chair: Twentieth Century British Chair Design, ICA, London 1988, pp. 12–13

4. **Isabelle Anscombe, Charlotte Gere**, Arts & Crafts in Britain & America, Academy Editions, London 1978, p.19

5. **Derek E. Ostergard**, Mackintosh to Mollino: Fifty Years of Chair Design, Barry Friedman Ltd., New York 1984, p. 8

6. **Graham Dry**, Bent Wood and Metal Furniture: 1850–1946, The American Federation of Arts, New York 1987, p. 58

7. **Isabelle Anscombe, Charlotte Gere**, Arts & Crafts in Britain and America, Academy Editions, London 1978, p. 169

8. **Derek E. Ostergard**, Bent Wood and Metal Furniture: 1850–1946, The American Federation of Arts, New York 1987, p. 255

9. **Reyner Banham**, Theory and Design in the First Machine Age, Architectural Press, London 1960, p.30

10. **The Whitechapel Art Gallery**, Modern Chairs 1918–1970, Lund Humphries, London 1970, p. 5

11. Ibid., p. 7

12. **Derek E. Ostergard**, Bent Wood and Metal Furniture: 1850–1946, The American Federation of Arts, New York 1987, p. 283

13. **Kathryn Hiesinger, George Marcus**, Design Since 1945, Thames & Hudson, London 1983, p. 221

14. **Eric Larrabee & Massimo Vignelli**, Knoll Design, Abrams, New York 1981, p. 44

15. **Fulvio Ferrari**, Carlo Mollino Cronaca, Stamperia Artistica Nazionale Editrice, Torino 1985, p. 19

16. **Tada Architectural Studio**, Finn Juhl Memorial Exhibition, Osaka 1990, p. 42

17. **Cherie & Kenneth Fehrman**, Postwar Interior Design: 1945–1960, Van Nostrand Reinhold, New York 1987, p. 24

18. Ibid., p. 63

19. **The Whitechapel Art Gallery**, Modern Chairs, 1918–1970, Lund Humphries, London 1970, p. 29

20. **The New Furniture Group, press release**, Laverne Originals, New York 1953

21. **The Whitechapel Art Gallery**, Modern Chairs, 1918–1970, Lund Humphries, London 1970, p. 116

22. **Cherie & Kenneth Fehrman**, Postwar Interior Design: 1945–1960, Van Nostrand Reinhold, New York 1987, p. 25

23. Ibid., p. 82

24. **Virgilio Vercelloni**, The Adventure of Design: Gavina, Jaca Book, Milan 1987, p. 15

25. **Christopher Wilk**, Design 1935–1965. What Modern Was, Abrams, New York 1991, p. 357, see foot notes 587–592

26. **The Whitechapel Art Gallery**, Modern Chairs, 1918–1970, Lund Humphries, London 1970, p. 56

27. **Ann Lee Morgan**, Contemporary Designers, St. James Press, London 1985, p. 142

28. **Ignazia Favata**, Joe Colombo & Italian Design of the Sixties, Thames & Hudson, London 1988, p. 6

29. **Virgilio Vercelloni**, The Adventure of Design: Gavina, Jaca Book, Milan 1988, p. 16

30. **Ann Lee Morgan**, Contemporary Designers, St. James Press, London 1985, p. 486

31. **Ann Lee Morgan**, Contemporary Designers, St. James Press, London 1985, p. 10

32. **The Whitechapel Art Gallery**, Modern Chairs, 1918–1970, Lund Humphries, London 1970, p. 94

33. **Mario Mastropietro**, An Industry for Design – The Research, Designers and Corporate Image of B&B Italia, Edizioni Lybra Immagine, Milan 1986, p. 246

34. **Albrecht Bangert**, Italian Furniture Design: Ideas Styles Movements, Bangert Verlag, Munich 1988, p. 41

35. **Institute of Contemporary Arts**, The Modern Chair: Twentieth Century British Chair Design, ICA, London 1988, pp. 12–13

36. **Nigel Whiteley**, Pop Design: Modernism to Mod, The Design Council, London 1987, p. 88

37. **Andrea Branzi**, The Hot House: Italian New Wave Design, Thames & Hudson, London 1984, p.144

38. **Peter Dormer**, The New Furniture: Trends & Traditions, Thames & Hudson, London 1987, p. 32

39. **Institute of Contemporary Arts**, The Modern Chair: Twentieth Century British Chair Design, ICA, London 1988, p. 51

40. **Deyan Sudjic**, From Matt Black to Memphis and Back Again, Architectural Design and Technology Press, London 1989, p. 202

41. **Le Musée des Arts Décoratifs de Montreal**, Frank Gehry: New Bentwood Furniture Designs, Exhibition catalogue – 1992, pp. 42–43

42. **Moroso Spa**, Spring Collection Catalogue, Milan 1992, p. 2

43. **Vitra GmbH**, Sipek Collection, Press Information – April 1992

Anscombe, I., Gere, C., Arts and Crafts in Britain and America, Academy Editions, London 1978

Bangert, A., Italian Furniture Design: Ideas Styles Movements, Bangert Verlag/Bangert Publications, Munich 1988

Banham, R., Theory and Design in the First Machine Age, Architectural Press, London 1960

Branzi, A., The Hot House. Italian New Wave Design, Thames & Hudson, London 1984

Dormer, P., The New Furniture: Trends & Traditions, Thames & Hudson, London 1987

Dry, G., Bentwood and Metal Furniture: 1850–1946, The American Federation of Arts, New York 1987

Eidelberg, M., Design 1935–1965: What Modern Was, Le Musée des Arts Décoratifs de Montreal/Harry N. Abrams, New York 1991

Favata, I., Joe Colombo and Italian Design of the Sixties, Thames & Hudson, London 1988

Fehrman, C. & K., Postwar Interior Design: 1945–1960, Van Nostrand Reinhold, New York 1987

Fiell, C. & P., Modern Furniture Classics since 1945, Thames & Hudson, London 1991

Friedman, M., De Stijl 1917–1931. Visions of Utopia, Phaidon, Oxford 1982

Ferrari, F., Carlo Mollino Cronaca, Stamperia Artistica Nazionale Editrice, Torino 1985

Hayward, H., World Furniture, Hamlyn, London 1965

Hiesinger, K. & Marcus, G., Design Since 1945, Thames & Hudson, London 1983

Katz, S., Plastics: Designs and Materials, Studio Vista, London 1987

Klein, D. & Bishop, M., Decorative Art 1880–1980, Phaidon/Christie's, Oxford 1986

Kras, R., Gerrit Rietveld Centenary Exhibition, Barry Friedman, New York 1988

Larrabee, E., Vignelli, M., Knoll Design, Abrams, New York 1981

MacCarthy, F., British Design since 1880: A Visual History, Lund Humphries, London 1982

Mastropietro, M., An Industry for Design: The Research, Designers and Corporate Image of B&B Italia, Edizioni Lybra Immagine s.n.c., Milan 1982

Morgan, A.L., Contemporary Designers, St. James Press, London 1985

Nelson, G., Chairs, Whitney Publications Inc., New York 1953

Neuhart, J. & M., Eames, R., Eames Design: The Work of the Office of Charles & Ray Eames, Harry N. Abrams, New York 1989

Ostergard, D.E., Mackintosh to Mollino: Fifty Years of Chair Design, Barry Friedman, New York 1984

Russell, F., Garner, P. & Read, J., A Century of Chair Design, Academy Editions, London 1980

Sembach, K.J., Contemporary Furniture: An International Review of Modern Furniture 1950 to the Present, The Design Council, London 1982

Sembach, K.J., Leuthäuser, G. & Gössel, P., Twentieth Century Furniture Design, Benedikt Taschen Verlag, Cologne

Spark, P., Furniture: Twentieth-Century Design, E.P. Dutton, New York 1986

Sudjic, D., From Matt Black to Memphis and Back Again, Architectural Design and Technology Press, London 1989

Vercelloni, V., L'avventura del design: Gavina, Jaca Book, Milan 1987

Whiteley, N., Pop Design: Modernism to Mod, The Design Council, London 1987

Exhibition Catalogues

Institute of Contemporary Arts, The Modern Chair: Twentieth Century British Chair Design, ICA, London 1988

Le Musée des Arts Décoratifs de Montreal, Frank Gehry: New Bentwood Furniture Designs, Le Musée des Arts Décoratifs de Montreal, Montreal 1992

Tada Architectural Studio, Finn Juhl Memorial Exhibition, Tada Architectural Studio, Osaka 1990

The Whitechapel Art Gallery, Modern Chairs, 1918–1970, Lund Humphries, London 1970

36, main: Besitz: Die Neue Sammlung, Staatliches Museum für angewandte Kunst, Munich; Photo: Angela Bröhan, Munich; archival: Gebrüder Thonet, Vienna; © Photo Thomas Römer, Vienna

37, main: Besitz: Die Neue Sammlung, Staatliches Museum für angewandte Kunst, Munich; Photo: Angela Bröhan, Munich; archivals: Shaker, London

38, main: Besitz: Die Neue Sammlung, Staatliches Museum für angewandte Kunst, Munich; Photo: Angela Bröhan, Munich; archival: Nordenfjeldske Kunstindustrimuseum, Trondheim

39, main: The Fine Art Society, London; archival, left: from: Entwurfsunterlagen zur Ausschreibung, «Haus eines Kunstfreundes», Darmstadt 1901; archival, right: Huntarian Art Gallery, University of Glasgow, Glasgow

40, main: Courtesy Fischer Fine Art Ltd., London; archival: Postcard, 1899

41, main: The Museum of Modern Art, New York (Gift of Liberty & Co., London); archival, top: Dekorative Kunst, IV, 1899; archival, centre: Architektursammlung der technischen Hochschule, Munich; archival, bottom: Museum für Industriekultur, Nürnberg

42, main: Galerie Metropol, Wien; archival, top left: Deutsche Kunst und Dekoration, XIX, 1906/07; archival, bottom left: Dekorative Kunst, VII, 1903/04; archival, bottom right: Marianne Haller, Südstadt

43, main: Sotheby's, London; archival, centre: Christie's, Scotland; bottom: T.R. Annan & Sons, Glasgow

44, main: Christie's, London; archival, bottom left: Courtesy The Frank Lloyd Wright Foundation; archival, bottom right: Barry Friedman Ltd., New York

45, main: Christie's, New York; archival, top left: The Frank Lloyd Wright Foundation; archival, bottom left: Whitechapel Art Gallery, London; archival, bottom right: Courtesy The Frank Lloyd Wright Foundation

46, main: Fiell International Ltd., London; archival, top left: Deutsche Kunst und Dekoration, III, 1898/99; archival, bottom left: Galerie Metropol, Wien; archival, bottom right: Barry Friedman Ltd., New York

47, main: Besitz: Die Neue Sammlung, Staatliches Museum für angewandte Kunst, Munich; Photo: Angela Bröhan, Munich; archival, bottom left: Whitechapel Art Gallery, London; archival, bottom right: Sotheby's, New York

48, main: Deutsches historisches Museum, Berlin, Photo: Lepkowski; Archiv des Verlags; archival, bottom left: W. von Debschitz-Kunowski, BHA Inv.-Nr. 8783; archival, bottom right: Bauhaus-Archiv, Berlin

49, main: Sotheby's, Monaco; archival, bottom left: Ecart International, Paris

50, main: Gebrüder Thonet, Frankenberg; archival: Courtesy Stuhlmuseum Burg Beverungen

51, main: Bauhaus-Archiv, Berlin; Photo: Lepkowski; archival, bottom left: Sotheby's, New York; archival, bottom right: Courtesy Fischer Fine Art Ltd., London

52, main: Bauhaus-Archiv, Berlin; Photo: Lepkowski; archival: Gebrüder Thonet, Frankenberg

53, main: Sotheby's, New York; archival, bottom left: Cassina, Milan; archivals, bottom centre & right: Courtesy Fischer Fine Art Ltd., London

54, main: Sotheby's, London; archivals: Cassina, Milan

55, main: Christie's, Amsterdam; archival, bottom left: Knoll Group, New York; archival, bottom right: Photo: Klaus Frahm, Hamburg

56, main & archivals: Courtesy Fischer Fine Art Ltd., London

57, main: Besitz: Fiell International Ltd., London; Photo: Paul Chave; archival: Mathsson International, Värnamo

58, main: Besitz: Die Neue Sammlung, Staatliches Museum für angewandte Kunst, Munich; Photo: Angela Bröhan, Munich; archival, left: Courtesy Fischer Fine Art Ltd., London; archival, right: Cassina, Milan

59, main & archivals: Zanotta, Milan

60, main: Stöhr Import-Export GmbH, Biesigheim; Photo: Kriwanek; archival: Knoll Group, New York

61, main: Besitz: Die Neue Sammlung, Staatliches Museum für angewandte Kunst, Munich; Photo: Angela Bröhan, Munich; archival, from «Landesausstellung Catalogue», 1939

62, main & archivals, bottom left & right: Galerie Bischofberger, Zurich; archival, top left: Christie's, London

63, main: Galerie Bischofberger, Zurich; archival: Photo: Aldo Ballo, Milan

64, main & archivals: Fiell International Ltd., London; Photos: Paul Chave

65, main & archival, bottom: Knoll International, Murr/Murr; archival, top right: Knoll Group, New York

66, main & archival centre: Johannes Hansens Mobelsnedkeri, Copenhagen; archival, left: Fritz Hansen, Copenhagen; archival, right: Fiell International Ltd., London; Photo: Paul Chave

67, main & archivals: Arflex, Milan

68, main: Besitz: Die Neue Sammlung, Staatliches Museum für angewandte Kunst, Munich; Photo: Angela Bröhan, Munich; archivals: Race Furniture, Bourton-on-the-Water

69, main & archival: Fischer Fine Art Ltd., London

70, main: Fiell International Ltd., London; Photo: Peter Hodsoll; archival: Knoll Group, New York

71, main & archival, bottom: Fiell International Ltd., London; Photo: Paul Chave; archival, top left: Courtesy Fischer Fine Art Ltd., London

72, main: Fiell International Ltd., London; archival: Laverne Originals, New York

73, main: Besitz: Die Neue Sammlung, Staatliches Museum für angewandte Kunst, Munich; Photo: Angela Bröhan, Munich; archival: Tecno, Milano

74, main & archival, top left: Fiell International Ltd., London; Photo: Paul Chave; archivals, bottom left & right: Fritz Hansen, Copenhagen

75, main: Besitz: Die Neue Sammlung, Staatliches Museum für angewandte Kunst, Munich; Photo: Angela Bröhan, Munich; archivals: Knoll Group, New York

76, main: Besitz: Die Neue Sammlung, Staatliches Museum für angewandte Kunst, Munich; Photo: Angela Bröhan, Munich; archival: Alessandro Mendini, Milan

77, main: Artery, Miami

78, main: Fiell International Ltd., London; archivals: Fritz Hansen, Copenhagen

79, main: Fiell International Ltd., London; Photo: Peter Hodsoll; archival, bottom left: Fiell International Ltd., London; Photo: Peter Hodsoll; archival, bottom right: Fifty/50, New York

80, main: Sotheby's, London; archival: Herman Miller, Zeeland

81, main & archival, bottom: Fiell International Ltd., London; Photo: Paul Chave; archival, top left: Herman Miller, Zeeland

82, main: Besitz: Die Neue Sammlung, Staatliches Museum für angewandte Kunst, Munich; Photo: Angela Bröhan, Munich; archivals: Zanotta, Milan

83, main & archival: Fiell International Ltd., London; Photo: Peter Hodsoll

84, main: Besitz: Die Neue Sammlung, Staatliches Mu-

seum für angewandte Kunst, Munich; Photo: Angela Bröhan, Munich; archivals: Fritz Hansen, Copenhagen

85, main: Fiell International Ltd., London; Photo: Paul Chave; archival: Fiell International Ltd., London; Photo: Peter Hodsoll

86, main: Fiell International Ltd., London; Photo: Peter Hodsoll; archivals: Herman Miller, Zeeland, Michigan

87, main: Besitz: Die Neue Sammlung, Staatliches Museum für angewandte Kunst, Munich; Photo: Angela Bröhan, Munich; archival, bottom left: Fiell International Ltd., London; Photo: Paul Chave; archival, top & bottom right: Verner Panton, Basel

88, main: Bernini, Milan; archivals: Gavina, Milan

89, main: Herman Miller International, Zeeland Art Ltd., London

90, main: Fiell International Ltd., London; Photo: Paul Chave

91, main: Fiell International Ltd., London; Photo: Peter Hodsoll; archival: Fiell International Ltd., London; Photo: Paul Chave

92, main: Fiell International Ltd., London; Photo: Paul Chave; archivals: Hille Executive Furniture & Seating Ltd., London

93, main: Finlandcontact GmbH, Dinslaken; archival, left: Stendig, New York; archival, right: Fiell International Ltd., London; Photo: Paul Chave

94, main: Besitz: Die Neue Sammlung, Staatliches Museum für angewandte Kunst, Munich; Photo: Angela Bröhan, Munich; archival, top: Courtesy Fischer Fine Art Ltd., London; archival, bottom: Bayer AG, Leverkusen

95, main & archival left: Courtesy Fischer Fine Art Ltd., London; archival, right: Whitechapel Art Gallery, London

96, main: Fiell International Ltd., London; Photo: Paul Chave; archival: Knoll Group, New York

97, main: Besitz: Die Neue Sammlung, Staatliches Museum für angewandte Kunst, Munich; Photo: Angela Bröhan, Munich; archivals: Knoll Group, New York

98, main & archival right: Poltronova, Milan; archival, left: Archizoom Associati

99, main & archival: Knoll Group, New York

100, main: Galerie Objekte, Munich; archival: Günter Belzig Playdesign, Hohenwart-Deimhausen

101, main: Fiell International Ltd., London; Photo: Peter Hodsoll; archivals: Artifort, Lanaken

102, main: Besitz: Die Neue Sammlung, Staatliches Museum für angewandte Kunst, Munich; Photo: Angela Bröhan, Munich; archivals: Zanotta, Milan

103, main: Kunstmuseum, Düsseldorf; Photo: Walter Klein

104, main: Courtesy Fischer Fine Art Ltd., London; archivals, left & centre: Whitechapel Art Gallery, London; archival, right: Sormani Spa, Milan

105, main: Fiell International Ltd., London; Photo: Paul Chave; archival: Stendig, New York

106, main & archival, left: Zanotta, Milan; archival, right: Gufram, Turin

107, main & archivals: B&B Italia, Padua

108, main: Fiell International Ltd., London; archival: Castelli, London

109, main & archival: Fiell International Ltd., London; Photos: Paul Chave

110, main: Fiell International Ltd., London; archival: Stendig, New York

111, main: Poltronova, Milan

159

Credits . Fotonachweis . Crédits photographiques

112, main: Besitz: Die Neue Sammlung, Staatliches Museum für angewandte Kunst, Munich; Photo: Angela Bröhan, Munich

113, main: Don Treadway Gallery, Cincinnati; archival: Fred Hoffmann Gallery, Los Angeles

114, main & archival: Fiell International Ltd., London; Photo: Paul Chave

115, main & archival, left: Alessandro Mendini, Milan; archival, right: Alias, Milan

116, main: Fiell International Ltd., London; Photo: Paul Chave; archival: Vitra, London

117, main: Besitz: Die Neue Sammlung, Staatliches Museum für angewandte Kunst, Munich; Photo: Angela Bröhan, Munich; archival, top: Alias, Milan; archival, bottom: Artemide GB Ltd., London

118, main: Verlagsarchiv; Photo: Peter Strobl, Cologne; archival: Archiv Philippe Starck, Paris

119, main: Michele de Lucchi, Milan

120, main & archival: Stiletto Studios, Berlin; Photos: Idris Kolodziej

121, main & archivals: Danny Lane/Hanna Browne, London

122, main: Vitra, London; archival: Hiroyuki Hirai, Tokyo

123, main: Cappellini, Arosio

124, main & archival: A. Dubreuil Decorative Arts, London

125, main: Besitz: Die Neue Sammlung, Staatliches Museum für angewandte Kunst, Munich

126, main & archival: One Off Ltd., London

127, main: Fiell International Ltd., London; Photo: Paul Chave; archival, top: Cappellini, Arosio; archival, right:

Besitz: Die Neue Sammlung, Staatliches Museum für angewandte Kunst, Munich; Photo: Angela Bröhan, Munich

128, main: Photo Keiicki Tahara; archival: Photo: Bin Asakawa

129, main & archival: Photo: Nacasa

130, main: Fiell International Ltd., London

131, main: Knoll International; Photo: Jay Ahrend; archivals: Knoll Group, New York

132, main & archival, bottom: Vitra, London; archival, left: Fiell International Ltd., London; Photo: Paul Chave

133, main: Fiell International Ltd., London; Photo: Paul Chave; archival: Vitra Ltd., London

136, left: Whitechapel Art Gallery, London; centre: Finlandcontact, Dinslaken; right: One Off Ltd., London

137, left: B&B Italia, Padua; right: Knoll Group, New York

138, left: Tecno, London; centre, left: Mario Botta, Photo: Gitty Darugar; centre, right: Whitechapel Art Gallery, London; right: B&B Italia, Padua

139, Whitechapel Art Gallery, London

140, left: Hille, London; right: Space, London

141, left & right: Herman Miller, Zeeland

142, Knoll Group, New York

143, Fritz Hansen, Copenhagen

144, left: OMK, London; centre: Vitra, London; right: Danny Lane, London

145, left & right: Cassina, Milan

146, left: Vico Magistretti, Milan; right: B&B Italia, Padua

147, top: Knoll Group, New York; bottom: Artemide GB, London

148, top: Herman Miller, Zeeland; bottom: Peter Murdoch, London

149, left: Verner Panton, Basel; right: Artifort, Maastricht

150, left: Cassina, Milan; centre: Knoll Group, New York; right: © Collection Fulvio Ferrari, Turin

151, Sally Race, Powys

152, left: Whitechapel Art Gallery, London; top right: Knoll Group, New York; bottom right: Vitra, London

153, left: Vitra, London; right: B&B Italia, Padua

154, Gebrüder Thonet, Vienna

155, left: Cassina, Milan; right: Arflex, Milan

We are grateful to those individuals and institutions who have allowed us to reproduce illustrations. We regret that in some cases it has not been possible to trace the original copyright holders of photographs in earlier publications. We would also like to thank the numerous designers, manufacturers and institutions that have kindly supplied images for the biographical section.

Acknowledgement . Danksagung . Remerciements

Paul Chave, Photographer
Marre Moerel, Research Assistant
Mark Thomson, Design

A. Dubreuil Decorative Arts, London
Arflex spa., Milan
Artek, Helsinki
Artemide, London
Artifort, Belgium
B&B Italia, Padua
Barry Friedman Ltd., New York
Bauhaus-Archiv, Berlin
Christina and Bruno Bischofberger Collection, Zurich
Brüder Siegel GmbH + Co KG, Leipheim/Donau
Bundes-Mobilien-Verwaltung, Vienna
Cappellini, Arosio
Cassina spa., Milan
Castelli (UK) Ltd., London
Christie, Manson & Woods, Amsterdam
Christie, Manson & Woods, Geneva
Christie, Manson & Woods, New York
Collection of Alan Carter, Blackpool
Collection of Nick Dine, London
Collection of R.C. Hopkins, London
Collection of John and Jan McLean, London
Collection of Mr. Noritsuga Oda, Kyoto
Design Council, London

Design Museum, London
Driade, Milan
Fifty/50, New York
Fischer Fine Art Ltd., London
The Frank Lloyd Wright Foundation, Scottsdale
Fritz Hansen, Allerød, Annette Tingstrup
Galerie Metropol, Vienna
Galerie Objekte, Munich, Wolfgang Mauer
Gebrüder Thonet, Vienna
Graphic Acumen Ltd., London
Yoshio Hayashi, Kyoto
Herman Miller, Bath
Hille International Ltd., London
Peter Hodsoll, London
Richard Hollis, London
Interior Marketing, Bishop's Stortford, Mr. & Mrs. Paul Beauchamp
International Design Press Agency, Barcelona
Johannes Hansen, Mobelsnedkeri, Copenhagen
Douglas Kelley, London
Knoll Group, New York, Dennis Flannagan
Knoll Group, Paris, Chantal Sanglier
Kohseki Co. Ltd., Kyoto, Søren Matz
Danny Lane, London
Vico Magistretti, Milan
Alessandro Mendini, Milan
Metropolitan Museum of Art, New York
Jasper Morrison, London
Musée des Arts Décoratifs, Paris

Musée des Arts Décoratifs de Montreal, Montreal, Diane Charbonneau
Museum für Industriekultur, Nuremberg
Museum of Modern Art, New York
Nordenfjeldske Kunstindustrimuseum, Trondheim
O.M.K. Design Ltd., London
One Off Ltd., London
Österreichisches Museum für Angewandte Kunst, Ruperta Pichler, Vienna
Verner Panton, Basel
Gaetano Pesce, New York
Poltronova, Milan
Mrs. Sally Race, Powys
Race Furniture Ltd., Bourton-on-the-Water
Sotheby's, London
Sotheby's, Monaco
Sotheby's, New York
Space, London
Stendig, New York
Victoria & Albert Museum, London, Gareth Williams
Vitra Limited, London, Laura Hatton
Whitechapel Art Gallery, London
The William Morris Gallery, Walthamstow
Yale University Archives
Zanotta, Milan